Organisational Theory

David Crowther
Miriam Green

D1078031

Miriam Green is Senior Lectu~~rer in~~ Organisation Studies, London Metropolitan University.
David Crowther is Professor of Corporate Social Responsibility, London Metropolitan University.

The CIPD would like to thank the following members of the CIPD Publishing Editorial Board for their help and advice:

Pauline Dibben, Middlesex University Business School
Edwina Hollings, Staffordshire University Business School
Caroline Hook, Huddersfield University Business School
John Sinclair, Napier University Business School

The Chartered Institute of Personnel and Development is the leading publisher of books and reports for personnel and training professionals, students, and all those concerned with the effective management and development of people at work. For details of all our titles, please contact the publishing department:
tel: 020-8263 3387
fax: 020-8263 3850
e-mail publish@cipd.co.uk
The catalogue of all CIPD titles can be viewed on the CIPD website:
www.cipd.co.uk/bookstore

Organisational Theory

David Crowther
Miriam Green

Chartered Institute of Personnel and Development

Published by the Chartered Institute of Personnel and Development, CIPD House, Camp Road, London, SW19 4UX

First published 2004

Design by Fakenham Photosetting, Fakenham, Norfolk
Typeset by Fakenham Photosetting, Fakenham, Norfolk
Printed in Great Britain by The Cromwell Press, Trowbridge, Wiltshire

British Library Cataloguing in Publication Data
A catalogue of this book is available from the British Library

ISBN 0 85292 999 4

The views expressed in this manual are the authors' own and may not necessarily reflect those of the CIPD.

The CIPD has made every effort to trace and acknowledge copyright holders. If any source has been overlooked, CIPD Enterprises would be pleased to redress this for future editions.

Chartered Institute of Personnel and Development, CIPD House,
Camp Road, London, SW19 4UX
Tel: 020 8971 9000   Fax: 020 8263 3333
Email: cipd@cipd.co.uk   Website: www.cipd.co.uk
Incorporated by Royal Charter.   Registered Charity No. 1079797

Contents

List of figures and tables

Abbreviations

AMT	advanced manufacturing technology
AQL	acceptable quality levels
BPR	business process re-engineering
CAD	computer-aided design
CAM	computer-aided manufacturing
CIM	computer-integrated manufacturing
CIMA	Chartered Institute of Management Accounting
CNC	computer numerically controlled
CSR	corporate social responsibility
EU	European Union
FMS	flexible manufacturing systems
IS	information systems
ISM	intervention strategy model
JIT	just-in-time manufacturing
KM	knowledge management
MRP	materials requirement planning
MRPII	manufacturing resources planning
NIE	newly industrialising economy
NIMBY	'not-in-my-backyard'
NPV	net present value
OPT	optimised production technology
RBV	resource-based view
SVM	shareholder value management
TQM	total quality management
TQM	total quality marketing
VBM	value-based management

To our families and colleagues

Introduction

CHAPTER 1

INTRODUCING ORGANISATION THEORY

Almost all activity in any society takes place through people acting together. This is certainly true of all business activity, and we all enjoy the fruits of this business activity in terms of the goods and services provided by such organisations. Most of us are also employed by organisations and receive an income in return for our contribution to the activity of that organisation. It is important therefore to understand how organisations operate and why they are structured in the ways in which they are. Organisations do not evolve by chance – nor are they structured in a random manner. To provide the goods, services and employment that they do requires some planning and organisation.

Much attention has been devoted since the mid-nineteenth century to a consideration of how such organisations can be structured to improve the contribution they make to society and to the improvement (or otherwise) of all our lives. The knowledge and experience gained about this has been collectively termed as organisation theory – the subject matter of this book. In studying the theory in this book, however, it is important to remember that organisations do not 'organise' themselves and have no feelings. It is people who organise themselves and others, and people who apply any theory developed.

THEMES AND TOPICS

In this book therefore we seek to look at various topics or themes about organisations – some regularly found in many textbooks about organisations, some more unusual. This book has several themes that are not necessarily common to all textbooks on organisations and to what has been loosely called 'organisation behaviour'. The topics chosen are also differently 'sized' – ranging from micro-organisational processes to broader societal and global issues. We have also treated topics from different theoretical perspectives. We regard all the topics discussed as important for organisations and for the people working in them. They also have wider implications for the society in which the organisations are placed and for inter-relationships with societies more generally in a global context.

We ourselves have sought to take a critical view on theories and practices in the field of organisation studies. This has meant that we have included opposing or different views by other theorists and occasionally by practitioners, with comeback at times by the original theorists. The book also includes ideas from Critical Theory itself – a school of theorists incorporating writers from the 'Frankfurt school' and those influenced by them. Their views stem in part from radical theoretical perspectives originating from Marx, and from other non-mainstream ideas such as hermeneutic and psychoanalytical approaches.

BROADER CONTEXT

We have attempted to show how organisation theory stems from and is linked to a broader context. First, organisation theory itself is derived from some of the great 'fathers' of sociology, writing in the nineteenth and early twentieth centuries. These are normally thought to be Marx, Weber and Durkheim. Apart from Weber's analysis of bureaucracy, these theorists did not concern themselves specifically with organisations but with society in general. Their analyses were about the future of industrial societies, and capitalist societies in particular. They considered, for example, what the social and occupational structures of societies would look like as they became more industrialised; the congruence in values and social norms in technologically changing societies between those running factories and offices and their employees; and whether there would be a convergence or divergence in power, wealth, status and ideology among the general population.

Later theorists in the 1960s and 1970s also concerned themselves with these questions, either from an optimistic view according to certain interpretations of Durkheim's theories, or from a more pessimistic view arising from Marx and Weber's ideas. Some theorists like Clark Kerr *et al* saw a convergence of wealth, skill and status among the populace in industrial societies and then eventually in third world countries; Blauner saw industrial manual work as having passed through its harshest stages in the industrialised world and thought it would in future be more pleasant, skilled and rewarding. On the other hand Braverman, taking his ideas from Marx, predicted a worsening of conditions not only for manual workers but office workers as well. He argued that white-collar work would become 'proletarianised', involving further de-skilling, with decisions made increasingly by management at the expense of the workforce.

Transposed to organisations, Weber's work on bureaucracy encouraged the development of theories of structure and hierarchy, as, for example, in the classical management school. Clear lines of command were seen as desirable for efficient management, as were clear procedures and regulations, including rules for recruitment regarding the various positions in large organisations and their job descriptions. On the other hand, Weber's reservations about bureaucracy also encouraged a critique of such systems in terms of their controlling elements and restrictions on creativity. Additional criticisms of bureaucracy, linked to these, were concerned with inflexibility and slowness (Weber 1970).

Interpretations of Durkheim encouraged in organisation theory an interest in people's feelings of social harmony and its opposite – 'anomie', to use Durkheim's language. Human relations theories have emphasised the importance of emotional and social well-being among employees and their commitment to the organisation, and the importance for managers to ensure this. Motivation theories have been linked to these ideas, and have taken concepts of social well-being further to encompass intrinsic interest and challenge in the work, and increased responsibility for employees (Clegg and Dunkerley 1980).

From Marx came criticisms of organisation theories based on managerialist values: the idea that managers should be in control of the information and decision-making; and that managers' aims and strategies were necessarily for the good of all employees, and indeed for the good of the organisation as a whole. Marx's theories, which were never about organisations *per se* but about capitalist society based on his analysis of nineteenth-century Britain, emphasised the exploitative nature of relations between the dominant and subordinate classes in capitalist societies. Organisation theorists taking up these ideas have made their focus the exploitative nature of managerial practices in organisations (Braverman 1998).

We argue in various parts of the present book that one cannot separate societal and organisation theories from their global context. Thus critics of Clark Kerr *et al* have argued that the trend to convergence and more equal and better societies, if they exist at all in the West, will not necessarily be replicated in third world societies, especially in the poorer societies in Africa and South America. They claim, as is outlined in this book, that the wealth of Western societies has at least in part been derived from exploitation of 'developing' countries in terms, for example, of their natural resources – human, mineral and agricultural – and, currently, of their debt repayments. Thus when organisation theorists argue that organisations are becoming better places for workforces, one should bear in mind the possibility that this, where true, may be at the expense of people in other societies.

It is possible that in the future there may be other theorists who will also be regarded as founding 'fathers' or 'mothers' of organisation theory. Wittgenstein may be one such person, primarily for his later theory about language and reality. In *Philosophical Investigations* (Wittgenstein 1967) Wittgenstein argued against his earlier views in the *Tractatus Logico-Philosophicus* (Wittgenstein 1922) that language represented reality. In his later work, he argued that it is through language that we create reality/realities (Bogen 1972). This raises issues about what reality is and about whether or not there is an 'objective reality' or whether there are multiple realities created through language, or 'languaging' as Becker (1991) has conceived it. Postmodern theorists have taken up these issues and, as will be discussed below, they are pertinent to organisations. The term 'organisation' itself begs the question as to what kind of reality it constitutes, as do various aspects commonly attributed to organisations, such as structure, hierarchy and culture.

DIFFERENT THEORETICAL PERSPECTIVES

The theoretical perspectives used most frequently in this book are what have been categorised as functionalist, radical and postmodern approaches. Functionalist theories, which appear mostly in the early chapters, are managerialist in orientation, assume an objective reality that includes organisational characteristics such as structure, and within it lines of command and communication. Many theorists have concentrated on analysing structure and prescribing what they regard as the one most fitting for organisations in particular circumstances. Functional organisation theorists have also written about people and recommended certain strategies, which they argue would result in optimum performance by employees. These theories are often based on the assumption that people are in their core or essence a certain way and thus are similarly open to managerial strategies such as those giving cultural direction to increase motivation and commitment among the workforce.

Radical theorists, taking their views initially from Marx, have adopted a different line. Rather than deal with how best to make organisations more productive and employees more committed, radical theorists have often started their analyses from the opposite end of organisations – employees at various levels in the organisation, starting from the lowest. Because they are interested in questions of exploitation, they have engaged with different issues: types and levels of managerial control; trends and degrees of up-skilling or de-skilling in job design; and workplace resistance or, as some writers have described it, survival strategies. Radical theorists often start and permeate their analyses with relations of power in organisations, where functional theorists might look at power as something more technical and not influencing other areas of organisational life.

Those following ideas of the Critical Theory or Frankfurt school have been more interested in the power of ideology. One of the main questions they have sought to answer is why it is that in democratic societies the majority of the population vote in governments that, according to critical theorists, override their interests in favour of more powerful interests in the dominant classes. Similar questions have been asked by them of the workplace, in terms of why employees may put up with uncongenial situations at work, under conditions that probably serve the interests of their employers more than their own.

Postmodern approaches have drawn partly on radical ideas and also on the hermeneutic tradition, which emphasises the different perceptions, interpretations and enactments by the actors in whatever situations they find themselves, including in organisations. They also emphasise the importance of context and how the same action can have different significance depending on the place and time. These ideas have been developed by some postmodern theorists to emphasise the significance of relational factors. They have addressed the issue of relational and contextual factors with regard to people, their personalities and their potential, arguing against the idea of people having an essential core and thus being able to be categorised in various ways, such as having 'it' in them, or not to achieve certain things – being management 'material', for example. They argue instead that people have different potentialities and different personalities, and behave differently according to the situation and context they're in, and with which they interact.

Those studying organisations from postmodern perspectives have focused on process, particularly local micro-processes. One example is Foucault's (1980) ideas about the existence of many types of power (other than top-down 'sovereign' power), which operate at all levels in many forms. Postmodernists reject the idea of organisation structure being 'real' and 'objective' in any sense. In fact, they reject the notion of 'objective reality' in the sense of people seeing things the same way, or seeing the same things as being significant. In organisations, formal structure may, for example, be regarded as 'real' by senior management, yet as irrelevant by people lower down the hierarchy who have found more 'useful' informal channels which for them are much more 'real'. Thus postmodern theorists work on the assumptions that there are different realities for different people, on which they 'act' – in organisations as anywhere else. They also recognise that things change, that perceived realities are fragile and shifting, and that there is ambiguity and diversity in people's perceptions of hitherto taken-for-granted aspects of organisations such as hierarchy, lines of communication, culture and many other areas.

ORGANISATIONAL PRACTICE

We have shown in many instances how theory is related to organisational practice. Case studies have been used in some instances to discuss 'real' situations and to show how they can be analysed in greater depth and sophistication using organisational theory. We also have sought to demonstrate how certain theories have been applied to organisational contexts, and the results – the successes, failures, ways of implementation, opportunities and constraints, and their significance. By doing this we have sought to make the theory clearer and more accessible, and also to give a flavour of how organisational strategies based on these theories have worked out in practice in organisational life. We have also aimed at making more concrete the different theoretical perspectives we have used, and how they can be harnessed to understand and analyse organisational and other situations from different viewpoints. For example, after discussing the postmodern concept of 'social constructionism' we have shown how education policies and practices in England and Wales can be conceived and analysed using social constructionist theories. A further aim is to provide readers with a theoretical framework with which to position and evaluate theory, including unfamiliar ideas and those yet to be developed.

ACADEMIC PRACTICE

In our presentation of theory and organisational practice we have also engaged in issues around the academic 'industry'. We have mentioned the different theoretical perspectives used by academic writers to understand and analyse organisation theory, organisation systems and workplace practices. We have also highlighted academic debates and disputes on several issues and dealt extensively with academic critiques of various theoretical positions. We have touched on academic practices in the sense of when and how certain authors and ideas get taken up and disseminated, and how ideas are developed and taken further within the broader social and political context as well as within the framework of 'the academy'. Issues around publication are important here, as what gets published has a better chance of being accepted as authoritative 'knowledge'. Thus editorial policies in academic journals or with academic book publishers can have a strong influence on what knowledge is produced and what becomes epistemologically valid.

ORGANISATION OF THE BOOK

Most books on organisation theory treat the development of this theory in a linear historical manner. The implication of this approach is that as new theory is developed it replaces older theory because it is better theory – better in the way in which it explains the operation of organisations. We have taken a different approach to our discussion of theory, because we do not believe that any of the theory has been replaced by subsequent theory. Rather, we believe that new theory has been developed to address some of the deficiencies of earlier theory, but it has not replaced it, as the older theory has also continued to develop. Different theory is based upon different perspectives. We argue that there are certain schools of thought and practices about organisations arising from different theoretical, political and ethical perspectives which are present at any one time, albeit in different guises and with changing names, 'in vogue' for the moment. Similarly the critiques about these theories also keep recurring from the several theoretical perspectives of those making critical evaluations.

We have sought to show how each school of theory still has relevance in the present. Our perspective is that *all* of the theory we consider in this book is relevant and has something to say about organising. In doing so, although our personal preferences might be apparent, we make no statements that some theory is better than other – only that it addresses different problems and issues. The organisation of this book therefore is based upon schools of thought with the theory grouped into what we consider – and hope you do too – to be logical groupings.

FURTHER READING

CLEGG, S. and DUNKERLEY, D. (1980) *Organization, class and control*. London: Routledge & Kegan Paul.

REFERENCES

BECKER, A.L. (1991) A short essay on languaging. In F. Steier (ed) *Research and reflexivity*. London: Sage.

BOGEN, J. (1972) *Wittgenstein's philosophy of language: some aspects of its development*. London: Routledge & Kegan Paul.

BRAVERMAN, H. (1998) *Labor and monopoly capital: the degradation of work in the twentieth century*. 25th anniversary ed. New York: Monthly Review Press.

CLEGG, S. and DUNKERLEY, D. (1980) *Organization, class and control*. London: Routledge & Kegan Paul.

FOUCAULT, M. (1980) *Power/knowledge: selected interviews and other writings 1972–1977* (ed C. Gordon). New York: Pantheon Books.

WEBER, M. (1970) Class, status, party (Wirtschaft und Gesellschaft, part III, chap. 4, pp631–640). In H.H. Gerth and C. Wright Mills (eds) *From Max Weber: essays in sociology*. London: Routledge & Kegan Paul.

WITTGENSTEIN, L. (1922) *Tractatus logico-philosophicus*. London: Routledge & Kegan Paul.

WITTGENSTEIN, L. (1967) *Philosophical investigations* (trans G.E.M. Anscombe). 3rd ed. Oxford: Basil Blackwell.

The foundations of organisation theory

INTRODUCTION

Commercial organisations have existed for as long as civilisation has existed. We know of early organisations primarily from their accounting records. Accounting records dating back to ancient civilisations have been located, including building accounts for the Parthenon in Athens, which have been found on marble tablets. Similarly, ancient Greek records exist illustrating an early form of stewardship accounting known as 'charge and discharge accounting': charge representing the amounts received and discharge being the amount expended (de Ste Croix 1956). This system was further developed in Italy throughout the thirteenth and fourteenth centuries.

These organisations were, however, essentially very small and the need for theories of organisation did not exist. For example, the process outputs for a textile business include spinning, weaving and finishing. In the past each of these activities had been carried out by separate craftsmen operating in their own right and with their process outputs being exchanged in the market via merchants. It was only from the late 1700s onwards that a number of influencing factors on the development of commercial organisations resulted in change. Entrepreneurs believed that bringing the various processes associated with a single activity, such as textiles, within the control of one centrally organised hierarchy would result in greater profits. In so doing, however, a need was created to control the efficiency of the processes when combined and to attach an internal price, or more precisely a cost, to the processes now performed within the hierarchy. These systems thus provided quasi-market metrics that enabled managers to gauge the efficiency of the economic activity taking place within the organisation.

MEASURING EFFICIENCY

This ability to measure efficiency was predicated in the certainty arising from the Copernican idea of the clockwork universe in which time was itself a certainty that could be measured. This point was argued by Sombert (1915), who stated:

> Thought in economic activities then becomes more definite and conscious, in other words, more rational, and modern science has tended to make it so. But it has also helped to make it more exact and punctual, by providing the necessary machinery for measuring time.

Other factors were influencing the form of organisations in society, and affecting not just commercial organisations but also government – which up to this time had also been small. Thus the Napoleonic Wars placed a huge financial burden on the UK. The government response to this was the introduction of taxes on income, including that of businesses. This new tax burden created an incentive for businesses to maintain detailed accounting records.

Secondly, the coming of the transport systems – canals and then the railways – in the eighteenth and nineteenth centuries created the demand for substantial funding, beyond the resources of any individual. To satisfy this demand, companies were formed whose shares

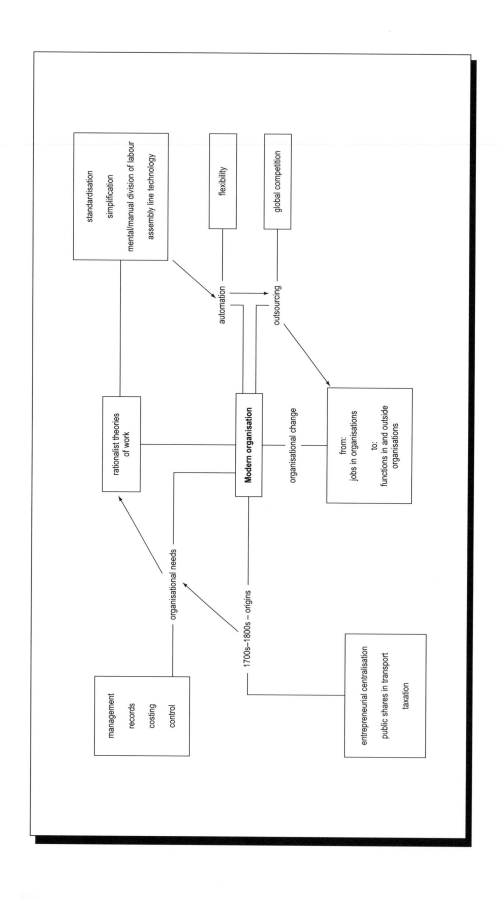

were sold to the wider public. Widespread ownership of shares in the canal and railway companies meant that it was no longer feasible for all shareholders to be involved in the active management of the enterprise: this task was delegated to professional company managers.

Nineteenth-century entrepreneurs arranged for processes that had previously been organised and priced in the market to be brought within the control of one organisation. This influenced the development of cost management systems (Johnson and Kaplan 1987), which emphasised the need to control the level of input resources consumed, particularly labour, per unit of output. Different industries developed control measures to match and serve their own particular requirements: railways used cost per ton-mile; distributors/retailers used gross margins and stock turnover. Johnson and Kaplan describe how cost accounting developments were created to serve the needs created by other organisational and procedural changes that were occurring in the late nineteenth and early twentieth centuries.

THE DEVELOPMENT OF ORGANISATION THEORY

The preceding explanation might suggest that the development of modern organisations was driven entirely by accounting. While accounting is important to an understanding of this development it is by no means the only factor. At a similar time Adam Smith produced his famous book *The Wealth of Nations*, which argued for the division of labour as a means of increasing industrial efficiency. Indeed Adam Smith (1776) questioned the ability and motivation of the directors of such a company to conduct the oversight of the assets of the company in an honest manner, stating:

> being the managers rather of other people's money than of their own, it cannot well be expected that they should look over it with the same anxious vigilance with which the partners of a private copartnery frequently watch over their own.

Recently there has also been much talk in the business press concerning managerial behaviour, with a suggestion that managers tend to pursue their own interests rather than those of the shareholders upon whose behalf they are employed to manage a business.

Given that managers have both the ability to commit the organisation to whatever contracts and transactions they feel appropriate and a responsibility towards the owners of the business, there was a need to ensure that this responsibility was exercised. It is normally accepted that agency theory provides a platform upon which this can be ensured. Agency theory suggests that the management of an organisation is undertaken on behalf of the owners of that organisation – in other words, the shareholders.

This view of an organisation has, however, been extensively challenged by many writers, who argue that the way to maximise performance for society at large is both to manage on behalf of all stakeholders and to ensure that the value thereby created is not appropriated by the shareholders but is distributed to all stakeholders. Others such as Kay (1998) argue that this debate is sterile and that organisations maximise value creation not out of concern for either shareholders or stakeholders but by focusing upon the operational objectives of the firm and assuming that value creation and equitable distribution will thereby follow.

RATIONAL ORGANISATION

Just as the use of professional managers motivated and rewarded according to agency theory was seen as a rational approach to dealing with the increasing size of firms, so too were other organisational theories. The earliest of these were concerned with what has become known as scientific management – an approach developed by Frederick Winslow Taylor. Taylor is best known for his notion of 'one best way' of utilising labour and material resources, measured in terms of physical units. He aimed to standardise and simplify jobs by breaking them down into individual elements which could then be distributed among workers so that each performed one job – but performed it efficiently and without thought. As Taylor (1911, p59) stated:

> Now one of the very first requirements for a man who is fit to handle pig iron as a regular occupation is that he shall be so stupid and phlegmatic that he more nearly resembles in his mental make up the ox than any other type. The man who is mentally alert and intelligent is for this very reason entirely unsuited to what would, for him, be the grinding monotony of work of this character.

Taylor's scientific management was based upon a clear ideological position that placed a sharp division between physical and mental work. Over time this became established as a division between manual labour and clerical/administrative work – with different pay and conditions for each.

Taylor's work led to a whole field of study of operations in organisations. This field was known as work study or as time and motion study. The objective of this work was to place the operations involved in the work process on a scientific basis by devising the best (ie most efficient) way of doing each task. A further area of organisational development that came from Taylor's work was the organisation of operations into an assembly line production system. This method was devised by Henry Ford and is related in that it is concerned with attempting to find the most efficient form of organising.

It is often forgotten that Taylor was concerned not just with the most efficient form of work organisation but also with how the financial rewards of this increased efficiency were distributed. For him the workers involved should share in the increased profit resulting from increased efficiency. Thus in the Bethlehem Steel company in which he was employed, the results of his scientific approach to organisation were that productivity per person increased by 350 per cent but the pay of the employees also went up by 65 per cent. This can be contrasted with more modern approaches to designing cost reductions by more efficient operations. The results of similar changes in the 1980s were that productivity per person increased while remuneration decreased – with all the benefit accruing to the employers rather than being shared.

THE NEW FORMS OF ORGANISING

A logical extension of this concern with rational forms of organising and the consequent increases in efficiency has been the development of automation in the production process. Automation has the joint aims of reducing direct labour and ensuring consistency of output. However, whilst automation may reduce the requirements for direct employees it increases the demand for employees with the ability to programme and maintain the equipment. So as direct labour decreases with automation, back-up staff, categorised as overhead, actually increase in proportionate terms. There are varying degrees of automation, ranging from the isolated use of computer numerically controlled (CNC) machines and robotics through to the use of computer-integrated manufacturing (CIM) (see later for explanations of these terms). Manufacturing is moving inexorably towards CIM and 'dark factory' production and thus the trend towards continued replacement of direct labour by skilled software staff seems inevitable. We will consider these aspects of automation in detail later in this chapter. Automation inevitably requires increasing capital investment in the operational processes of a plant and increases costs in this respect. Automation, however, also reduces the amount of labour necessary to operate the various processes involved in the firm's operations and so the direct labour component of product cost has been diminishing as firms increasingly automate.

These changes have had the effect of changing the nature of operating a business and have helped it meet the modern requirements of flexibility and customisation. The modern environment can be characterised by:

- shorter production runs
- increasing product development and customisation
- shortening product life cycles
- continuous improvement and innovation.

These changes have been to a large extent imposed upon business in seeking to respond to an increasingly global marketplace and to respond to the challenges posed by the economies of the Far East, which are characterised by capital intensiveness and low labour costs. Responding to this challenge has posed many problems to business managers involved in production, but also in other areas of management activity such as marketing. The techniques that have evolved are collectively known as advanced manufacturing technology (AMT) and can be classified into two types:

- techniques of manufacture using more advanced technology
- techniques of production planning and scheduling.

Advanced manufacturing technology

Rather than being a technique itself, AMT is a collective expression encompassing a variety of techniques that have been introduced into manufacturing. As stated previously these techniques include both those designed to change the way in which a product is manufactured and techniques to assist in the planning and implementation of production. Thus the techniques include both equipment and planning tools. The use of AMT enables a firm to be more responsive and to:

- produce high-quality goods at low cost
- be innovative and flexible
- be able to deal with shortening product life cycles
- reduce levels of stock-holding.

These techniques thereby enable a firm to provide increasing levels of customer satisfaction.

The AMT techniques are based upon the consideration of the process of manufacturing rather than a consideration of the products produced. This approach enables a firm to be more responsive to the market needs and flexible in its product mix and production processes.

Techniques of manufacture

Computer-aided manufacturing (CAM)

Computers have increasingly been introduced into manufacturing for the control of production machinery. This can be seen in its most basic form as CNC machines but increasingly is manifest in the use of robotics. These machines have the advantage of being able to perform many functions and having reduced set-up and tool-changing times. Such machines have therefore increased the flexibility of manufacturing and reduced the need for direct labour. CAM has also had the effect of introducing greater control into the manufacturing process, which has led to better and more consistent quality and less wastage through scrap and the need for the reworking of items of output. It has also resulted in fewer machines being needed to perform the various production processes and in reduced machine set-up times, thereby increasing productivity.

Flexible manufacturing systems (FMS)

A flexible manufacturing system is a highly automated manufacturing process capable of producing components in an automated manner, moving these components from tool to tool as needed and assembling them to form finished products. Such a system contains a combination of CNC machines and robots, linked together by automated materials handling equipment. In an FMS environment therefore there is less need for human intervention and the direct labour component of a product made in this environment is extremely low. The ultimate aim of FMS is the complete automation of a whole factory, known as computer-integrated manufacturing (CIM).

Computer-integrated manufacturing (CIM)

This is the 'dark factory' concept mentioned earlier. The concept of CIM is that raw materials are introduced at the appropriate point in the manufacturing process but that this process operates as a whole without manual intervention up to the stage at which finished products roll off the end of the process. Such a concept therefore involves no direct labour in the manufacturing process and substitutes instead indirect labour in the form of production controllers, often located in a separate room, who oversee the manufacture at a distance through the use of computer monitoring systems. Although major steps have been taken in this direction in a variety of industries it is probably realistic to state that this ultimate system, totally devoid of direct labour input, has not yet been achieved in any production environment. The rate of progress of technology is however such that it can only be a matter of a limited amount of time before a true CIM system is implemented.

Computer-aided design (CAD)

Computers are increasingly being used both to design finished products and to plan and design the components that make up that final product. CAD speeds up the design process by allowing the design to be modified as needed throughout the process without the need to start again. It also enables a database of standard parts to be incorporated into the design process and this can lead to simplified design and reduced costs by the use of standard components, thereby minimising stock-holding. CAD thus speeds up the design process, simplifies product development and speeds up the rate at which new products can be introduced. It also increases the range of variations which can be designed into the product range to meet the individual needs of customers, thereby enabling the mass customisation concept needed in the current global market. It is common for firms to integrate CAD with CAM, thereby reducing the lead time from product design to its manufacture and introduction into the market.

Techniques of planning production

Just-in-time manufacturing (JIT)

Just-in-time manufacturing, which will be discussed in more detail in Chapter 5, aims to match the usage of raw materials with their delivery from suppliers, thereby reducing the levels of raw materials and work in progress stocks to a minimum with the ultimate aim of reducing such stock-holding to zero. JIT production works on a demand pull basis, which seeks to ensure that components are not made until required by the next process, working backwards from the finished product through the various processes to the raw materials. This method eliminates (or at least almost totally eliminates) work in progress as it ensures that components are not completed until needed for the next process and reduces the need for raw materials held in stock to a minimum. Reduced costs are achieved by a firm using JIT due to the reduced investment in stock, space savings from inventory reduction and reduced manufacturing time through the elimination of waste at intermediary stages in the production system. JIT is an approach that attempts to move the manufacturing environment away from a job or batch processing environment towards a repetitive processing environment and hence is only appropriate when this type of environment exists. This technique is considered in detail later in this chapter.

Materials requirement planning (MRP)

Materials requirement planning is a computerised scheduling tool, with the objective of maintaining a smooth flow of production. Its aim is to schedule the production of components and the ordering of raw materials by ordering the schedule of processing for each machine tool within the factory so that the final output is maximised from minimal stock levels and with maximum speed. It thereby ensures that the various machines used in production are utilised to best effect. At the same time MRP has the effect of reducing work in progress, as components are not manufactured and left waiting for the next stage in the processing cycle for the completion of other jobs. It also has the effect of reducing stock holding by maximising the efficiency of the timing of orders for parts and raw materials from external suppliers. MRP is designed to be used in any manufacturing environment rather than merely the continuous processing environment for which JIT is suitable. It is therefore more flexible and suitable to job and batch processing environments.

Manufacturing resources planning (MRPII)

MRP has been extended by MRPII which is designed to integrate the materials resource planning with machine capacity planning, factory capacity and labour scheduling. Its aim is to schedule the whole resources of the factory to achieve maximum output from the resources available and to minimise wastage, work in progress and cost while maintaining quality. MRP and MRPII therefore are techniques particularly suitable to complex manufacturing environments such as job processing or made-to-order environments when the simplifications of JIT techniques are not appropriate.

Optimised production technology (OPT)

Optimised production technology is a technique that recognises that some processes in the production cycle cause bottlenecks and limit the production capacity of the firm while others are not so critical, as they do not affect production capacity. OPT concentrates upon these bottleneck processes in the production cycle and attempts to manage the operations of the factory to best effect by managing the scheduling of work within the bottleneck processes. The objective is to manage the operations in these processes by scheduling the order of work to be processed in such a way that it enables work flow through the other production processes, and hence total output of the factory, to be maximised.

THE GROWTH OF OUTSOURCING

Global competition has ensured that Western business has had to respond to the challenge outlined above. It did this by extending the presumed rational approach to organisation and management in adopting the manufacturing techniques and philosophies applied so successfully by the Japanese. The result has radically changed the face of and restored the importance of manufacturing, which is now seen as a means of providing competitive advantage. The imperatives now emphasised are:

- quality
- reduced inventory levels
- continuous improvement of processes
- removal of all forms of waste
- an improved quality of workforce committed to the achievement of company goals.

A further extension to the seeking of a rational form of organising has developed more recently, and this is concerned with what should be handled within the firm and what is better handled by other organisations. Consequently there has been a trend for organisations to reduce their activities to core activities and to buy in other functions and services. So there has been a trend for organisations to diminish in size (ie to downsize) and to buy services from other organisations (ie to outsource) in the belief that this is more efficient (ie less costly) and therefore more rational.

What is outsourcing?

Outsourcing is defined as 'having an outside vendor provide a service that you usually perform in-house' (Laabs 1997). It is described as deciding to obtain selected goods or services from outside your company, and finding new suppliers and new ways to secure the delivery of raw materials, goods, components and services by utilising knowledge, experience and creativity of new suppliers not used previously (Kraker 1995). This transfer usually involves the transfer of operational control to the suppliers.

Outsourcing has been viewed as a form of predetermined external provision with another enterprise for the delivery of goods and/or services that would previously have been offered in-house (Domberger 1998; Finlay and King 1999)

Zhu et al (2001) define outsourcing as the process of transferring specific business functions from an employee group to a non-employee group. They also raise the question of how outsourcing can save money for a firm. Savings can be achieved because outsourcing offers certain leverages that internal departments cannot offer (Bendor-Samuel 1998). The leverage can be many-dimensional, including economies of scale, process expertise and access to expensive technology. Savings occur because the outsourcer specialises in the function that is being outsourced and is able to perform the task more efficiently and better than the internal departments of organisations.

The definitions above refer to the concept of looking for outside expertise to handle existing internal functions. The decision-making process that management must undergo when considering outsourcing hinges on a 'make or buy' philosophy. Many other variables come into the equation when management considers outsourcing any of the activities in its value chain. In today's business environment it is now possible to outsource virtually any part of an organisation's business. This possibility has led to the creation of virtual companies. These virtual companies outsource all of their activities and processes and manage the outsourcers in order to gain competitive advantage.

The rise of outsourcing

Outsourcing of non-core services by organisations has been in existence for many decades. In the postwar period, managers were encouraged by academics and consultants to conglomerate, and horizontally and vertically integrate. The reason for this was because economies of scale could be achieved. They also suggest that another reason this was encouraged was because horizontal integration provided the opportunity to exercise greater market power. The third reason given for conglomeration was that they offered the potential for greater security through increased product range. The final reason given for conglomeration was that it gave companies greater control over the cost of raw material sources and distribution channels.

By the 1970s many large and diverse companies were continually reporting disappointing financial performance and were underperforming the market. This underperformance continued into the 1980s. The continuing trend and the onset of a global recession in the 1980s led to the emergence of a consensus that corporate strategies should focus on fewer activities.

Before this economic downturn, only peripheral services such as cleaning were outsourced. It was not a service that senior managers in organisations paid much attention to. Since the 1980s outsourcing has grown rapidly. It was during the recession of the 1980s that many companies questioned the wisdom/rationale of having non-core activities in-house. Some even questioned the need to have all of their core activities in-house. Many companies soon began to outsource these services. The primary objective of this action was to reduce costs and to give these organisations competitive advantage over their rivals through lower costs. These actions were often viewed as short-term cost reductions and often these services were brought back in-house when these organisations became more profitable. Blumberg (1998) suggests that there is an underlying assumption being made that outsourcing can, by itself, reduce costs and improve efficiency.

According to Winkleman et al (1993) there are two basic drivers behind the growth of outsourcing: cost reduction and a strategic shift in the way organisations are managing their business. Gupta and Gupta (1992) suggest that there are two additional drivers behind the growth of outsourcing: market forces and technical considerations. Aarts et al (1995) added that outsourcing is led by strategic considerations to concentrate on core business activities.

Finlay and King (1999) suggest that the major influence affecting the outsourcing of product and/or services is the consideration of scale and costs. Boston Consulting Group conducted a study of more than a hundred key companies with extensive outsourcing practices to find the reasons for outsourcing and concluded that most Western companies outsource primarily to achieve savings on their overheads, or induce short-term savings. McFarlan and Nolan (1995) echoed this conclusion in their research. They argue that until the 1990s, the major reasons for outsourcing IT were primarily cost-effective access to specialised or occasionally needed computing power or systems development skills, and the avoidance of building in-house IT skills at very high costs. Others argue that the growth in indirect overhead costs which represent 'non-core competences' is the reason for the growth of outsourcing (Chalos 1994; Branda 1999).

Many other scholars and practitioners argue that global competitive pressures have positioned large companies to adopt greater market discipline (Grant 1995). As a result, companies have divested 'peripheral or supplementary' businesses in order to focus upon their 'core' business and, in turn, have vertically 'de-integrated' by increasingly outsourcing their requirements for components and business services (Grant 1995). The drive for greater efficiency has led to an increase in the number of services being outsourced by many companies.

Decisions to outsource non-core activities are now growing in importance in many companies. The drivers for these remain the same, but decisions to outsource are now viewed as longer-term decisions. Many organisations now view outsourcing as necessary in order to improve the competitive pressures that squeeze profit margins and eliminate investments in fixed infrastructure. By concentrating on core activities, organisations are better able to meet customer needs at lower costs, and this enables organisations to remain competitive.

Outsourcing now takes place in the global environment (see Chapter 14) in which firms operate, as much outsourcing consists in finding alternative sources from other parts of the world. At present many British and other Western firms are in the process of using the resources of the East for this purpose. Thus many skills are currently outsourced primarily from India but also increasingly from China. The basis for doing so is concerned with cost – particularly the minimisation of cost – because it is cheaper to employ skilled people in these Eastern countries. This obviously represents a scientific approach to the organisation of firms, which assumes that people are just a resource for a business to be used in the optimum way from the perspective of the business itself. Such outsourcing has been shown, however, to be a source of conflict for businesses and also for societies themselves.

CONCLUSIONS

The earliest approach to organisation theory was based upon the assumption that there was a single best way of organising the factors of production, and was brought about by the increasing size and complexity of these organisations. Initially it was based upon the organisation of jobs within an organisation and was known as scientific management – on the basis that science equated to rationality. Although other approaches to management and organisation have been introduced since, as we will see in subsequent chapters, this approach has not been superseded and still plays a significant role in organisation theory. Over time, however, the emphasis has changed from that of organising jobs within the organisation to organising functions – either within the organisation or within the wider environment in which the organisation operates.

SUMMARY

- The development of commercial organisations with varied processes controlled centrally led to a need to control processes through measurement.
- Modern production is concerned with product innovation, product development and short product life cycles. Its emphasis is on short product runs and rapid changes in manufacturing times.

- As the manufacturing environment has changed so have processes of organising needed to change to meet the changed business needs.
- This led to the development of rationalist management approaches:
  - measurement and standardisation
  - distinctions between mental and manual work
  - automation, with replacement of direct labour by computer-skilled staff
  - advanced manufacturing technology (AMT) responding to global markets, requiring flexibility and customisation
  - outsourcing to reduce costs and improve efficiency.
- AMT is a term used to describe manufacturing methods that have been introduced into modern businesses. Such techniques include:
  - computer-aided manufacture (CAM)
  - flexible manufacturing systems (FMS)
  - computer-aided design (CAD)
  - just-in-time manufacturing (JIT)
  - materials requirement planning (MRP)
  - manufacturing resources planning (MRPII)
  - optimised production technology (OPT).

FURTHER READING

CLUTTERBUCK, D. and CRAINER, S. (1988) *The decline and rise of British industry*. London: W.H. Allen & Co.

JOHNSON, H.T. and KAPLAN, R.S. (1987) *Relevance lost: the rise and fall of management accounting*. Harvard, Mass: Harvard Business School Press.

MEREDITH, J.R. (1992) *The management of operations: a conceptual emphasis*. London: John Wiley & Son Inc.

REFERENCES

AARTS, J.C., CHEON, M.I. and GROVER, V. (1995) Decisions to outsource information systems functions: testing a strategy-theoretic discrepancy model. *Decisions Sciences*, Vol. 26, No. 1, pp. 75–103.

BENDOR-SAMUEL, P. (1998) *The brave new world of outsourcing*. Available at http://www.outsourcing-journal.com/issues/may1998/html/everest.html.

BLUMBERG, N. (1998) Beyond outsourcing: managing IT resources as a value centre. *Sloan Management Review*, spring, Vol. 39, No. 3, pp. 51–64.

BRANDA, D. (1999) More firms outsource high-availability systems. *Computing Canada*, Vol. 25, No. 34, 26–27.

CHALOS, G.C. (1994) Costing control and strategic analysis in outsourcing decisions. *Journal of Cost Management*, Vol. 8, No. 4, 31–37.

DE STE CROIX, G.E.M. (1956) Greek and Roman accounting. In A.C. Littleton and B.S. Yamey (eds) *Studies in the history of accounting*. London: Sweet & Maxwell.

DOMBERGER, S. (1998) *The contracting organisation: a strategic guide to outsourcing.* Oxford: Oxford University Press.

FINLAY, P.N. and KING, R.M. (1999) IT outsourcing: a research framework. *International Journal of Technology Management*, Vol. 17, No.1–2, 109–128.

GRANT, R.M. (1995) *Contemporary strategy analysis*. Cambridge: Blackwell Business.

GUPTA, U.G. and GUPTA, A. (1992) Outsourcing the IS function: is it necessary for your organisation? *Information Systems Management*, summer, 44–50.

JOHNSON, H.T. and KAPLAN, R.S. (1987) *Relevance lost: the rise and fall of management accounting*. Harvard, Mass: Harvard Business School Press.

KAY, J (1998) Good business. *Prospect*, Vol. 28, March, 25–29.

KRAKER, F. (1995) *The truth about outsourcing* (eds B. Roherty and I. Robertson). Aldershot: Gower.

LAABS, J. (1997) *Why HR is turning to outsourcing*. Workforce On-line Research Centre. Available from www.workforce.com.

McFARLAN, F.W. and NOLAN, R.L. (1995) How to manage IT outsourcing alliance. *Sloan Management Review*, Vol. 36, No. 2, Winter, 9–23.

SOMBERT, W. (1915) *The quintessence of modern capitalism*. New York: E.P. Dutton & Co.

TAYLOR, F.W. (1911) *Principles of scientific management*. New York: Harper.

WINKLEMAN, L., FITZGERALD, G. and FEENY, D. (1993) Outsourcing IT: the strategic implications. *Long Range Planning*, Vol. 26, No. 5, pp. 59–70.

ZHU, Z., HSU, K. and LILLIE, J. (2001) Outsourcing – a strategic move: the process and the ingredients for success. *Management Decision*, Vol. 39, No. 5, 373–378.

Rationalist theories of organisational behaviour

INTRODUCTION

As organisations became more complex there was an obvious need for the organisation of the management of these complex organisations. This in turn led to academics developing theories concerning organisations. One of the earliest of these theorists was Max Weber (1864–1920). Weber was a sociologist who thought that it was necessary to attempt to provide a theoretical basis to the social sciences by studying modern industrial society and the increasing importance of large organisations in society. He emphasised the effects of these organisations on individuals in society. He argued that individuals would become increasingly bound by rules and therefore uncreative as they pursued the narrow specialised tasks required of these organisations. This led to his development of the theory of bureaucracy.

A bureaucracy is characterised by a number of features:

- a set of rules
- the specialisation of functions within the organisation
- the keeping of written records and documents
- a salaried staff who are distinct from the production staff and who manage the administration of the organisation
- authority being derived from the formal role within the organisation rather than from the person.

Nowadays the term is often used in a disparaging manner, but Weber saw bureaucracy as the ultimate form of rational organisation for any large enterprise. As organisations grew in size they developed into hierarchical structures with many layers of management. In such an organisation responsibility could easily be placed upon an appropriate person. Thus in the first half of the twentieth century there was a tendency for organisations in the West to increase the size of their hierarchical structure, and this was considered to be desirable. With the onset of competition from the Far East (primarily from Japan) in the 1970s, however, such an organisation was shown to be slow to change and to respond to threats from the external environment. Thus the bureaucratic form of organisation became unfashionable as new forms of organisation, based upon newer theories, were developed to respond to the newer environment. Nevertheless the idea of a rational form of organisation has continued to exist and in recent years this type of theory has been developed into the various forms of programmed change that exist.

Additionally, many of Weber's ideas concerning bureaucracy have been brought to prominence in recent years by George Ritzer (1993, 1998), who applied these theories in the development of his 'McDonaldization' thesis in which he argued that increasingly society was being broken down into narrow, specialised activities.

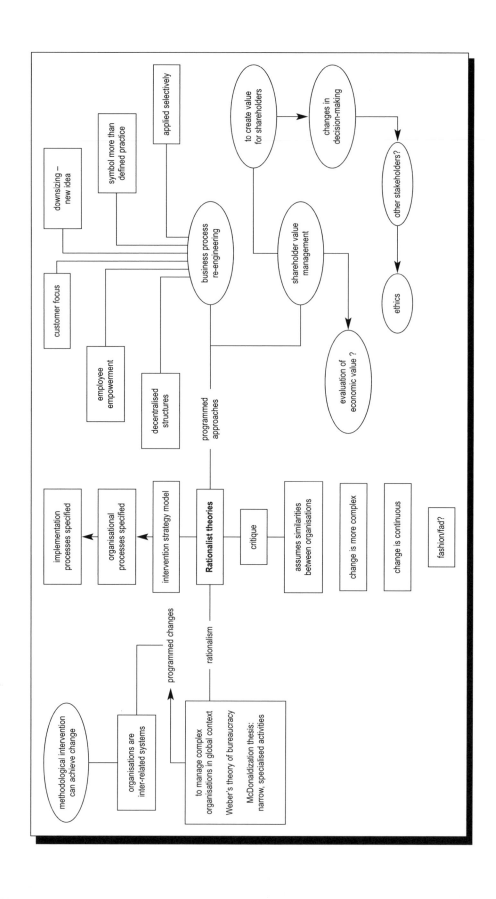

PROGRAMMED CHANGE

One way of understanding an organisation is to view the organisation as a system. A system can be defined as a set of components or activities related in such a way that the behaviour of any component will affect the status of the system. By thinking of the organisation as a system we can see that we can effect change in the organisation by affecting one part of that organisation. Moreover it enables us to think about interventions in terms of a programmed approach, in that we can effect the change that we desire through a methodical approach. This is known as a programmed approach to change and in this chapter we are going to consider three such approaches. These are known generically as programmed change initiatives, and the two we are going to consider are:

- business process re-engineering (BPR)
- shareholder value management (SVM).

We will consider the particular features of each of these initiatives and how they might be implemented. We will also consider some of the problems with such a programmed approach to managing an organisation, as well as some of the benefits. The initial benefit is of course obvious – that such a programme gives us a structured set of steps that enables us to decide how to begin any change process. Before that, however, we will consider the systems approach to change in terms of the intervention strategy model (ISM), a generic approach to considering change within an organisation.

THE INTERVENTION STRATEGY MODEL

In order to understand an organisation as a system it is necessary to understand the aspects of the organisation:

- the physical processes of the operational system
- the communications process between different parts of the system
- the monitoring process needed to maintain system stability.

The method of implementing an intervention depends upon knowing these and can be considered as three phases, each with several parts:

1 The problem definition phase
   - clarification of objectives
   - collecting all relevant data

2 The evaluation (or design) phase
   - systems analysis
   - identifying alternative solutions
   - evaluation of alternatives

3 The implementation phase
   - solution implementation
   - monitoring and appraisal.

These stages can be represented in Figure 3.1. This diagram shows that the various stages in the process operate sequentially; at each stage there is a need for evaluation and feedback that might necessitate a reworking of previous stages in the model. The environmental iteration loop, however, is designed to show that the process is never complete and an investigation of the effects of the change overall may necessitate the commencement of the process again.

This process is explained in detail by Paton and McCalman (2000) as a continuously iterative process of change, on the basis that any initiative is never complete but needs to be continually monitored and improved upon. For our purposes, however, it is sufficient to consider the change initiative in isolation as a discrete process. This understanding provides us with a means of looking at the programmed change initiatives that follow. It is argued that such initiatives provide the theory and practice to enable organisations to meet the expectations of their owners.

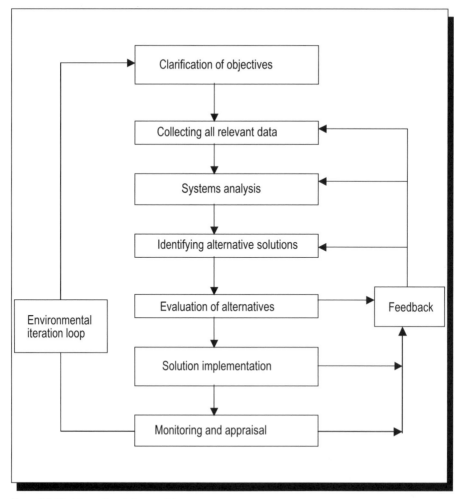

Figure 3.1 *The intervention strategy model*

BUSINESS PROCESS RE-ENGINEERING

The concept of business process re-engineering (BPR) is a relatively recent phenomenon in the business management world. Its origins can be seen to reside in the work of Hammer (1990), which was subsequently followed by Hammer and Champy's definitive text *Reengineering the corporation* (1993). Indeed the term re-engineering was trademarked by Hammer at the start of the decade. In the relatively short space of time since then, the technique has become firmly embedded within the repertoire of managerialist techniques. Indeed the concepts which underpin the practice have become centrally positioned within the power/knowledge discourse of organisational theory. BPR claims to offer radical solutions to urgent competitive pressures, and proclaims that the alternative to BPR is 'for corporate America to close its doors and go out of business' (Hammer and Champy 1993, p1). More extravagantly, BPR protagonists suggest that BPR constitutes a reversal of the Industrial Revolution.

Broadly speaking BPR can be classified as a programmed change initiative viewing organisations as being unable to respond to the competitive pressures of a global economy because of the anachronistic nature of their current organisational design. The competitive pressures described by Hammer and Champy can be characterised by the need for mass customisation, which is in response to the rise in power of the consumer, something that Hammer and Champy argue differentiated stagnant American corporations from their dynamic Japanese counterparts. There is little new in this argument, however; for instance Abernathy *et al* (1983) developed the dematurity thesis in order to explain how markets which were previously considered 'mature', to draw upon the marketing lexicon, were in the process of fragmenting. BPR is a technique, or rather a programme incorporating a loosely defined set of techniques, created in America and subsequently taken up in Britain as of value to British industry. Indeed BPR can be considered to be an America-centric concept, which is an argument developed by Grint (1994, p94) who highlights that Hammer and Champy describe the concept in the following terms:

> Reengineering thrives on the juxtaposition of what are considered as cultural affinities with Americans and cultural differences from others, especially Japanese.

Furthermore, Grint argues that if this is indeed the case then only American corporations 'are likely to experience the full benefit of reengineering' (1994, p195). If Grint is right, and certainly it is possible to support his thesis, this adds confusion to an analysis of BPR in the UK. A logical extension of this argument regarding the American rationale of BPR could be posited as follows:

> The competitive pressures in the world economy are such that the organisation needs to be totally focused on the customer, which is currently not the case. This means that radical change in the organisation is necessary to facilitate this. However, in order to bring about this change an organisation will need to adopt the American qualities of being innovative, self-starting, able to change, and willing to take risks. Because a British organisation is unlikely to display such virtues, it is therefore unlikely to benefit fully from such a change initiative.

This America-centric view of corporate life is a reflection of the American view of life in general and the implicit acceptance that the ultimate state of the world will be in accordance with the American ideal. This can be seen also in other writings emanating from America, such as Fukuyama's (1992) argument concerning the end of history, which implicitly accepts that stability for the world will ensue from the arrival of the American political ideal of liberal democracy as the norm for the political organisation of any society. However, Fukuyama also argues that liberalism is not in itself sufficient for continuity and that traditional organisations have a tendency to atomise in the pursuance of the ends of the individuals who have aggregated for the purpose that the organisation fulfils. This can be contrasted with Hammer and Champy's view of BPR as the final state of history as far as organisational activity is concerned. Indeed BPR as expounded by its proponents can be considered to be the one metanarrative that not only explains organisational existence and behaviour but also leads the organisation into the future.

We can only imagine that this America-centric part of Hammer and Champy's (1993) text has been downplayed by management consultants as they hawk their BPR nostrums around the conceptual landscape of corporate Britain. In this respect BPR can be seen to differ significantly from previously promulgated change initiatives. Indeed one of the characteristics of such previously programmed change initiatives has been the lack of spatial imprinting, so that an initiative can come from nowhere to travel everywhere (see Clegg and Hardy 1996). Such was the case with total quality marketing (TQM) and other, earlier, programmed change initiatives.

The elements of BPR

BPR claims to offer radical solutions that embrace survival in the contemporary business environment. An examination of Hammer and Champy's text identifies ten elements of BPR, namely:

1 Process teams replacing functional departments
2 Multi-skilled workers instead of single-skilled workers
3 Employee empowerment instead of top-down power relationships
4 Education being regarded as more important than training
5 Payment being made for value added performance and not attendance
6 Advancement for individuals through an assessment of ability and not based on current performance
7 Customer focus replacing a management focus
8 Management style changing to resemble a coaching style rather than a supervisory style
9 The flattening of organisational structures
10 Executives becoming leaders rather than merely scorekeepers.

In many respects these elements comprising the distinguishing features of BPR are not new and all have been promulgated in the past; these elements are considered variously in the work of Drucker (1981, 1985), Peters and Waterman (1982), Handy (1994) and many other management experts. It is only the aggregated package of elements, when taken as a whole, that distinguishes BPR from other earlier initiatives. It is perhaps self-evident that any theory of organisational behaviour must take into account the fact that organisations consist of people who plan, control and manage a business and also interact with each other, and Likert (1967) advocates a recognition of the human element of management. Indeed Grint (1994) suggests that there is little originality in many of these activities, certainly not enough to substantiate the claims made on behalf of BPR. This view is supported by Blair et al (1997, p4) who view BPR as representing 'continuity in organisational theory rather than radical departure'. Indeed such is the resonance between BPR and initiatives such as TQM and the 'excellence' genre that Ball and Carter (1997) lump them together in the catch-all phrase of 'new managerialism'. Table 3.1 shows the resonance between BPR and earlier initiatives.

One respect in which BPR does differ from previous techniques, however, is in its emphasis on information technology in enabling the new organisational design. Another area of difference is the abandonment of the incrementalist position of TQM in favour of the radical implementation strategy overseen by a change agent. However, this hardly gives credence to the claims that BPR marks a radical rupture with the past.

Indeed even the central argument of Hammer and Champy that American corporations must change in order to succeed in competition with their Japanese counterparts is not a new argument. This argument has in fact pervaded the management literature for the past 20 years with various writers proposing methods of overcoming this perceived problem. Various solutions have been proposed and, for example, Ouchi (1981) advocates a change in management style to include communication, involvement of people and trust in relationships, suggesting that while these were present in the best-run American companies they were missing from others. He labelled this theory as theory Z to distinguish it from, and imply its superseding of, theories X and Y of McGregor (1960) concerning human behaviour, and implying that there was a logical progression in understanding human behaviour in the work place from theory X to Y to Z. In this respect his arguments ran counter to the prevailing

Table 3.1 *BPR and earlier organisational theory initiatives*

BPR	Earlier initiatives
Process teams	Matrix organisations
	TQM
Multi-skilled	Flexible specialisation
	Japanisation
Empowerment	TQM
	Quality circles
Education and training	Postmodernism
Customer focus	Marketing theory
Coaching	McGregor theory Y
	TQM
Flattening of structures	Tom Peters – bureaucracy is 'out'
Executives as leaders	Enterprise culture
	Peters
	Handy

concerns of the time; such concerns have not, however, died away and indeed have been resurrected by Hammer and Champy in order to provide an underlying justification for their new initiative. Again it can be seen to provide a reflection of the American view of the world as insular, isolationist and threatened by anything that challenges their hegemony.

Critiquing BPR

BPR was trademarked by Hammer and this in effect created BPR as a concept, although there is nothing new within the concept in terms of distinctive elements or routines. Nevertheless the concept exists and has entered the lexicon of management both in America and in the UK. In this respect it can be argued that the concept of BPR exists because it is believed to exist rather than because it is a clearly identified concept in its own right. This tendency to create new concepts and techniques through labelling and trademarking can be considered to be a characteristic of American capitalist society.

As BPR does not consist of a discrete set of unique activities to distinguish the concept from other change programmes it is unsurprising that organisations claiming to have adopted BPR tend to have in fact adopted their own version of BPR and selected techniques from within its repertoire that meet the needs of their own organisation. Indeed Hewitt and Yeon (1996) found from a study of UK companies undertaking re-engineering that they shared a common vision that they were undertaking BPR, which was desirable, but little in the way of techniques. More particularly Hammer and Stanton (1995) change the definition to compensate for the statement made by Hammer and Champy (1993) that 50–70 per cent of re-engineering efforts were not successful. This redefinition means that if the re-engineering fails it is because it is not done correctly. By implication therefore true BPR must succeed and is redefined as a symbol of success.

Thus BPR can be viewed as merely a symbol for change within an ambiguous context of reaction to the changing external environment – a symbol requiring no justification, as the justification is embedded in the symbol as representation of reality. In view of this lack of commonality of approach it is reasonable to argue that these techniques have been adopted for entirely different purposes and collated under the BPR banner in order to give legitimacy to activities which have been undertaken for other reasons. In this context therefore the concept of BPR tends to mean different things to different organisations, so the images, spectacles and signs of the concept dominate the actual content.

It is, for example, possible to argue that some of the rationale for the use of the techniques revolves around the creation of returns to shareholders in the present through downsizing the organisation, restructuring its processes and gathering power at the centre. Often this value creation is achieved, not through any changes in value-creating activities but merely through temporally externalising the consequent costs into the future. The myth-creating role of BPR, however, establishes an image of a more dynamic organisation that will perform better in the future, and as such BPR provides a legitimating vehicle for such changes that meet the needs of present management.

SHAREHOLDER VALUE MANAGEMENT

Finance theory has long assumed that the primary objective of the firm is to maximise shareholder wealth, and that a firm will seek to achieve this by making decisions that create shareholder value. Companies often pay lip-service, however, to shareholder value, and whilst they may publicly espouse their commitment to shareholders' interests, internal systems often remain driven by other rationales. It is perhaps for this reason that new techniques have been developed that are more explicitly concerned with the creation of value for shareholders. Thus in recent years there has been a shift towards a more explicit shareholder value-oriented approach to managing a business which has become known as shareholder value management (SVM) or value-based management (VBM). VBM has been defined as:

> an approach to management whereby the company's overall aspiration, analytical techniques and management processes are all aligned to help the company maximise its value by focusing on the key drivers of value.
>
> (Copeland *et al* 1996, p96)

SVM is an approach to managing an organisation that requires a change in the way decisions are made from the way they are normally made. It is for this reason that it has been classed here as a programmed change initiative – not because it is a way of managing change but rather because it is a way of managing a business which results in change. It is based simply upon the premise that all actions within the organisation must be made based upon the desire to maximise shareholder value. Thus it requires the application of appropriate measures of value to provide a 'shareholder value' perspective for all key internal planning and control systems: strategic decision-making, resource allocation, performance measurement and control, and managerial compensation.

An increasing number of US companies, including Coca-Cola and Quaker Oats, are reported to have adopted this approach, and it is attracting growing interest in the UK, where a significant number of large companies have embraced the concept and techniques of VBM. Evidence of this interest has been confirmed through recent survey evidence (Coopers & Lybrand 1996; Deloitte & Touche 1996; KPMG 1996; PA Consulting 1997; KPMG 1998).

As stated above, finance theory suggests that the primary objective of the firm is to maximise shareholder wealth. It has been argued that the pursuit of this objective not only benefits shareholders but also maximises, through the natural workings of the free market, the value created in a business for other stakeholders. There has been, however, increasing debate on the validity of this argument and it has been suggested that shareholder value is in fact actually maximised through an expropriation of value from other stakeholders in the business. This is to say that if shareholder value is maximised then this must be at the expense of the other stakeholders such as employees, consumers, government and community/society. If this latter view is accepted then, it has been further argued, firms are behaving unethically. There has as a result been an increased interest in ethics and stakeholder management theory, which suggests that the firm should be managed with reference to the needs of all of the different stakeholders. However, despite the attention stakeholders have received in theory, there appears to be limited work suggesting how stakeholder management can be achieved and how it would work in practice.

Internal planning for value maximisation

An important, if not fundamental, feature of all approaches to performance management is the alignment of objectives, measures, strategic decision-making and rewards intended to promote value creation at all levels of the business (Cornelius and Davies 1997). The need for this alignment of the internal planning and control systems is not new. If we firstly consider the alignment of objectives and measures we can see that in the management accounting literature Emmanuel *et al* (1990, p1) suggest that:

> In order to measure organizational performance, it is first necessary to discover what the organization is attempting to achieve.

Therefore the link between the aims/objectives of an organisation and performance measures needs to be made clear. In addition they suggest that the 'multiple nature of objectives' can generate the need for multiple performance measures. Furthermore, as objectives tend to be conflicting, the measures used can require trade-offs and composite measures. This in fact highlights one of the suggested advantages of the VBM approach, as it provides a single overriding objective that should not require any such trade-offs.

If we consider significant decision-making then this is an area that has already been aligned with the shareholder objective in finance theory. Brignall and Ballantine (1996) suggest that the Fisher–Hirshleifer model (Fisher 1930; Hirshleifer 1958) has shown that shareholder wealth is maximised 'by investing in all projects offering a positive Net Present Value (NPV)'. It is important to note here that many organisations have shareholder value as an objective, and many (80 per cent according to a 1997 UK survey; Arnold 1998) also use NPV as a decision-making criterion because it is consistent with shareholder value, but this is not sufficient to make them a VBM company. As mentioned above, VBM goes further in terms of requiring shareholder value to be the primary, if not the only, objective and that the whole internal planning and control system should be consistent with this, not just the decision-making. This may seem technical, and the techniques of SVM can become very complicated, but this is sufficient for our needs. All we need is to understand the rationale for the techniques and the implications for the management of change.

Rappaport (1986) considered the concept of shareholder value and how this can be created and sustained. He developed a methodology of shareholder value based upon his previous work, where he argues (1992) that a shareholder value approach is the correct way of evaluating alternative company strategies. He states that the ultimate test of a corporate plan is whether it creates value for the shareholders, and that this is the sole method of evaluating performance. This is based upon the assumption that maximising the value of a firm to its shareholders also maximises the value of that firm to society at large. Within the discourse therefore the concept of shareholder value is frequently mentioned and there is acceptance of the need to account for shareholder value within the practitioner community. Indeed the annual reports of companies regularly expound the virtue of creating value for shareholders and it is frequently cited as a corporate objective. This objective can simply be defined as being achieved when the rate of return obtained within a business exceeds the cost of obtaining funds.

Shareholder value in practice

The concept of shareholder value as an objective appears to be widely accepted within the business community but its use as a quantified evaluation is less often found in practice. A recent development in the quest for a tool to measure shareholder value has been the concept of economic value added, which has been developed by Stewart (1991) as a better measure to assess corporate performance and the creation of shareholder value than conventional accounting measures. Indeed Stewart (1994, p73) states that:

> Economic value added is an estimate, however simple or precise, of a business's true economic profit.

Mechanisms for calculating economic value added are described by Stewart (1991), who elaborates the standard adjustments needed to transform accounting information into an economic value added[1] calculation. A definition of economic value added can be given simply

---

1 The term 'economic value added' is copyrighted as the property of Stern Stewart & Co.

as operating profits after tax less a charge for capital used to generate these profits. The residual from this calculation is the measure of economic value added, and if positive, demonstrates that the company has earned a greater return on its capital employed than the opportunity cost of the capital employed, and has hence added value to the company from the viewpoint of shareholders. Opportunity cost is defined in this context simply as the market cost of capital, appropriately weighted between equity and debt capital. If negative, the opposite is the case and value has been lost.

Associated with economic value added is the measure market value added[2] which is defined by Stewart (1991) as the market value of the company (ie stock price x shares outstanding) minus the economic book value of the capital employed. Stewart argues that this measure is superior to just using market value as a means of assessing the value-creating performance of a company because market value can be increased simply by investing as much capital as possible, without consideration of the returns to be achieved from this investment. In theory, market value added should reflect the present value of expected future value added and thereby provide a measure of the expectation of shareholder value created. In practice, this relationship is not as simple as this, because of the factors affecting the operation of the market. It is therefore argued by proponents of these kinds of shareholder value analysis techniques that both measures need to be considered together in order to evaluate the value of the techniques of shareholder value analysis in assessing company performance. The two measures together are therefore taken as a representation of shareholder value.

Govindarajan and Gupta (1985) argue that long-run criteria contribute to organisational effectiveness rather than short-term criteria, whereas Rappaport (1986, 1992) suggests that shareholder value analysis addresses both and maximises both. There is, nevertheless, a considerable body of evidence that suggests otherwise and that a concern with shareholder value added and returns to shareholders leads to a short-term focus and lack of regard for the longer term (eg Coates *et al* 1995). Indeed some managerial actions taken to boost short-term valuations (eg de-layering and outsourcing) can be argued to actually reduce long-term value, particularly when the product and market development capability are externalised.

The market value added concept recognises the fact that the market value of equity, and changes therein as a result of changed expectations by existing and potential investors, is an important part of the measurement of performance for investment purposes. It equally recognises, however, that the market value of equity does not by itself constitute a reliable measure of shareholder wealth creation. It does, though, seek to measure how much a firm has added to or subtracted from its shareholder investment and as such seeks to measure one factor that is of significance to this group of shareholders. It does of course fail to take into account the level of dividend return to shareholders, and in this respect can be considered as completely contrasting with more traditional measures such as EPS (earnings per share), which is concerned entirely with profit attributable to ordinary shareholders. Dividend returns are of course a potentially significant source of wealth creation for shareholders, and for certain companies that adopt high dividend pay-out policies the ignoring of such dividends would significantly distort their actual wealth creation potential.

Improving performance through VBM

The proponents of shareholder value techniques would argue that the use of the techniques by an organisation will inevitably lead to better performance by that organisation, both for shareholders and for other stakeholders. Moreover they would argue that the use of the

2 The term 'market value added' is copyrighted as the property of Stern Stewart & Co.

techniques would imply the use of different measures of performance management from the traditional accounting measures used in a traditional environment. It is therefore appropriate at this point to examine these differences.

VBM has been defined by a variety of people, including Copeland, Koller and Murrin (1996), in a variety of ways which all reflect a change in approach to the management of a company which focuses on the key drivers of value within the business.

Thus this implies a different approach to management and therefore a change in organisational behaviour, as it also requires the application of appropriate measures of value to provide a 'shareholder value' perspective for all key internal planning and control systems, ie strategic decision-making, resource allocation, performance measurement and control, and managerial compensation. An important, if not fundamental, feature of all VBM approaches is this alignment of objectives, measures and rewards intended to promote shareholder value creation at all levels of the business. Advocates of VBM techniques have advanced strong claims on its behalf, the chief of which is that its use will lead to the creation of shareholder value. McTaggart *et al* (1994, p51) for example argue that VBM will:

> greatly improve the quality of decision-making, by improving the quality of the alternatives that management has to consider as well as building a bias for choosing and implementing the best available alternatives.

Stern Stewart (1995), meanwhile, claim that: 'The major benefit EVA (economic value added) firms can expect is a higher market value.' They also cite other significant benefits that will accrue from the use of the technique, stating (p5) that these are:

> a common language for planning and managing, more accountability for delivering value, a greater concern for managing assets, a greater willingness to rationalise and redirect resources, better bridges to link operations and strategy with financial results, more collaborative long-term planning.

As a further example, Copeland *et al* (1996, p98) argue that:

> the management processes ... provide decision-makers at all levels of the organisation with the right information and incentives to make value creating decisions.

These claims are extremely positive concerning the effects of VBM implementation within an organisation, but it must be remembered that the literature in this area has largely originated from the leading shareholder value consultants (ie Rappaport 1986; Stewart 1991; McTaggart *et al* 1994; Copeland *et al* 1996) who arguably stand to gain the most from the widespread adoption of their preferred techniques. If we now consider the use of VBM techniques in practice we see that little is known about how these concepts are in fact applied, and the problems practitioners experience in trying to implement a VBM approach. An international survey of shareholder value management issues, conducted by Coopers & Lybrand in 1996, for example, found that in the UK there is still great uncertainty on how to apply VBM principles throughout a company. Key issues identified included the perceived complexity of the techniques, the need for cultural change to coincide with adoption of the techniques, implementation difficulties and perceived problems with the application in both corporate headquarters and particular types of business such as research and development-driven companies. More generally recent survey evidence (Coopers & Lybrand 1996; Deloitte & Touche 1996; KPMG 1996; PA Consulting 1997; KPMG 1998) indicates that whilst there is a growing interest in VBM/shareholder value and a recognition of its importance, it is neither widely used nor well understood. These surveys have found that contrary to 'VBM theory' few companies have successfully applied 'full VBM' and also that profit-based measures are often used alongside shareholder value measures. The failure to apply 'full VBM' refers to companies in practice not applying VBM techniques consistently across all of the key internal planning and control systems, from decision-making through to managerial compensation.

CRITIQUE OF PROGRAMMED CHANGE

A programmed approach to change starts from the assumption – as the name suggests – that change can be programmed and implemented by following a set of steps. This is particularly the case for the techniques we have considered in this chapter. This implies that all organisations are basically similar and thus change can be implemented in the same manner. The systems approach is based upon this cause–effect approach, assuming that if we understand the variables of a situation we can predict the output from a given input. Thus we can implement change successfully if we understand our organisation and its environment sufficiently. In reality things are not of course that simple and so successful change management cannot be reduced to a few common steps within a programme of change. If it were that simple then we would not need to study this in depth. For each of the techniques we have considered in this chapter we have shown that they are developed by consultants (who perhaps have a vested interest in promoting their own creations) and there is questionable evidence concerning how successful the techniques have been.

Of further concern perhaps is that such techniques come into fashion very quickly but are readily supplanted by newer techniques. Thus TQM has been supplanted by BPR while SVM is currently becoming more popular. What will happen in the future? If these techniques were really able to help us all manage change then they would not need to be replaced by newer techniques.

A further problem with these techniques is that they are premised on a belief that one single large-scale change is all that is needed in an organisation, followed by a period of reaping the benefits of that change. Change is of course a continuous process, and we shall return to this in later chapters.

CONCLUSIONS

The rational approach to organisation was developed to meet the needs of the larger, more complex organisations that were coming into existence at the end of the nineteenth century. These approaches were essentially complementary to the scientific approaches considered in the last chapter. Like these approaches they are still in use today, as there is still a general belief that there is a best way of organising that is suitable for all organisations. Nevertheless, these approaches have been shown to be deficient in some respects. In particular these approaches ignore people, or at least the fact that people are different and have different objectives and motivations. Scientific and rational approaches tend to treat people just as factors of production who can be manipulated and employed to the benefit of the organisation in just the same way as raw materials or machinery.

This view of the people within organisations is obviously untrue but is still prevalent in the way people are treated in many organisations. This factor has resulted in many of the industrial conflicts that have taken place throughout the last century and still continue to take place. Nevertheless, the fact that people are individuals with needs and motivations which need to be taken into account had been recognised by organisation theorists by the middle of the twentieth century, and this led to the development of theories concerning motivation, which we shall consider in the next chapter.

SUMMARY

- The need to manage large, complex organisations led to rationalist theories.
- Weber predicted a rule-bound system – bureaucracy, with its advantages of rationalism and disadvantages of inflexibility.
- Programmed change views organisations as systems that can be changed through methodological approaches.
- We considered two programmed change initiatives:
  - business process re-engineering (BPR) – involves horizontal teamworking, multi-skilling, worker empowerment, customer focus, IT, radical change
  - shareholder value management (SVM) – aims to maximise shareholder value through performance management, alignment of objectives, measures, decisions and rewards.
- Critique: programmed change is managerialist, ignores organisation processes and employee agency.

FURTHER READING

ARNOLD, G. and DAVIES, M. (eds) (2000) *Value based management*. London: Wiley.

COOPER, S., CROWTHER, D., DAVIES, M. and DAVIS, E.W. (2001) *Shareholder or stakeholder value? The development of indicators for the control and measurement of performance*. London: CIMA.

REFERENCES

ABERNATHY, L., HIRSCHHEIM, R. and LACITY, M. (1983) *Industrial development in mature markets*. London: Kogan Page.

ARNOLD, G. (1998) *Corporate financial management*. London: Financial Times/Prentice Hall.

BALL, K. and CARTER, C. (1997) *He came, he saw, he reengineered*. Paper presented at the 15th International Labour Process conference.

BLAIR, H., TAYLOR, S.G. and RANDLE, K. (1997) *A pernicious panacea – a critical evaluation of business reengineering*. Paper presented at the 15th International Labour Process conference.

BRIGNALL, S. and BALLANTINE, J.A. (1996) *Interactions and trade-offs in multi-dimensional performance management*. Research Paper No. 247. Warwick: Warwick Business School.

CLEGG, S. and HARDY, C. (1996) Representations. In S.R. Clegg, C. Hardy and W.R. Nord (eds) *Handbook of organization studies* (pp676–708). London: Sage.

COATES, J.B., DAVIES, M.L., DAVIS, E.W., ZAFAR, A. and ZWIRLEIN, T. (1995) *Adopting performance measures that count: changing to a shareholder value focus*. Research Paper No. RP9510. Birmingham: Aston Business School.

COOPERS & LYBRAND (1996) *International survey of shareholder value management issues*.

COPELAND, T., KOLLER, T. and MURRIN, J. (1996) *Valuation: measuring and managing the value of companies*. 2nd ed. New York: John Wiley & Sons.

CORNELIUS, I.G. and DAVIES, M.L. (1997) *Shareholder value.* Financial Publishing.

DELOITTE & TOUCHE (1996) *Financial management survey.*

DRUCKER, P.F. (1981) *Managing in turbulent times.* Oxford: Butterworth-Heinemann.

DRUCKER, P.F. (1985) *Innovation and entrepreneurship.* Oxford: Butterworth-Heinemann.

EMMANUEL, C.R., OTLEY, D.T., and MERCHANT, K. (1990) *Accounting for management control.* London: Chapman & Hall.

FISHER, I. (1930) *The theory of interest.* New York: Macmillan.

FUKUYAMA, F. (1992) *The end of history and the last man.* New York: Free Press.

GOVINDARAJAN, V. and GUPTA, A.K. (1985) Linking control systems to business unit strategy: impact on performance. *Accounting, Organizations and Society*, Vol. 10, No. 1, 51–66.

GRINT, K. (1994) Reengineering history: social resonances and business process reengineering, *Organization*. Vol. 1, No 1.

HAMMER, M. (1990) Reengineering work: don't automate, obliterate. *Harvard Business Review*, July/August.

HAMMER, M. and CHAMPY, J. (1993) *Reengineering the corporation: a manifesto for business revolution.* London: Nicholas Brealey.

HAMMER, M. and STANTON, S.A. (1995) *The reengineering revolution.* London: HarperCollins.

HANDY, C. (1994) *The empty raincoat.* London: Random House.

HEWITT, F. and YEON, K.H. (1996) BPR perceptions, practices and expectations – a UK study. *Business Change and Re-engineering*, Vol. 3, No. 3, 47–55.

HIRSHLEIFER, J. (1958) On the theory of optimal investment decisions. *Journal of Political Economy*, 329–372.

KPMG (1996) *Value based management: a survey of European industry.* Brussels.

KPMG (1998) *Value based management: the growing importance of shareholder value in Europe.*

LIKERT, R (1967) *The human organisation.* New York: McGraw-Hill.

McGREGOR, D. (1960) *The human side of enterprise.* New York: McGraw-Hill.

McTAGGART, J.M., KONTES, P.W. and MANKS, M.C. (1994) *The value imperative.* New York: Free Press.

OUCHI, W.G. (1981) *Theory Z: how American business can meet the Japanese challenge.* Reading, Mass: Addison-Wesley.

PA CONSULTING. (1997) *Managing for shareholder value.*

PATON, R.A. and MCCALMAN, J. (2000) *Change management: a guide to implementation.* London: Sage.

PETERS, T.J. and WATERMAN, R.H. (1982) *In search of excellence.* New York: Harper & Row.

RAPPAPORT, A. (1986) *Creating shareholder value.* New York: Free Press.

RAPPAPORT, A. (1992) CFO's and strategists: forging a common framework. *Harvard Business Review*, May/June, 84–91.

RITZER, G. (1993) *The McDonaldization of society*. London: Pine Forge Press.

RITZER, G. (1998) *The McDonaldization thesis*. London: Sage.

STERN STEWART & CO. (1995) *The EVA company*. New York.

STEWART, G.B., III. (1991) *The quest for value: a guide for senior managers*. New York: HarperCollins.

STEWART, G.B., III. (1994) EVA, fact and fantasy. *Journal of Applied Corporate Finance*, Vol. 7, No. 2, 71–87.

A concern for people

CHAPTER 4

INTRODUCTION

The human relations approach to organisation theory arose because of dissatisfaction with the rational and scientific approaches that had preceded it. These approaches tended to assume that people all behaved in the same way and that organisations could therefore be programmed to the single best way of organising. This was recognised to be problematic, which led to the development of further theory. Unlike the theories in the previous chapters, therefore, human relations and motivation theories are about people's behaviour and feelings, and about their informal rather than formal organising.

The human relations school arose in unexpected circumstances. The main theorist in the school was Elton Mayo (1880–1949). His most famous investigation, which proved to be one of the bases for his theory, was carried out between 1927 and 1932 at the Hawthorne branch of the Western Electric Company in Chicago, where he continued a previous experiment to implement Taylor's theory of scientific management, in the sense of 'scientifically' working out the optimal lighting conditions for workers and their productivity. He set up a control group and used for his research a group of women working in the factory. He took the perhaps unusual step at that time of sharing the information about his research with the women he was investigating. Mayo performed various experiments with the lighting in order to establish the optimal situation for the highest productivity. He found that however he varied the lighting, the productivity of the women in both the research and the control group kept on rising (Pugh and Hickson 1996).

THE HUMAN RELATIONS SCHOOL

A second stage of the investigation was then undertaken by Mayo's Industrial Research team under his direction. A group of six women whose work was to assemble telephone relays was selected and subjected to various changes in their conditions of work, payment, rest pauses and refreshments. This research was known as the 'Relay Assembly Test Room'. The researchers communicated throughout with the workers and found that productivity kept on rising, even when workers returned to their original, inferior working conditions. To explain this Mayo undertook a series of interviews with employees. From this he came to the first important statement of his theory – that people's productivity was not determined by 'objective', 'scientific' factors, as had been claimed by Taylor. Mayo found that it was emotional factors that were important to workers, such as communicating with them well, helping them become involved in the organisation and making them feel wanted and important (Pugh and Hickson 1996).

The next part of the investigation was done in a natural work situation. Roethlisberger and Dickson (1939) in the 'Bank Wiring Observation Room' investigated the productivity of a number of male workers whose job it was to set up internal telephone exchanges in organisations. They investigated workers' productivity in a non-unionised and anti-union company, and found that there was an informal agreement among the workers as to what their productivity would be, and no financial incentives by the company would persuade them

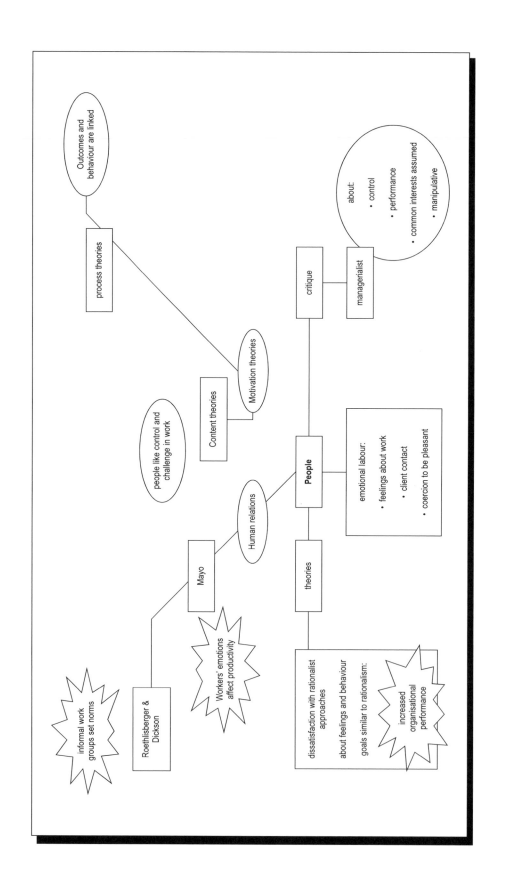

to deviate from their previously agreed standard. This has been explained in terms of the economic and job environment of the time. It was the time of one of the most serious global economic depressions of the twentieth century and unemployment was very high. Roethlisberger and Dickson's explanation for the unwavering level of productivity was that a higher output was seen as a threat to jobs (Hollway 1991).

From this came the second important precept of the human relations school: the informal social workgroup was important in setting work norms and standards. It was therefore management's task to get such groups 'on side', so that their values and goals would be in line with management's. Mayo's studies during the Second World War into absenteeism and labour turnover in a small east coast industrial city and later in aircraft plants in Southern California strengthened these ideas, and according to Clegg and Dunkerley (1980) it was this work which contributed most to the development of the human relations school. In *The Social Problems of an Industrial Civilization*, Mayo's major work, he wrote that every social group had to secure for its individual and group membership:

1   The satisfaction of material and economic needs.
2   The maintenance of spontaneous co-operation throughout the organization.
                                                    (Cited in Clegg and Dunkerley 1980, p124)

These ideas have had and are still having an enormous influence on organisation theory and management practice. It brought to the forefront the 'humanistic' aspects of work, the importance of workers' emotions and social groupings, and the importance of good communication between workers and management. There is something attractive and commonsensical about fostering workers' social and psychological needs in the workplace. It shares many ideas in common with the organisation motivation theorists' ideas in terms of the importance of social and esteem needs. Also, many later theories have based their ideas on human relations theories. The 'excellence' theories including concepts such as 'empowerment', written by 'management gurus' such as Peters and Waterman, have taken some of their important ideas from human relations approaches, as has the 'quality' movement's various strategies, such as quality circles, total quality management and 'just-in-time'.

Critique of human relations approaches

Various criticisms have been made of human relations theory. Some flaws have been found in Mayo's research. The research has been thought to have been badly designed; the experiment was not conducted rigorously with regard to the control group's conditions; output in some cases was dependent on financial incentive – the contrary to what the theory claims to be the case (Clegg and Dunkerley 1980). There are also criticisms based on the values lying behind these ideas. Although they have been represented in some textbooks as encouraging employees to be empowered in their work and organisations, the theory in fact limits involvement to good communication from managers to subordinates – so that workers feel their managers know and care about them, and so that employees are in the know about their managers' goals and strategies. There is no suggestion that there should be any serious devolution of decision-making down to the shop floor or general office. This of course raises political and ethical questions about who holds power and control, and what effect this has on the working lives of those who do not – which radical theorists are keen to explore (see eg Alvesson and Willmott 1996).

A second criticism, similar to that levelled against motivation theories, is the assumption of unitarist goals and interests between people at all levels within organisations. The importance of harnessing informal groups' values to management's organisational objectives has been disputed on moral grounds by radical theorists, who claim that there are conflictual interests between management and the workforce. The difficulties inherent in such harmonisation have been suggested by a wider group of theorists, both those in mainstream organisation theory such as Weber, Merton and Dahrendorf, who have shown dysfunctional effects in organisations of unequal power relations (Burrell and Morgan 1979), and by hermeneutic theorists, who would see difficulties in similar understandings being achieved, except with the help of time and discussion; by postmodern theorists such as Foucault, who believe that there is much activity to achieve and resist power at all interstices of organisations; and by poststructuralists, who believe that structures and processes are ambiguous and open to various interpretations and enactments, and are never as clear as they might look on paper (Alvesson and Skoldberg 2000).

Cynics have pointed out that this theory is likely to be welcomed by managers because it comes cheap. Unlike Taylor's and some of the motivation theorists' ideas mentioned below, workers are here supposedly motivated without having to be paid more for increased productivity. Radical theorists have linked the importance placed on psychological factors with attempts to manipulate workers. Human relations approaches are seen by such theorists as a more sophisticated form of control than the earlier ones (direct supervision, and technological and bureaucratic control; see Edwards 1979) by encouraging the manipulation of employees through psychological means – the reverse, in fact, of their having common interests. It can also be argued that there are similarities between human relations ideas and later theories on culture and cultural control, which are also about getting employees involved in their organisations and psychologically committed to them. These later ideas will be discussed in more detail in later chapters.

MOTIVATION THEORY

Motivation theory for the workplace was developed in the middle of the twentieth century. The main idea behind the theory was that in order to achieve organisational goals, managers should find a way of taking workers' 'hearts and minds' along with them. This was at a time when organisations were growing in size and complexity and the new breed of managers (rather than the original owners of smaller-scale firms) were looking for ways of controlling the workforce and also getting maximum productivity from it.

Motivation theories were in some ways very different from the classical and scientific management approaches discussed earlier and much more similar to human relations theories, as they focused on human feelings and desires, rather than on the more impersonal, technical aspects of organisations such as organisation structure and lines of command, or job design and employee selection. Although the means were different, these theories share the common goals of increased productivity, profitability or cost-effectiveness for the organisation. Some theorists, usually looking at organisational strategies from a radical point of view, have viewed motivation theories as they have human relations ideas – essentially as a different, more subtle strategy for control, and as primarily serving the interests of managers and their objectives for the organisation.

Various motivation theories were developed from the early 1940s, and variants of the idea have continued to be developed throughout the twentieth century to the present. As well as theories grouped under 'motivation', which will be discussed next, human relations, and later 'soft' human resource management approaches, neo-human relations ideas, Japanese management strategies and the management of organisational culture can all be shown to have taken their ideas from the original concept of motivating employees.

Origins of the theory

There were different strands to motivation theory, but all theories had as their basis Abraham Maslow's (1954) ideas about what he considered to be factors motivating people generally, rather than in organisations in particular. He developed the idea of a hierarchy of needs starting from physical needs and continuing onto less tangible and more intrinsic concepts to do with emotional fulfilment and achievement. Maslow argued that people would be motivated by a higher level need only when the lower one had been fulfilled. He suggested that there were five levels of need. The first or lowest level was *physiological* needs such as food, shelter, clothing and other bodily needs. It was only when these were satisfied that a person would then be motivated to secure those permanently. He called this second level *safety*. His third level was *social* – the need for acceptance, friendship and to be part of a group. His fourth was *esteem*, the feeling of self-worth and also respect from others. He called his final level *self-actualisation* – full achievement of one's potential in every sphere (Carter and Jackson 1993).

Maslow himself was not rigid about these categories. They were a suggestion for how people might feel and act. He recognised that there were strong exceptions to this model. For example, people who were very dedicated to a cause, such as a political or religious one, might well ignore the lower-level factors and give everything of themselves to their cause. Similarly an artist might prefer to starve rather than give up his or her art for a job that would get in the way of his or her true work. Maslow also did not think that self-actualisation was easily achievable, and believed probably only a very few would reach that level.

Content theories

Several theories were developed using Maslow's ideas. McGregor (1960) developed his ideas from his administrative experience as head of Antioch College in the USA. McGregor was primarily concerned with motivation from the viewpoint of managers and in his book, *The Human Side of Enterprise* (1960), stated:

> Every managerial decision has behavioural consequences. Successful management depends – not alone, but significantly – upon the ability to predict and control human behaviour.

McGregor argued that managers' behaviour towards others was influenced by their assumptions regarding human nature. He separated these assumptions into two categories and called them theory X and theory Y. These were based on Maslow's lower- and higher-level needs respectively. McGregor moved away from the classical management ideas, which assumed that it was management's role and prerogative to control employees. McGregor claimed that this approach (theory X) assumed certain characteristics among employees: that they would only work hard according to 'carrot and stick' or reward-and-penalty principles, as they disliked working, did not want responsibility and would not work well unless there were tangible, external factors driving them (Pugh and Hickson 1996).

An alternative management approach (theory Y) was that people actually liked working, could exert discipline and self-control over their work and, if they were encouraged to, would of their own accord seek out responsibility and contribute creatively if the work was interesting and challenging. The best rewards would be Maslow's higher-level self-actualising needs. Theory

Y would also serve to eradicate conflict between line and staff, as the staff would act in a supportive rather than the controlling role congruent with theory X (Pugh and Hickson 1996). McGregor was careful, however, to warn against universally classifying theory X as 'bad' and theory Y as 'good' as this culture, structure or technology could play an important part in determining appropriateness (Hollway 1991).

Herzberg (1966) was also interested in what motivated people, as he suspected that the way things were organised was not promoting welfare and happiness at work. With colleagues, he surveyed 200 engineers and accountants in Pittsburg, USA. The workers were asked to remember good and bad times at work and the reasons for these – in other words what led to job satisfaction, and what led to job dissatisfaction. Herzberg found that people were motivated and demotivated by different things. The absence of what motivated them was not the same as what actively demotivated them.

Herzberg called the first 'motivators' and the second 'hygiene factors'. Motivators consisted of the intrinsic factors relating to the job and the organisation, such as increased challenge and interest in the work, responsibility, achievement and advancement. Hygiene factors were to do with the extrinsic aspects of the job, such as the administration, one's supervisor, and conditions of work, including pay, social factors and the working environment. Herzberg concluded that because they were different and not the opposite of each other, they addressed different needs. They correspond quite clearly to Maslow's higher- and lower-level needs; to intrinsic and extrinsic rewards; or, in terms of Herzberg's biblical analogy, Abraham's achievements of development and growth as compared with Adam's needs of food, warmth, safety and security after his expulsion from the Garden of Eden. Herzberg then carried out further studies on over 1,600 employees and found similar results in the vast majority of cases (Pugh and Hickson 1996).

Job redesign

In order to increase the motivation and well-being of employees at work, Herzberg advocated that jobs be redesigned so that they were challenging and more interesting, using more employees' talents to a greater degree and giving them more responsibilities. This he called job enrichment, which was the very opposite of the job design advocated by Taylor, which, as discussed earlier on, was a narrow fragmentation of the different components of a job and the specialisation by workers in only one of its parts. Herzberg also distinguished his proposal from one where the number of jobs done by employees was increased (job enlargement) or varied (job rotation) (Pugh and Hickson 1996).

Successful examples of job enrichment noted by Herzberg include allowing clerks to be wholly responsible for replying to letters from clients instead of using set formats with extensive supervision. Other employees who had their work 'enriched' included laboratory technicians, sales representatives and factory supervisors. In all these instances people felt more job satisfaction and were more productive. Herzberg claimed that this led to less supervision and left the supervisors in turn to have more interesting, demanding and rewarding work (Pugh and Hickson 1996).

Herzberg's theory is designed to lead to a greater co-operation in working and is based upon gaining commitment through an understanding of corporate goals. This work was extended by Emery and Thorsrud (1963) who identified six criteria a job needs to have in order to maintain the interest of an employee. Such a job must:

- be reasonably demanding in terms other than sheer endurance, yet provide a certain amount of variety

- allow the person to learn as he or she works

- give the person an area of decision-making or responsibility that can be considered to be his or her own

- increase the person's respect for the task he or she is undertaking

- have a meaningful relationship with outside life

- hold out some sort of desirable future, and not just in terms of promotion, because not everyone can be promoted.

Argyris (1962), a theorist who has made important contributions to aspects of organisation theory such as organisational learning, emphasised the importance of allowing employees to engage in work that was intellectually stimulating, where employees could realise more of their potential. This would benefit not only the employees themselves, but also the organisation in terms of increased benefits. Because employees did not have these opportunities they become narrow in their work attitudes, avoid responsibility and challenge, encouraging managers to become even more controlling, in turn encouraging further defensiveness and opaqueness on the part of employees. This is detrimental to the organisation as well as to employees themselves.

Argyris claimed that people who were given responsibility would do a better job and would thereby make the organisation more profitable (Pugh and Hickson 1996). His ideas went further than other approaches mentioned so far, as he was interested in change and development of the whole person rather than what he regarded as manipulative techniques to bring about a desired change by others. He recognised the difficulty of steering a course between democratic choice and influences upon people to change (Hollway 1991).

Process theories

One of the criticisms of content theories of motivation is that they are fixed and universalised – based on the assumption that everyone's psyche works in the same way and is motivated or demotivated by the same factors. There is also the assumption that managers would determine what kind of work was motivating, or 'enriching' in Herzberg's terminology, and how to deliver that to employees. These ideas fit very comfortably into a modernist, functionalist theoretical perspective, with the belief in universal categories or rules, the idea that managers are best placed to make decisions for their workforce and unitarist assumptions about shared goals between management and the workforce (Burrell and Morgan 1979). Carter and Jackson (1993) point out that because the goal ultimately was increased productivity for the organisation, the measure of motivational success was assessed purely in terms of performance for the organisation.

Process theories allow for a much more individual choice about what drives people, and concentrate instead on explaining motivation in terms of whether people see themselves as able to achieve their goals. Their goals may include job satisfaction, but this is no longer a necessary precondition for motivation. Similarly, people may regard the same job differently, and some may perceive work as fulfilling their desire for a particular outcome; others may not; others may have entirely different desires in any case. Thus the assumptions underlying content theories of motivation that people will be motivated by the same factors and will behave in similar ways if presented with them do not hold with process theories.

Process theories include equity theory (Adams 1965) and expectancy theory (Vroom 1964). Equity theory involves cognitive (thinking) social comparison and exchange. It is essentially a comparative theory, as it states that a person's motivation is dependent upon his or her rewards for effort expended to achieve a task in comparison with what is believed about another person's effort/reward relationship. This of course implies that everyone will evaluate this comparison differently and thereby be differently motivated.

Expectancy theory

One type of process theory discussed here is expectancy theory (Vroom 1964), which is based on a comparison of outcomes with preferences, based on behaviour. In other words the assumption is that people will expect a certain outcome, such as a certain reward, if they behave in a certain way. Involved in this is the prediction of people's behaviour, and the assumption that people will behave in a way that is thought-through and rational.

This takes the decision as to what constitutes satisfactory performance away from the judgement of managers to that of the employees themselves. Similarly, all assumptions based on the premise that it is managers' understanding alone of what constitutes satisfying or challenging work also no longer hold. Expectancy theory, through its emphasis on individuals' understanding and perceptions, allows the workers themselves to make such decisions. Vroom pointed out that people would be motivated according to 'desired' rather than 'prescribed' goals. The very assumption that work is a good in itself and, given the right conditions, that workers would view it as such was also challenged by Vroom (Carter and Jackson 1993). However, as with content theories, goals are often seen in terms of organisational rewards or recognition.

The expectancy theory of motivation was developed further by Lawler (1973), who stated that a person will be motivated to undertake a task by a combination of his or her expectation that he or she will be able to complete the task and the value which he or she personally attaches to the completion of that task. In other words, the more important the task is to a person the greater the effort which will be put into its completion provided that the person considers that it is possible to complete the task. Lawler went further, arguing that this was reducible to a mathematical formula that would enable the extent of motivation to be precisely calculated. There are objections to this. Langer (cited in Thompson and McHugh 2002, p228) for example, highlighted unconscious motives or 'scripts' that affected people's behaviour.

Because motivating factors are not in any way predetermined by the theorists, process theories are seen by some writers, such as Carter and Jackson (1993), to lie outside the dominant orthodox paradigm, and instead to be part of a hermeneutic approach in which meaning in organisations is complex and cannot be determined by theorists or managers alone, and certainly cannot be universalised. Even if one could assume common interests and goals, it has been pointed out that people come to organisations with their own previously constructed identities, from different backgrounds. This makes it more difficult to predict how people will behave in the workplace, as it adds to the number of variables that have to be taken into account in trying to predict people's behaviour. Hermeneutic approaches emphasise the possible multiplicity of meanings given to events and processes in organisations and elsewhere because of the different identities, backgrounds and interpretations people bring to them (Hatch and Yanow 2003).

Expectancy theory also includes ideas that fit into postmodern ways of thinking. The emphasis on the subjectivity of people's perceptions and desires, which Vroom points out may be irrational and dysfunctional from the point of view of management's goals, attacks the idea of rationality, now seen as subjective and contrary to the notion of universalisable goals, let alone universalisable rules of needs or desires and behaviour. Emphasis has shifted from the functionalist focus on the relationship between the organisation and management on the one hand with the workforce on the other, to individuals in their own right. Expectancy theory illustrates:

the end of the meta-narrative, of the attempt to produce totalizing explanations of organizational existence, which end is so much the epitome of postmodernism.   (Carter and Jackson 1993, p96)

Critique of motivation theories

Motivation theories can be regarded as a step forward from the previous, more 'mechanistic' prescriptions in classical and scientific management theories. Like human relations ideas, they placed on the agenda human feelings, desires and perceptions instead of the less personal recommendations in terms of organisation structure and hierarchy on the one hand and job design on the other. In all these examples of motivation theory there is a concern to allow employees to enjoy upgraded work, which would allow them to exercise various talents to meet its challenges and responsibilities.

However, it is also clear that these recommendations are also aimed at senior management's own goals and objectives. In all these theories there is present the agenda of increasing productivity for the organisation. Mainstream organisation theorists regard this as a happy conjunction of corporate or organisational interests with those of employees. Indeed unitarist theorists, as mentioned earlier, believe that everyone in an organisation, be they owner, senior manager or humble employee, all have the same goals and interests, and that everyone's future is dependent on the well-being, efficiency and profitability of the organisation.

Radical theorists, as mentioned above, take a more cynical view. Unlike unitarist theorists, who see no conflict between the goals and interests of different 'stakeholders' and people in different positions in the organisation, radical theorists see such interests as irreconcilable, given that we are living in what they regard as a society with unequal relations of power, wealth and status. They would therefore see attempts to motivate people by offering them more power and responsibility as ultimately a contradiction in terms – as real power must remain in the hands of those in control of the assets and power in organisations (Burrell and Morgan 1979).

This strengthens radical theorists' scepticism about the true motives behind these and later theories. They see motivation theories as primarily designed to foster corporate objectives and to help managers get the most out of their workforce, albeit in a kinder way. They see motivation theories as no less a means of control than other types of control, such as the technological control stemming from job design, and the bureaucratic control through rules and procedures as recommended in classical management theory. The type of control motivation theory offers is more of a psychological control, and doesn't necessarily guarantee satisfying or interesting work (Alvesson and Willmott 1996).

The other side of this argument is from the perspective of employees at various levels in the organisation. If unitarist assumptions are incorrect and there is no congruence in the interests of all stakeholders in an organisation, employees' rationalities may not be unidirectional and consistent with corporate goals. People might behave in what to them is a rational way, for example to further their own, narrow political objectives, which might be at variance with those of the senior managers of the organisation.

Because motivation theories essentially come from a mainstream orthodox theoretical perspective, they contain assumptions firstly about the possibility of classifying and universalising factors motivating human action. Most motivation theories are part of a closed-system view characterised by the belief that 'objective' factors can exert a direct influence on human behaviour (Clegg and Dunkerley 1980). Secondly, the possibility of motivational factors in the workplace conflicting with corporate objectives is not seriously envisaged. Just as different personal contexts leading to different meanings and behaviours are not problematised, so too the context of the workplace is not taken greatly into account, with the major responsibility for the stimulus for motivation coming from the individual. Maslow's theory in particular places the onus for being motivated on the employee and absolves management of any responsibility for poor practice (Cullen 1997).

Another weakness in content theories of motivation is their culture bias. It can be argued that Maslow's theory is Western-oriented, as self-actualisation is an individualised, Western concept, not necessarily prevalent in other cultures. Jaya (2001) contrasted the universalistic, achievement-oriented, inner-directed assumptions of Maslow's and Herzberg's theories with different philosophical underpinnings of non-Western cultures, where a collective ethos would find the concept of self-actualisation as a higher-order need to be inconsistent with local cultural and social values.

EMOTIONAL LABOUR

Emotional labour is a relatively new field within organisation theory. It has meant different things in the context of the workplace. Some writers such as Terkel (1975) have looked at how employees feel about their work – as stressful, a form of drudgery or a source of joy or passion (Fineman 1996). With the development of human relations approaches, the concept of the worker as a 'sentimental' or feeling being became very important and was linked to the notion of motivation. Roethlisberger and Dickson (1939) described ideas such as the right to work, fairness and a living wage as 'deeply rooted in sentiment and feeling' (Fineman 1996, p544). According to Fineman, the effects of negative emotions on work performance were stressed more than the possibility of positive feelings among employees. Psychoanalytically inspired approaches from the Tavistock Institute of Human Relations in the 1950s looked at unconscious emotions and how these influenced people in the work situation. They also emphasised the negative aspects (such as anxiety, powerlessness and feelings of threat to one's identity, envy, shame, guilt or political ambition) that influence organisation processes such as leadership and the working of groups (Fineman 1996).

The relationship between emotion and rationality has been discussed in the organisation literature for a long time. Rationality has been defined as the achievement of goals through systematic study, evaluation, measurement and calculation, all of which involve cognitive or thinking processes, as opposed to desire and emotion. Taylor's (1947) theory of scientific management is a good example of rationality in that he believed in systematically studying work and worker control in order to arrive at 'laws, rules and even to mathematical formulae' to achieve greater productivity for management and greater well-being for the workforce (Pugh 1997, p276).

Emotion has been regarded as interfering with rationality, as serving rationality or as being inseparable from rationality. In the first case, people will act irrationally for similar reasons to those given by the Tavistock Institute of Human Relations. Continuing involvement in the Vietnam War has often been cited, for example by Schwenk (1986) and Staw (1981), as an example of the entrapment of the US administration into escalating commitment to a lost cause (Fineman 1996). To avoid negative or destructive emotions in certain types of work situations, such as the distasteful and intimate tasks which nurses have to carry out, Fineman has pointed to what he describes as 'institutionalised irrationality' – work routines to achieve minimal emotional involvement with patients (Fineman 1996, p549).

Menzies-Lythe (1988, 1991) researched a London teaching hospital where she observed the depersonalisation of patients by referring to them by number or illness rather than name; rotas that resulted in more nurses doing specific tasks on a larger number of patients to minimise personal contact; the emphasis on keeping up routines that might be to the detriment of the patient such as waking them up for medication even if they would have been better left to sleep. This may have minimised emotional relationships with patients, but many nurses left precisely because they were missing the close patient contact they wanted both professionally and personally (Fineman 1996).

Emotion and rationality

Some writers have argued that emotions can help rationality. Examples given include the intuitive hunch that can solve a problem or result in an unexpected beneficial result for the organisation. Creativity in organisations, in science and in other areas of human activity such as music has often been ascribed partly to emotional factors. Writers in Europe and North America, following Peters and Waterman (1982) and Kanter (1983), have often recommended participative management as this:

> encourages subordinates to be involved in innovative decisions and to feel able to suggest novel ideas without fear
> of censure.   (King and Anderson 1995, p97)

This stems from human relations approaches which, as will be shown in Chapter 5, have continued to permeate organisation and management theory, particularly through the institution of strong corporate cultures that employees are expected to identify with fully.

Postmodern writers have argued that one cannot separate the rational from the emotional. A central argument is that emotion cannot exist apart from the thought processes of language and the meanings inherent in language. The argument is taken further to claim that all decisions and use of information in organisations cannot stand alone, but are inextricably linked with emotions and feelings, driven for example by anger, competitiveness, fear of upsetting powerful players and so on (Fineman 1996). The inseparability of reason and emotion also in research is argued by Jaggar (1989), who connects emotions with cultural expectations and norms and therefore with evaluation and judgement (Alvesson and Skoldberg 2000).

A different view of emotional labour has been put forward particularly by labour process theorists – the requirement on employees to be continually pleasant and responsive to customers. Common examples are getting 'friendly' with potential customers or clients by dealing with them on first-name terms, asking them how they are and always being equable in the face of any provocation. Emotional labour has been regarded as the exploitation of human beings who are required to display emotions in order to satisfy customers and organisational goals, and to carry out what some might argue are unreasonable demands from management. Fineman (1996) has pointed out that emotional labour demands are accelerating in terms of the hierarchical control exercised and increasing in terms of the number of employees, particularly those who are casual workers, being subjected to it. Radical theorists such as Noon and Blyton (1997) have used the term to describe it as another form of control and coercion over employees.

Employees having to engage in emotional labour include flight attendants, fast-food workers, insurance staff at the interface with customers, and people working in call centres. Taylor's principles are often applied to this kind of work, in that employees are sometimes required to have scripted conversations and responses and standardised, coerced, displays of emotion through verbal, facial and body language. Collinson (1994) has written about a situation where staff, who happened to be mostly black women, were put in this position in a hotel in the United States of America. They were having to stand for many hours a day, be pleasant to the hotel guests no matter how they were treated, and ask scripted questions while at the same time avoiding real personal contact.

Hochschild, who coined the phrase 'emotional labour', defined it in 1983 as a corporate resource, like money, expertise or physical work. She pointed out that it could also apply to people required to withhold feelings of friendliness or empathy to their clients, such as debt collectors. Some writers have argued that such demands to display false emotions in the interests of commercial goals can have a serious effect on people's emotional well-being. In forcing themselves to exhibit 'appropriate' emotions to accommodate clients in various situations, people can lose touch with their real emotions, which can lead to serious problems with their mental health and their own social relationships. Some employees, however, enjoy emotional labour. If they are friendly to customers this may elicit friendly responses back and may be part of the positive side of the work (Noon and Blyton 1997). However, not all situations demanding emotional labour are employee-friendly, as shown above.

People have rebelled against this type of emotional work. A now famous quotation by Hochschild (1983, p127) illustrates this:

> A young businessman said to a flight attendant, 'Why aren't you smiling?' She ... said, 'I'll tell you what. You smile first, then I'll smile.' The businessman smiled at her. 'Good,' she replied. 'Now freeze and hold that for fifteen hours.'
>
> (Cited in Noon and Blyton 1997, p132)

CONCLUSIONS

The theories considered in this chapter are very much in opposition to the rational theories of the preceding chapters and were developed because of a recognition of the deficiencies of those previous theories. They led directly to the type of job-enrichment approaches that were fashionable in the 1970s as well as to the approaches to be considered in the next chapter. They were highly popular during the 1960s and 1970s, and in some respects their very popularity was a cause of the problems they created. These problems result primarily from an abandonment of the rational theories preceding them, although this abandonment was only temporary, because they are still currently a basis for much organisation theory, as we considered in the last chapter. This tension between scientific and rational modes of organising and a concern for people is an ongoing feature of organisation theory. We shall return to this conflict in subsequent chapters.

SUMMARY

- Human relations theories differ from rationalist theories in their concern with people – their behaviour, emotions, and social and psychological needs.

- Critique: research flawed; employee empowerment limited; assumption of common goals; rewards psychological rather than material.

- Motivation theories similar in conception to human relations theories – content and process theories.

- Critique: improvement on rationalist approaches in emphasising human angle, encouragement of upgraded work for employees; negative criticisms include the agenda being managerialist rather than employee-centred, difficult to achieve in terms of congruence with employee perceptions and interests.

- Emotional labour – employee feelings about work; strategies for employees to reduce emotion or display it to please customers.

FURTHER READING

CLEGG, S. and DUNKERLEY, D. (1980) Organization, class and control. London: Routledge & Kegan Paul.

FINEMAN, S. (1996) Emotion and organizing. In S.R. Clegg, C. Hardy and W.R. Nord (eds) Handbook of organization studies. London: Sage.

HOLLWAY, W. (1991) Work psychology and organizational behaviour: managing the individual at work. London: Sage.

PUGH, D.S. and HICKSON D.J. (1996) Writers on organizations. 5th ed. Harmondsworth: Penguin Books.

REFERENCES

ADAMS, J.S. (1965) Injustice in social exchange. In L. Berkovitz, Advances in experimental social psychology, vol. 2. New York: Academic Press.

ALVESSON, M. and SKOLDBERG, K. (2000) Reflexive methodology: new vistas for qualitative research. London: Sage.

ALVESSON, M. and WILLMOTT, H. (1996) Making sense of management: a critical introduction. London: Sage.

ARGYRIS, C. (1962) Interpersonal competence and organisational effectiveness. London: Tavistock Publications.

BURRELL, G. and MORGAN G. (1979) Sociological paradigms and organisational analysis. Aldershot: Ashgate.

CARTER, P. and JACKSON, N. (1993) Modernism, postmodernism and motivation, or why expectancy theory failed to come up to expectation. In J. Hassard and M. Parker (eds) Postmodernism and organizations. London: Sage.

CLEGG, S. and DUNKERLEY, D. (1980) Organization, class and control. London: Routledge & Kegan Paul.

COLLINSON, M. (1994) Through the keyhole? Organization, Vol. 1, No. 1.

CULLEN, D. (1997) Maslow, monkeys and motivation theory. Organization, Vol. 4, No. 3, 355–373.

EDWARDS, R. (1979) *Contested terrain: the transformation of the workplace in the twentieth century*. USA: Basic Books Inc.

EMERY, F.E. and THORSRUD, E. (1963) *Form and context in industrial democracy*. London: Tavistock.

FINEMAN, S. (1996) Emotion and organizing. In S.R. Clegg, C. Hardy and W.R. Nord (eds) *Handbook of organization studies*. London: Sage.

HATCH, M.J. and YANOW, D. (2003) Organization theory as an interpretive science. In H. Tsoukas and C. Knudsen (eds) *The Oxford handbook of organization theory*. Oxford: Oxford University Press.

HERZBERG, F. (1966) *Work and the nature of man*. Staple Press.

HOCHSCHILD, A.R. (1983) *The managed heart: commercialization of human feeling*. Berkeley: University of California Press.

HOLLWAY, W. (1991) *Work psychology and organizational behaviour: managing the individual at work*. London: Sage.

JAGGAR, A.M. (1989) Love and knowledge. *Inquiry*, Vol. 32, 51–176.

JAYA, P.S. (2001) Do we really 'know' and 'profess'? Decolonizing management knowledge. *Organization*, Vol. 8, No. 2, 227–233.

KANTER, R.M. (1983) *The change masters*. New York: Simon & Schuster.

KING, N. and ANDERSON, N. (1995) *Innovation and change in organizations*. London: Routledge.

LAWLER, E.E. (1973) *Motivation in work organisations*. London: Wadsworth.

MASLOW, A.H. (1954) *Motivation and human personality*. New York: Harper & Row.

McGREGOR, D. (1960) *The human side of enterprise*. New York: McGraw-Hill.

MENZIES-LYTHE, I. (1988) *Containing anxiety in institutions: selected essays*. London: Free Association Books.

MENZIES-LYTHE, I. (1991) Changing organizations and individuals: psychoanalytic insights for improving organizational health. In M.F.R. Kets de Vries (ed) *Organizations on the couch: clinical perspectives on organizational behavior and Change*. San Francisco: Jossey Bass.

NOON, M. and BLYTON, P. (1997) *The realities of work*. Basingstoke: Macmillan Press Ltd.

PETERS, T.J. and WATERMAN, R.H. (1982) *In search of excellence: lessons from America's best-run companies*. New York: Harper & Row.

PUGH, D.S. (ed). (1997) *Organization theory: selected readings*. Harmondsworth: Penguin Books.

PUGH, D.S. and HICKSON, D.J. (1996) *Writers on organizations*. 5th ed. Harmondsworth: Penguin Books.

ROETHLISBERGER, F.J. and DICKSON, W.J. (1939) *Management and the worker*. Cambridge, Mass: Harvard University Press.

SCHWENK, C.R. (1986) Information, cognitive biases and commitment to a course of action. *Academy of Management Review*, Vol. 11, 298–310.

STAW, B.M. (1981) The escalation of commitment to a course of action. *Academy of Management Review*, Vol. 6, 577–587.

TAYLOR, F.W. (1947) *Scientific management*. New York: Harper & Row.

TERKEL, S. (1975) *Working people talk about what they do all day and how they feel about what they do*. London: Wildwood House.

THOMPSON, P.N. and MCHUGH, D. (2002) *Work organisations*. 3rd ed. Basingstoke: Palgrave.

VROOM, V.H. (1964) *Work and motivation*. New York: John Wiley & Sons.

The application of the human relations approach

INTRODUCTION

Neo-human relations, total quality management (TQM) and other strategies that have been loosely and sometimes erroneously called Japanese methods of management have been influenced by the human relations approaches, which, as mentioned in Chapter 4, have had a long and lasting impact on organisation theory and practice.

These strategies have arisen in the context of the globalisation of markets and of competition between organisations, and these approaches have come to prominence since the successful incursion of Japanese businesses into Western markets from the 1960s onwards. The perceived threat from Japanese business led Ouchi (1981) to advocate a change in management style to include communication, involvement of people, and trust in relationships, suggesting that while these were present in the best-run American companies they were missing from others.[1] For the last few decades therefore it has been argued that a competitive edge is dependent largely on the motivation and creativity employees put into their work, rather than on price or quality of product, which, with modern technology and the internationalisation of the labour market, can be more difficult to achieve. Other factors considered essential for organisations to adopt in the context of global competition are flexibility and lean production models (Botti 1995).

General principles shared by these strategies include the notion of serving the customer. The customer (or client) must have good-quality services and/or products, preferably tailored to their particular requirements. In order for this to be achieved, there are various strategies, all of which involve the notion, mentioned above, of engaging employees in the process, often in teams, in such a way as to achieve this competitive edge. These strategies include some devolution of responsibility and decision-making to the employees actually involved in producing the good or delivering the service to customers. This can include how the product should be produced or the service carried out, and responsibility for checking on its quality, which should be being improved continuously.

Involving the employee

The influence of human relations ideas is clear. The notion of involving the employees in their work and making them feel that they are valued is taken further perhaps than in Mayo's ideas, where good communication with employees and engaging them as valued employees was sufficient. Neo-human relations ideas encourage some devolution of authority and decision-making, and hence the further changes required in relation to structure. Strategies requiring devolution of power and decision-making should have in place less hierarchical, more decentralised structures with stronger horizontal links than mechanistic structures allow.

---

1 He labelled this theory as theory Z to distinguish it from, and imply its superseding of, theories X and Y of McGregor (1960) concerning human behaviour, and implying that there was a logical progression in understanding human behaviour in the workplace from theory X to Y to Z.

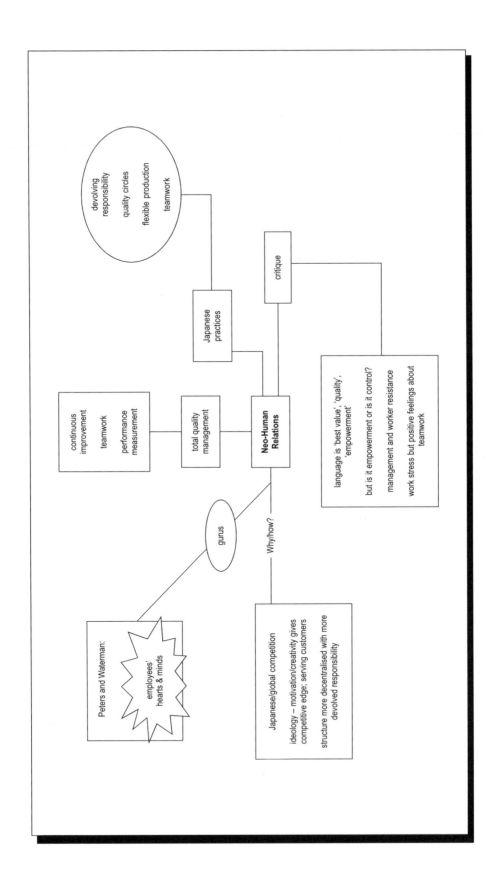

The ideological or symbolic languages that go along with these ideas are also reminiscent of human relations values. Concepts such as 'quality', 'best value' and 'empowerment' are often used to convey the main principles inherent in these strategies in terms of the product and service and the importance accorded to employees.

There are, of course, problems with these concepts in terms of their meanings and their use in practice, and also in terms of their intended methods and outcomes. Hermeneutic and postmodern theorists have shown up the problems in terms of how these concepts are understood and interpreted in different organisations and contexts. Radical theorists have pointed out, as they have regarding human relations and motivation theories, that they are essentially strategies of control, albeit usually psychological and cultural rather than overt technological and bureaucratic control. Where these strategies have been operationalised, it has been shown in some cases that political considerations have overruled the intentions of the policy in various ways. In the first place, the power devolved is often very limited and concerns only operational aspects of the job rather than wider policy issues. Attempts at even this limited devolution can be resisted by managers and supervisors who fear their power will be weakened, rather than seeing it as an opportunity to do more interesting things themselves. Managers have also used these strategies to fulfil some previous goal they had, which may not necessarily be part of the 'official' goals for the strategy.

NEO-HUMAN RELATIONS APPROACHES

Neo-human relations approaches include popularised and very popular writings by management 'gurus' such as Peters and Waterman. They also include what have been called management fads or fashions – which arise and are then replaced by others. Clark and Salaman (1996) have pointed out that management gurus have not concerned themselves specifically with structure or organisation systems. Their target has been the hearts and minds of senior managers, and in human relations style they have aimed to alter beliefs, attitudes and feelings of managers. Their focus has been on enthusing employees with the goals, mission and values of the organisation, which have often included the idea of the primacy of the customer, and the intention of paring the organisation down to a 'leaner' and, in some views, 'meaner' one. Much of the agenda on organisational restructuring in the 1990s, including culture change and delayering, according to Clark and Salaman (1996, p104):

owe much of their appeal and pervasiveness to the activities of a small number of management gurus.

Kieser (1997) has pointed out that management fashions can serve as an excuse for managers to implement changes they have been wanting to make anyway, or for interpreting the new strategy and its implementation to serve political ends. For example Carter and Crowther (2000) describe this process in a regional electricity company where the wish to change is wrapped up in the rhetoric of the latest management fashion for techniques; this migrated from TQM to BPR as the fashion changed (see Figure 5.1 overleaf). Other examples will also be given of the ways strategies such as TQM have been understood and how they have been implemented. Such fads and fashions also serve the purpose of legitimating the organisation by demonstrating that it is keeping up with changes and is engaged in the never-ending improvements themselves legitimised by the people and institutions that matter – consultancies, management gurus, business schools and the publishers of popular management texts.

> The Director of Corporate Development commented:
>
> *We were all agreed on the need to change, all we had to do was decide what to*
>
> *change.*
>
>
> A senior manager of Coastline Electric, reflecting on the decision to implement TQM,
>
> commented:
>
> *The idea came from the previous Board. The finance guy was from a TQM*
>
> *background and told us of the benefits it had brought his previous company. He had*
>
> *the idea and then set up a working group of 6 of us. We looked at 50 companies and*
>
> *decided to adopt TQM ... as that was the key to being successful.*
>
> From Carter and Crowther (2000)

Figure 5.1 *The introduction of TQM*

SEARCHING FOR EXCELLENCE

Peters and Waterman (1982) made a big splash and, doubtless, a great deal of money, with their book *In Search of Excellence*. In it they describe 'excellent' companies[2] as those where there is an unusual effort made on the part of 'apparently ordinary employees' in regard to the customer – in Peters and Waterman's case, the concierge of an hotel still remembering their names a year after they first met him. IBM's 'take' on excellence, according to Peters and Waterman, was to provide unparalleled customer service, speaking the customer's language and providing full guarantees and a local back-up service. Best quality could even be toilet paper, as in the case of Proctor and Gamble.

Another characteristic of some excellent companies is the care and promotion of 'product champions' – employees who believe so strongly in their ideas that they will bypass or railroad through any obstructive bureaucracy to achieve them, sometimes going to extraordinary lengths. An example to illustrate this is Boeing engineers spending a sleepless weekend redesigning the B-52, complete with a balsa model (Peters and Waterman 1982).

Linked with this is the idea of strong corporate cultures. Stories such as the one about the sleepless weekend, or about the chief executive of a company personally dealing with a

2 It is interesting to observe that the companies identified by Peters and Waterman as excellent companies have since experienced periods of financial hardship and would no longer be considered to be excellent performers. This of course raises a question as to what can be regarded as excellent and whether any example of excellence can be considered sustainable rather then merely based upon following the fashions of the time.

customer to right a misunderstanding, contributed to the development of strong cultures where the message would be about like company values (Peters and Waterman 1982).

In *In Search of Excellence* Peters and Waterman seek to explain how to achieve this kind of commitment and creativity from employees. They argue that it is not enough to motivate people as recommended by McGregor or Herzberg. Citing Becker, a psychologist, they claim people have the apparently contradictory needs (a) to be a part of something, but also (b) to show that they are different and can excel as individuals. Becker further argued that people would be happy to endure a boring, routine job if they saw it as playing a part in a greater cause.

Peters and Waterman saw the key to unlocking these aspirations in employees as consisting of three parts. The first was to give them some control over their working lives, or in their words (1982, pxxiii):

> even a modicum of apparent control over his or her destiny.

The example given in the preface of their book is of an experiment where people were given some puzzles to solve in a noisy atmosphere. The group who were given the means to turn off the noise did five times better than the control group, *even though* the first group did not actually use the mechanism. Secondly, employees should be made to feel important (their need for 'greatness'). Examples given by Peters and Waterman include the hiring of a football stadium by the sales branch of a company. As each employee ran through the players' tunnel their names lit up on the scoreboard to the accompaniment of cheers from colleagues, family and friends. The encouragement of a culture among employees congruent with that of the organisation is the third plank of Peters and Waterman's recommendations (1982, pxxv):

> Even management's job becomes more fun. Instead of brain games in the sterile ivory tower, it's shaping values and reinforcing through coaching and evangelism in the field – with the worker and in support of the cherished product.

Critiquing *In Search of Excellence*

There are of course comments one can make about these ideas. Some will be similar to those made about the original human relations and motivation theories. In the first place a unitarist ethos in organisations is assumed. There is no suggestion that employees do not or cannot be brought round to feeling identified with their organisation and with its goals and means of achieving them. Yet these ideas, as already mentioned, have been contested. Interpretive theorists would question whether the possibility of different meanings, interpretations and actions given to mission statements, aims or methods of operation can achieve the clear and tightly knit unitarism flagged up in *In Search of Excellence* (Hatch and Yanow 2003).

Radical theorists believe that power relations are important in organisations and underlie many of the structures and processes within them, and that these relations are ones of inequality and exploitation. They would therefore contest the assumption of everyone willingly pulling together to achieve corporate goals, let alone going to the extraordinary lengths to provide the kind of service suggested by Peters and Waterman (Alvesson and Skoldberg 2000). Critical theorists recognise that sometimes employees do go out of their way to provide such service, and suggest that it is due to the ideological manipulation of getting people to believe that their interests are the same as management's, which in turn are 'universal' (Alvesson and Deetz 1996).

Many, sometimes novel, ideas have been implemented to induce loyalty in employees. Peters and Waterman's suggestion is to foster their assumed need for 'greatness'. The example given above of having employees' names emblazoned in a sports stadium is reminiscent of similar, if less spectacular, conferrings of recognition on employees. In the case of UK water companies, charts of different departments' achievements were posted regularly to show off the best achievers, and, presumably, to show up the others in the hope they would do better in future. In one large American company the chairman would give a banana to the most deserving individual of the moment.

Another method, as Peters and Waterman suggested, is to give employees some control. Radical theorists would see this as a contradiction if genuinely offered, as they see the domination and subordination of senior and junior employees as one of the bases of organisational ideology and practice. But Peters and Waterman acknowledge that they are not offering real and significant control. They write about 'a modicum of apparent control' (1982, pxxiii). Also, the example they give – the power to turn a switch – is trivial and hardly offers any power at all.

There have been examples, particularly as part of organisational change programmes, where employees have been offered more control or 'empowerment' in their work. This is usually accompanied by structural changes, normally with less hierarchy, more de-layering of levels of management and often more work for the remaining employees. This has been a feature of the restructuring of UK utility companies, as described by Carter and Crowther (2000). The 'power' normally offered is operational – for example having the choice to make decisions within a broader policy that has been decided from higher up. For example, employees within 'Barsetshire' county council were given a budget within which they had to manage, and could make some decisions as to how it should be allocated. Some employees enjoyed their new-won powers of control, but others saw the limitations and also the tightness of the budgets within which they had to operate (Keen 1994).

In another case, the privatisation of the water industry in the UK in 1989, an analysis of the organisational change instituted showed that accountants were offered a measure of power over their budgets. This was part of a cultural change where the main mission of the industry changed from that of providing services to customers to that of bringing profits to shareholders. One can see that the 'empowerment' the accountants received was part of the equation to change the culture, for along with this new power came computerised control to ensure that accounts and budgets were being used to promote the new culture and value system (Ogden and Anderson 1999).

EVANGELISM AND CORPORATE CULTURE

'Coaching and evangelism' are also means to achieving a strong corporate culture. As with motivation theories many writers are critical of this approach and see it as a way of manipulating people to 'buy into' a way of thought. Some writers have shown that it can become a method of coercion. A case study has been written on Tandem, where employees were encouraged and given the space to be flexible and creative, as advocated by writers like Peters and Waterman. Deal and Kennedy (cited in Morgan 1989, pp166–8) described how all the employees in Tandem, including the founders and chief executive officer, were on first-name terms and how they all went to the pub on Friday evenings and shared other social events. Yet there is a suggestion in the 'subtext' that employees would not get very far in the company if they did not participate in these events and show that they were 'one of the boys and girls', in addition to the long hours of work put in for the company.

Casey (1996) analysed a large multi-national corporation (Hephaestus) involved in the design and manufacture of technological systems and in corporate restructuring. She showed how the organisation culture was changed in the wake of heavy market loss to Japanese companies and the firing of some 25,000 employees. The new culture and the redesign of work, made possible by computer-aided design and technologies, led to more generalised jobs including both technical and other corporate-related work such as management functions. These served to weaken employees' former loyalties and networks in the organisation – namely their occupational identities, trade union affiliations and informal social groupings – in favour of organisational 'teams' and 'families' with an agenda of employee 'involvement' and customer satisfaction. As in *In Search of Excellence*, the epitome of the Hephaestus employee was someone enthusiastic, passionately dedicated to customer needs and willing to 'go the extra mile' for the team (Casey 1996).

Senior management adopted coercive and totalitarian-type techniques further to enforce corporate conformity. Casey gives the example of an employee who, in his own time after a long day at a trade fair, went to repair a client's newly installed machine. Because of the circumstances he went to the client's premises dressed in informal clothes. When this was relayed back to senior management, the employee faced disciplinary action for breaching the company dress code.

Strong corporate cultures can have a deleterious effect on family life. Many people are increasingly spending most of their time and energy working in and for their organisations, as is happening both in the UK and perhaps more extensively and from earlier on in the USA. It has been pointed out that there comes a point where employees begin to identify more with their organisations and feel more comfortable there than with their families, who have become fed up with their lack of presence and consideration.

The real-life instances given by Peters and Waterman are contestable also. As with other theorists who have used examples of interested, creative and committed employees, it has been pointed out that this may apply only to a small minority of the people working in an organisation. Such criticisms were made of Blauner, who will be discussed below. His inverted 'U' curve predicted that work would become more skilled, intellectually challenging and require more responsibility. Critics pointed out that this might well be true of some employees, for example the people in Blauner's example of process industries (such as gas, petrol, milk), who would walk around in white coats with charts taking measurements from dials. However, many employees might still be engaged in traditional manual work – for example, (until recently) carrying sacks of coal to power the energy for these process industries.

Another optimistic portrayal of work in the future has been the idea that work is becoming more flexible, giving people greater choice and opportunity (Piore and Sabel's flexibility thesis 1984). However, similar points have been made as those regarding Blauner's vision. Atkinson (cited in Crompton *et al* 1996) pointed out how modern flexibility does not affect all employees equally or positively. He distinguished between a 'core' workforce which he saw as benefiting from such flexibility and from opportunities for further training and career development, and the 'peripheral' workforce which afforded flexibility for the organisation in that they could be hired and fired as needed, and who lacked other rights, as well as those of secure employment and career opportunities: for example social security, pension rights and holiday pay (until recent changes in legislation).

TOTAL QUALITY MANAGEMENT (TQM)

These ideas and the critiques of them are not of course peculiar to *In Search of Excellence*. Many management strategies, some of them fads lasting for only a few years, have much in common with Peters and Waterman's assumptions and recommendations. They include the concepts of 'best value', 'empowerment' as a central idea in its own right, BPR (see Chapter 3) and TQM.

TQM became popular in the 1980s for reasons of competitiveness in the globalising contexts mentioned earlier, the influence of the quality movement and Japanese management methods, the pressure on management to 'move with the times' fostered by consultants and management schools, and because other companies were adopting this strategy. The main principles on which TQM was based were similar to those mentioned in the introduction to this chapter: increased performance and productivity; the importance of delivering quality and appropriate services and products to the customer; and teamwork, with decisions for continuous improvements in quality delegated to the employees engaged in the process at the point of delivery to the customer. TQM is concerned with improving performance. In order to evaluate performance it is considered necessary to determine the constituents of good performance and the use of performance indicators as a means of determining this. Oakland (1989) states that, to be useful, a performance indicator must be measurable, relevant and important to the organisation's performance. Such indicators must also be meaningful to anyone seeking to evaluate performance, and the cost of obtaining the information must not outweigh its value.

Many large companies worldwide have attempted to implement TQM in the last few decades. The principles of continuous improvement to decrease waste, thereby enhancing productivity, have been taken up more widely than those of encouraging teamwork and employee involvement, which have had more varied responses. The monitoring of the performance of TQM teams, as happened for example in the New South Wales plant of Pirelli Cables after it was introduced in the 1990s, also contradicted the broader principle of increased trust in employees and the importance of their commitment to the TQM strategy (Dawson 2003).

There were problems with employees actually being given the control they were supposed to have. In Pirelli Cables (Australia) middle managers and supervisors were unwilling to hand over such control, fearing the vulnerability of their own positions (Dawson 2003). Similarly, there have been varied responses by employees to the empowerment strategies implemented. While some enjoyed having more power to make decisions about how the product or service was to be delivered, others saw it as additional hard work, with little actual increase in power. In the same Pirelli plant, workers felt they were not being remunerated for productivity gains made, and did not feel that involvement and pride in work done more efficiently was reward enough, perhaps in opposition to human relations ideas. They shifted their attitudes and found a way of resistance through joining more TQM teams and thereby reducing their time spent on the production line (Dawson 2003).

The interest and role of senior management also made a difference. Perhaps because TQM was adopted more as a 'fad' in the wake of other companies' implementations than because of a perceived need the strategy would meet, senior management did not always take an active role, nor did they always allow sufficient resources effectively to institute the changes needed. De Cock and Hipkin (1997) investigated two companies in the UK and found that senior management did not take an active part in the implementation of TQM. Lack of interest by management may, in the two companies investigated, have also resulted in a lack of interest among employees. Their attitudes may have included a general lack of trust in management initiatives, perhaps because of the many tried before, with varying degrees of success, and then discarded in favour of yet another strategy, or because of a lack of trust specifically regarding the devolution of power.

An overarching problem, which postmodern theorists would regard as entirely normal and unavoidable, is the fact that TQM, like other strategies, shifts in its meanings and significance, just as do organisations in their structures, processes, policies and symbols. Different organisational contexts also make for very different interpretations of enactments of policy, as Dawson (2003) concluded from his analysis of three different Pirelli plants in Australia. TQM has been interpreted in various ways. This is to an extent necessary, as different organisations have specific systems, needs and problems. However, postmodern and also interpretive theorists argue that because people perceive and understand things differently and then act on them according to their understandings, there are bound to be differences in definition and implementation.

De Cock and Hipkin (1997) add a political dimension to these differences in 'enactment'. Managers at different levels made sure that their implementation of TQM was congenial to their own 'parochial' political interest, and in some cases instituted changes they had been wanting to make for a long time under the TQM umbrella. Similarly Dawson pointed out that in one of the Pirelli plants the formation of TQM teams was used to bring to the fore longstanding disagreements among its members that had previously been left unsaid. Generally these degenerated into more protracted quarrels rather than serving to 'clear the decks' (Dawson 2003, p35).

Despite the difficulties outlined above, there were positive changes in some organisations. The implementation of TQM in Pirelli's Cable Processing Plant in South Australia resulted in increased daily communication between shop-floor employees, and generally improved relationships and collaboration. However, even where successful, it was limited, because the original pattern of work, based on one operator per machine, with monitoring and evaluation on that individual basis, remained rather than being changed to the teamwork ostensibly so important in TQM strategies (Dawson 2003). De Cock and Hipkin (1997) also found that there were positive effects from the introduction of TQM. They nevertheless concluded in the case of the two companies they analysed that TQM did bring about some changes for the benefit of the company, because of the efforts mainly of the employees and perhaps despite the input or lack of input of some levels of management.

'JAPANESE' METHODS OF MANAGEMENT: JIT, KANBAN AND THE QUALITY MOVEMENT

There has been some argument about whether these ideas do in fact come from Japan. According to Oliver and Wilkinson (1993) many of these practices are of Western origin but were developed in the 1950s in Japanese industry. Indeed two Americans are credited with the development of many of these ideas – W.E. Deming and J.M. Juran. Although they worked in the USA, it was Japanese companies who picked up on their ideas of quality control and put them into action, before the ideas were subsequently reimported back into the West as Japanese concepts (Clutterbuck and Crainer 1990). Certainly they share ideas in common with human relations and motivation theories. They are also part of the 'quality' movement and have many principles in common with TQM. There is the idea of devolving responsibility to employees at the 'coalface', and with some of these strategies similar issues and difficulties have arisen as in the case of TQM. Quality circles are a way of giving employees an opportunity to offer ideas as to how constantly to improve their work – its quality and/or efficiency. This gives people on the shop floor or at the service counter a way of having a say over their work. It is very similar to the concept of 'Kaizen' – the idea of involving all employees in teams in order to find continual ways of bettering their work, be it in quality, productivity, ease of working or a better environment (Oliver and Wilkinson 1993).

The traditional 'Japanese model' was an integrated set of manufacturing practices, management strategies and personnel policies. In Italy, according to Botti (1995), production was flexible, automated and quality-oriented, with workers relied upon to collaborate, and allowed their initiative. Personnel practices included job security, promotion according to seniority, participative decision-making and informal communication. Such employment policies are generally not emulated in the West, particularly now. They are also less common in Japan these days, and as will be shown below, certainly do not apply to all Japanese companies, nor to employees at all levels.

Just-in-time manufacturing (JIT)

Based on the work of Deming and Juran, the Japanese established their own quality gurus and also developed the notion of cycle time reduction – the minimisation of the time from receipt of an order from a customer to the delivery of the finished product. According to Monden (1983) the concept of JIT was developed by the Toyota Motor Company in Japan in the mid-1970s. Toyota turned the focus upon waste, inherent in quality management approaches, to a focus upon the waste of time. From this developed the just-in-time (JIT) philosophy. Just-in-time manufacturing aims to match the usage of raw materials with their delivery from suppliers, thereby reducing the levels of raw materials and work in progress stocks to a minimum, with the ultimate aim of reducing such stock-holding to zero, whilst also preventing any delays in the production process, so that raw materials are always available when needed.

JIT production works on a demand-pull basis, which seeks to ensure that components are not made until required by the next process, working backwards from the finished product through the various processes to the raw materials. Reduced costs are incurred by a firm using JIT due to the reduced investment in stock, space savings from inventory reduction and reduced manufacturing time through the elimination of waste at intermediary stages in the production system. JIT is an approach that attempts to move the manufacturing environment away from a job- or batch-processing environment towards a repetitive processing environment.

JIT is often viewed as simply a method of reducing stock levels (Blackburn 1988) by, for example, requiring suppliers to deliver components to the factory at the time and in the quantity that they are required. In this simplistic view of JIT the technique involves merely passing the cost of stockholding backwards up the value chain to suppliers. In fact, the successful application of JIT requires the adoption of a much wider management philosophy. Meredith (1992), for example, quotes the three tenets of JIT as:

- the minimisation of waste in all forms
- the continuous improvement of processes and systems
- maintaining respect for all workers.

In order to provide a contextual understanding of the changing environment created by JIT, it is helpful to provide an overview of the JIT philosophy. The differences between JIT and the more traditional production environment will be highlighted. The philosophies and procedures that underpin JIT can be envisaged as pieces of a jigsaw that collectively create a holistic strategy for improving the efficiency and reducing the cost of operations. JIT differs from traditional approaches to operations management in a number of ways.

The strategic emphasis of JIT is focused on competing in a clearly defined market rather than seeking to manufacture any product that the customer demands. Thus, product standardisation is a particular feature of the system. This does not necessarily mean a lack of luxury features; in fact the product may well be of a particularly high specification. For example, a motor car may be sold with air conditioning as standard. The aim is simply to remove the complexity of operations often associated with traditional production approaches. The simplified product range enables operations management to focus on both low costs and high quality. This concept commences at the design stage, where an emphasis is given to *design for manufacturing*. It is recognised that it is essential to pass to the manufacturing function a product design capable of being efficiently produced. This contrasts with the traditional approach of designing a product first and then passing the product onto manufacturing with a challenge to make it. It is naturally impossible for production to produce efficiently an ill-conceived product design, and so design and production need to be integrated for maximal benefit.

Total quality management and just in time

It is important to recognise that JIT stresses the importance of employees to the success of the business. Thus Hatvany and Pucik (1981) make the point that Japanese companies treat employees as their most valuable long-term assets rather than merely as a resource. As such, efforts are directed towards developing this crucial asset base through extensive training and development. The creation of a long-term perspective among employees is achieved by offering life-time employment and through reward and evaluation systems designed for long-term emphasis (Cope 1982). Flexibility amongst employees is attained through job rotation. The adoption of these human resource strategies encourages employees to take a longer-term view and to have active involvement in the operation. This in turn supports initiatives like TQM.

TQM forms an integral part of the JIT philosophy. The process is directed towards involving all employees in the quest for perfect quality. The inclusion of 'total' in the title emphasises that it embraces all processes from design until the product reaches the customer. TQM recognises that it is impossible to inspect quality into a product once it is manufactured and, therefore, places the responsibility for quality back with those who produce the product. This is referred to as *Jidoka* or the autonomous control of defects (Monden 1983). In certain plants workers are encouraged to halt the production process if a defect from the previous process is identified. This has the advantage of instantly highlighting the cause of the defect thus enabling rectification of the problem before further parts are produced and unnecessary costs incurred. An additional control mechanism aimed at ensuring quality is *Poke Yoke*. This mechanism incorporates mistake-proofing as an integral part of a production process.

Traditional production philosophy has acceptable quality levels (AQL) built into the process, which is a further illustration of the Western notion of accepting certain process variables as given. In the traditional production environment considerable efforts are expended in attempts to determine the optimum quality level by seeking to balance the cost of quality against the cost of defects. In contrast, the Japanese refuse to accept that any defect is tolerable. TQM supports the JIT philosophy, since uncertain product quality has to be compensated for both by holding safety buffer stocks and by longer lead times. Many companies that have introduced the autonomous control of defects have seen their costs reduced with the elimination of the dedicated inspection function.

JIT requires a smooth, steady flow of work through the production shop. Clearly, machine failures will cause interruptions to this flow, and so great importance is placed on the preventative maintenance of machines. Often operators will be trained to carry out simple maintenance tasks such as lubricating machines and in the detection of signs of impending machine failure. Machines will also be run at a steady pace, which is frequently below their rated capacity. In a traditional environment the emphasis is on corrective maintenance, stockholding to buffer machine stoppages and operating machines at full capacity.

In order to ensure the smooth flow of work, to avoid complexity of operations and to ensure the maximum flexibility of operations, the process logistics in a JIT environment will differ from traditional concepts. A key notion with JIT is that material should flow like water and hence not touch the floor. Accordingly, processes are organised to ensure the logical flow of goods. To reduce materials handling, machines are positioned close together: materials handling does not add value and should therefore be eliminated. Cellular production is also a common process layout adopted with JIT. Cells are generally U-shaped to increase visibility of operations, thereby assisting in the early detection of defects, the promotion of teamwork and accessibility of machines. In a traditional layout machines carrying out similar functions will be grouped together – this type of layout complicates material flow.

JIT adopts a control-based system, which pulls work through the system on an as-needed basis. It is actual customer demand for output from the final process in the production system that determines the demand for parts. That final process then signals the demand for components from the immediately preceding process. If demand for a part ceases, then machines may stop working. This immediately signals the need to reassign workers from those areas to alternative tasks. Since there is an absence of buffer stocks between processes, any defect that emerges from one process will cause the disruption of the subsequent process. This creates an immediate demand for attention to both overcome the problem and introduce corrective action to prevent a recurrence.

The kanban

The device used to pull work from one process to another is a kanban or card. The typical system uses two kanbans: a withdrawal kanban and a production kanban. Operation 2 receives a full container from operation 1 together with a withdrawal kanban. The withdrawal kanban is placed in a rack located at operation 2 and parts are withdrawn from the container for processing. When the number of withdrawal kanbans at operation 2 reaches a predetermined level, the operator takes an empty container, together with a withdrawal kanban, back to the store area at operation 1, where he locates a full container attached to which will be a production kanban. The production kanban is removed from the container, and placed in a rack located at operation 1. The withdrawal kanban is then placed in the full container, thereby authorising release of the container from the area. When the number of production kanbans in the rack at operation 1 reaches a predetermined level, this is taken as authority to produce additional parts.

A key concept in the JIT philosophy is that inventory represents waste and should thus be avoided or at least minimised. Not only is inventory seen as an idle resource, but it can also be a means of masking operational problems. Traditional production methods use inventory to buffer processes from (*inter alia*):

- demand uncertainties
- inefficiencies
- defective products
- poor load-balancing between processes
- machine downtime.

Inventory must then be held in sufficient quantities to avoid these problems affecting processes. In contrast, the Japanese approach is progressively to reduce stock levels in order to expose and then eradicate these operational problems. The Japanese consider inventory to be analogous to a lake below which operational problems are submerged. By reducing the water/stock levels these problems emerge and can be addressed.

JIT seeks to reduce machine set-up times, recognising that this is a non-value-adding activity. In the traditional production environment set-up takes a considerable time to accomplish. Thus, once machines have been set up, conventional logic suggests that there should be long production runs. The Japanese have sought and perfected ways to minimise set-up times and have achieved 'single-minute exchange of dies' (Shingo 1985) and more latterly 'one-touch exchange of dies'.

Finally, and this is perhaps the most recognised element of the system, is JIT purchasing. The concept is to move away from the adversarial role that has traditionally existed between supplier and purchaser. According to Lamming (1993) JIT recognises that suppliers can only be expected to pursue goals of quality and delivery performance if long-term partnerships between the supplier and the purchaser are created. In these partnerships suppliers may have to commit to hold prices over the life of the contract, or in some cases offer year-on-year price reductions. Suppliers are expected to ensure frequent deliveries in small lots to the purchaser on an as-needed basis. Suppliers are quality approved and, once approved, are responsible for guaranteeing that all parts delivered are of the required quality. This removes from the purchaser the burden of checking the quality of incoming materials. Suppliers are often offered sole-supplier status when entering into a partnership with the purchaser.

Critique of the Japanese approach

JIT involves employees, commonly on a production line, through all its stages, deciding when they need additional materials to complete their part in the production system, and ordering them only very shortly before they are needed. This saves storage space, the accumulation of stocks of spares that may become obsolete, and employee costs. It also makes more visible any problems in the production process. The Toyota production line, for instance, gets many deliveries each day, delivered to the exact point on the production line (Oliver and Wilkinson 1993). Of course the JIT philosophy involves the workers concerned working much harder at continuous tasks, and Toyota have more recently been accused of making assembly line workers work in conditions that could cause repetitive strain injuries. Another accusation made against the JIT philosophy is that it is an exploitation of the power relationship between large firms and smaller firms, as the focus upon keeping minimal stocks forces supplying companies to keep the stocks instead and deliver them when required. This accusation is made particularly against car manufacturers such as Toyota and against retail stores such as Sainsburys or Tesco. So, rather than JIT being a philosophy concerned with people it can be considered to be one of control, albeit full of such terms as 'empowerment'.

Like other managerial strategies JIT has been used politically. Jick and Peiperl (2003) have shown how one of the aims of one of the senior managers at the Apple computer company was to change from a departmental distributive system to a JIT system. A result of instituting this strategy would be to lose a whole department and its branches, presumably potentially saving the organisation considerable cost, aside from getting rid of a formidable possible rival in the organisation. Problems arising from the insecurity of the rung of managers immediately above employees who are supposed to be implementing a JIT policy have arisen in the same way as with TQM. Selto *et al* (1995) have shown this difficulty in a company where the system was not implemented as intended, with employees on the shop floor not being given the power to make these decisions.

Quality circles and other strategies where employees are encouraged to suggest improvements to the operational aspects of their work can sometimes backfire, in the sense of turning out to be the opposite of empowering for employees. What has sometimes happened is that employees, in thinking about how to make their work more efficient, actually come up with ideas as to how to make themselves work harder. There have certainly been instances where managers have used this to introduce policies surreptitiously which they know would be resisted if they were to suggest them, but would be much more acceptable if coming from employees themselves, as in Pirelli Cables Australia Ltd (Dawson 2003).

In one extreme case described by Junkerman (1982) employees at a Datsun plant run by Nissan Motor Company in Zama, near Tokyo, were expected among other things to participate in quality circles in their own time and to come up with suggestions for improved efficiency. One of their suggestions led not only to their working harder, but also to their working under far more dangerous conditions. The suggestion was that machinery on the assembly line be repaired without its being halted and switched off, in order that no production time should be lost. This was implemented, and tragically, a worker doing such repairs was killed. This policy was part of the implementation of a strong, one might say totalitarian, corporate culture, which did not stop short of verbal and physical intimidation where there was evidence of opposition or resistance to management (Junkerman 1982).

Not all Nissan workers are placed in such an extreme position as those working at the Datsun plant. Garrahan and Stewart (cited in Oliver and Wilkinson 1993, p35), in a study of Nissan workers in Sunderland, North-East England, pointed out that workers here too found the pace of work, which they agreed would be dictated by the moving assembly line, so difficult to keep up with that they had to do additional unpaid work to meet targets, in addition to forfeiting pay when they were ill and not believed by their supervisors. Nevertheless there were still some positive feelings largely because of teamworking and the 'togetherness' this created.

Examples like this encourage radical theorists to argue that the quality movement and the other strategies outlined above are essentially more subtle means of controlling workers and getting them to work harder under the guise of their ideas being valued and their being given more power over their work.

CONCLUSIONS

The approaches discussed in this chapter can in some ways be considered to be a development of the concern for people discussed in the previous chapter. In other respects, however, they are very clearly based on the scientific approaches of the previous chapter and are designed to enable organisations to extract greater value from their employees while at the same time providing work that is more interesting and satisfying. In itself, an attempt to marry together these two diverse approaches to organising is to be lauded – although not all theorists (as we will see) would agree with this.

SUMMARY

- Strategies influenced by human relations theories arose out of global markets and organisational competition.

- Principles: serving customer needs, teamworking, employee empowerment, quality of product/service, strong corporate culture.

- Peters and Waterman's 'excellent' companies.

- Critique: similar to those regarding human relations and motivation theories – assumption of congruence between employees' cultures and those of management; limitations on employee empowerment.

- Total quality management (TQM) – influence of quality movement and Japanese management methods.

- Difficulties: ceding of control by managers to operatives, lack of remuneration for additional work, commitment of senior managers, different agendas regarding implementation.

- Japanese management methods: just in time (JIT), kanban, the quality movement.

- Difficulties: similar to TQMs, with which closely connected.

FURTHER READING

CLARK, T. and SALAMAN, G. (1996) The management guru as organizational witchdoctor. *Organization*, Vol. 3, No. 1, 85–107.

CROMPTON, R., GALLIE, D. and PURCELL, K. (1996) *Changing forms of employment: organisations, skills and gender.* London: Routledge.

DAWSON, P. (2003) *Reshaping change: a processual perspective.* London: Routledge.

PETERS, T.J. and WATERMAN, R.H. (1982) *In search of excellence: lessons from America's best-run companies.* New York: Harper & Row.

REFERENCES

ALVESSON, M. and DEETZ, S. (1996) Critical theory and postmodernism approaches to organizational studies. In S.R. Clegg, C. Hardy & W.R. Nord (eds) *Handbook of organization studies.* London: Sage.

ALVESSON, M. and SKOLDBERG, K. (2000) *Reflexive methodology: new vistas for qualitative research.* London: Sage.

BLACKBURN, J.D. (1988) The new manufacturing environment. *Journal of Cost Management*, Summer, 4–10.

BOTTI, H.F. (1995) Misunderstandings: A Japanese transplant in Italy strives for lean production. *Organization*, Vol. 2, No. 1, 55–86.

CARTER, C.J.G. and CROWTHER, D. (2000) Unravelling a profession: The case of engineers in a regional electricity company. *Critical Perspectives on Accounting*. Vol. 11, No. 1, 23–49.

CASEY, C. (1996) Corporate transformations: designer culture, designer employees and 'post-occupational' solidarity. *Organization*, Vol. 3, No. 3, 317–339.

CLARK, T. and SALAMAN, G. (1996) The management guru as organizational witchdoctor. *Organization*, Vol. 3, No. 1, 85–107.

CLUTTERBUCK, D. and CRAINER, S. (1990) *Makers of management*. London: Macmillan.

COPE, R.E. (1982) Japanese productivity: can it work here? *Modern Casting*, 122–127.

CROMPTON, R., GALLIE, D. and PURCELL, K. (1996) *Changing forms of employment: organisations, skills and gender*. London: Routledge.

DAWSON, P. (2003) *Reshaping change: a processual perspective*. London: Routledge.

DE COCK, C. and HIPKIN, I. (1997) TQM and BPR: beyond the beyond myth. *Journal of Management Studies*, Vol. 34, No. 5, September, 659–675.

HATCH, M.J. & YANOW, D. (2003) Organization theory as an interpretive science. In H. Tsoukas & C. Knudsen (eds) *The Oxford handbook of organization theory* Oxford: Oxford University Press.

HATVANY, N. and PUCIK, V. (1981) An integrated management system: lessons from the Japanese experience. *Academy of Management Review*, July.

JICK, T. and PEIPERL, M. (eds). (2003) *Managing change: cases and concepts*. 2nd ed. New York: Irwin/McGraw-Hill.

JUNKERMAN, J. (1982) 'We are driven,' Mother Jones. In G. Morgan (1989) *Creative organization theory: A resource book* (pp21–23, 38–40). Newbury Park: Sage.

KEEN, L (1994) Middle management experiences of devolution in Barsetshire County Council Social Services Department. In D. Adam-Smith and A. Peacock (eds) *Cases in organisational behaviour*. London: Pitman Publishing.

KIESER, A. (1997) Rhetoric and myth in management fashion. *Organization*, Vol. 4, No. 1, 49–74.

LAMMING, R. (1993) *Beyond partnerships: strategies for innovation and lean supply*. Hemel Hempstead: Prentice Hall.

McGREGOR, D. (1960) *The human side of enterprise*. New York: McGraw-Hill.

MEREDITH, J.R. (1992) *The management of operations: a conceptual emphasis*. London: John Wiley & Son Inc.

MONDEN, Y. (1983) *Toyota production system*. Norcross: Industrial Engineering and Management Press.

MORGAN, G. (1989) *Creative organization theory: a resource book*. Newbury Park: Sage.

OAKLAND, J.S. (1989) *Total quality management*. Oxford: Butterworth-Heinemann.

OGDEN, S.G. and ANDERSON, R. (1999) The role of accounting in organisational change: Promoting performance improvements in the privatised UK water industry. *Critical Perspectives on Accounting*, Vol. 10, 91–124.

OLIVER, N. and WILKINSON, B. (1993) Japanization in the UK: experiences from the car industry. In D. Gowler, K. Legge and C. Clegg (eds) *Case studies in organization behaviour and human resource management*. 2nd ed. London: Paul Chapman Publishing Ltd.

OUCHI, W.G. (1981) *Theory Z: how American business can meet the Japanese challenge*. Reading, Mass: Addison-Wesley

PETERS, T.J. and WATERMAN, R.H. (1982) *In search of excellence: lessons from America's best-run companies*. New York: Harper & Row.

PIORE, M.J. and SABEL, C.R. (1984) *The second industrial divide: possibilities for prosperity*. New York: Basic Books.

SELTO, F.H., RENNER, C.J. and YOUNG, S.M. (1995) Assessing the organizational fit of a just-in-time manufacturing system: testing selection, interaction and systems models of contingency theory. *Accounting, Organizations and Society*, Vol. 20, No. 7, 665–684.

SHINGO, S. (1985) *A revolution in manufacturing: the SMED system*. Stamford, Conn: Productivity Press.

Optimistic approaches

CHAPTER 6

INTRODUCTION

One way of dividing up theorising about organisations is on the optimistic/pessimistic spectrum. From the beginning of organisation theory, and also in the writings of the great sociologists before a discipline called 'organisation theory' became accepted, there were writers who were optimistic about the future of society, work and the workforce; and there were those who foresaw increasing conflict in society and increasing misery and enslavement for most. In this chapter we will concentrate upon those who have taken an optimistic view.

Durkheim, one of the three 'fathers' of sociology (with Marx and Weber), has been quoted as approving of modern industrial society. He saw it as being far more liberating than were traditional communities, or what he called societies which had a 'mechanical solidarity', whose self-sufficiency and relatively low-level technology allowed far fewer differences in occupation and social conventions, and thus far less freedom of choice in major areas of life. Modern societies were more complex and could not maintain this kind of solidarity. Durkheim saw modern societies as being much larger-scale, with a far greater division of labour, and with people having more opportunities for diverse occupations, social mobility and social choices. This could, in Durkheim's view, lead to a new solidarity, which he called 'organic solidarity', consisting of contractual relationships created through the wider interdependence of a more extended division of labour (Clegg and Dunkerley 1980, p25).

DURKHEIM'S SOLIDARITY

An organic solidarity would need 'proper regulation', including moral education and a moral commitment, achievable because of the commonality of interest between occupations (Clegg and Dunkerley 1980, p24). There needed to be socially imposed norms in order to curb excessive individualism. If this did not happen, Durkheim predicted, a society where social norms would not be upheld and a condition of normlessness or *anomie* would obtain, with social insecurity and instability (Blauner 1964). He predicted that if the technological development of the industrial revolution moved so fast that social patterns were disrupted and new ones could not be established to keep pace with these changes, there would be a lack of social cohesion (Clegg and Dunkerley 1980).

However, according to Eldridge and Crombie (1974), Durkheim included one large proviso for the success of industrial society – a qualification often ignored by later theorists using and developing his ideas. Durkheim considered that modern societies could be successful and socially cohesive only if everyone in the society started at birth on a level playing field in terms of wealth and opportunities (cited in Clegg and Dunkerley 1980, pp28–29). This would have involved a complete revolution of the economic and social organisation of all the societies in Western Europe and the United States, the societies that were industrialising and that were Durkheim's examples of organic societies

As we know, Western societies did not revolutionise to become level playing fields, and there are debates as to how much social cohesion there is in our societies. In this chapter we shall

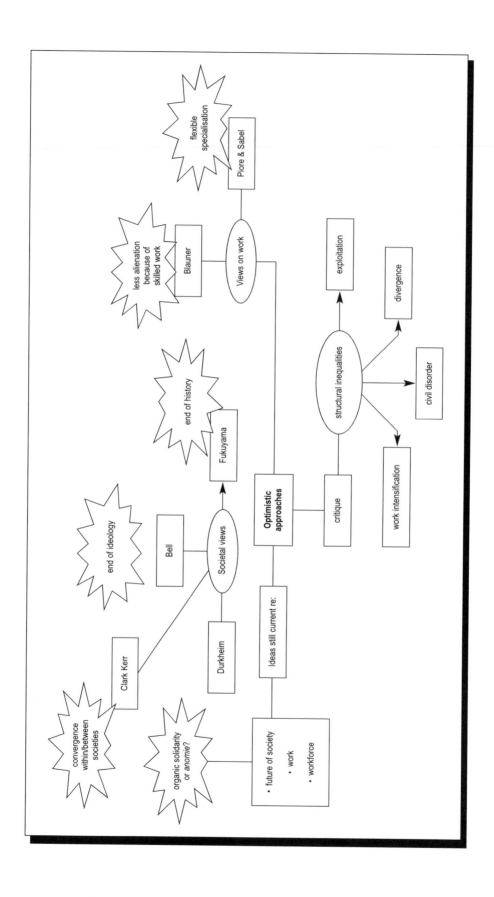

be considering those theorists who have been optimistic about Western societies and also about all other societies, seeing them as linked into one global system of progress. (Later on we shall be considering opposing theories that see the interlinkage of the world as one where richer, more industrialised countries exploit impoverished, less technologically developed ones.) Optimism has centred on the quality and conditions of work. Much of this writing has come from the United States, from the 1960s onwards; some of it is in opposition to the class-based, conflict-laden ideas of Marx and of labour process theorists who based their ideas on those of Marx.

Another way in which theorising about organisations has been divided is into theorists who on the one hand take a wider societal view. Some of these writers, the best-known perhaps being Kerr *et al* (1964), have argued that the very process of industrialisation will perforce bring about a world in which workers will become more skilled and better off because of the requirements of successful industrialisation, effects which will, as industrialisation spreads, reach all societies. Some theorists in the United States predicted that societies would improve so much that conflict would disappear, as would class and the ideology of class (Bell, 1962; Fukuyama, 1992). On the other hand, and particularly prevalent in the study of organisations in the 1970s and 1980s in the USA, are theorists who focus more narrowly on work and organisations (Lounsbury and Ventresca 2003). The first and last set of theories are in this last category. Work has been adjudged to be becoming less tedious, tiring and alienating, and more skilled, interesting and empowering (Blauner 1964). In the 1980s the flexible specialisation thesis followed in the same vein: work would be flexible and would be geared to allowing employees to develop, gain skills and have more independence, making for a happier, more empowered workforce (Piore and Sabel 1984).

So let us look at some of the key theorists and theories, which can be collected together into what we are labelling the Optimistic school, to see both their strengths and some of their weaknesses.

BLAUNER

Blauner (1964) surveyed developments since the early industrial revolution and concluded that the harshness, tedium and de-skilling that had accompanied technological developments were on the way out as technology advanced even further. There would be more skilled, more comfortable jobs with increased worker control and discretion likely in the future. He developed an 'inverted U-curve', which plotted the position of the worker and the degree of skill and involvement or alienation as industrialisation progressed, the type of technology used and the degree of control by the worker.

Blauner isolated four phases of the industrialisation process, each with distinctive technologies and varied levels of skill and discretion by workers. In his study, Blauner compared four industries each representing, in his eyes, different types and stages of industrialisation. The first, the printing industry, was in those days characteristic of a *craft* technology: little standardisation; low mechanisation, with much work done manually. More highly mechanised industries with more standardised work procedures are characterised for Blauner by the textile industry. This he called *machine-minding* technology, as the bulk of the work was done by workers minding machines. Further standardisation and automation, reaching the top of Blauner's inverted U-curve, were typified by the motor-car industry, characterised by an *assembly-line* technology with highly structured work, done by workers who had the least control over any part of the job, as they were dominated by the technology in terms of how, when and at what pace they carried out the work. The latest and most advanced type of technology according to Blauner, typified by the industrial chemical industry, was *continuous-process* production, in which all production processes were done automatically, with workers monitoring panel instruments and repairing the machinery. Here, workers would be skilled, much more comfortable in their work, and monitoring rather than being monitored by their machines (Blauner 1964, p7).

Blauner linked these four stages to his concept of alienation, which he described in terms of workers' feelings towards their work and workplace. He used the concepts of *powerlessness* (taken from Marx's writings), *meaninglessness, social alienation* (echoing Durkheim's idea of *anomie*) and *self-estrangement* to highlight the feelings that workers had when they were alienated (Blauner 1964, pp16–32). Blauner argued that workers experienced different types of alienation largely according to the technology they were working with. Worker alienation reached its highest intensity with the rigours of assembly line work, which, as mentioned, he plotted at the height of his inverted U-curve.

This, as will be seen in Chapter 8, is very different from Marx's concept of alienation. Blauner recognised Marx's ideas of loss of control over and separation from the work process by workers and the alienating effects of this, but he thought that actual ownership of the work process was less important in terms of workers' alienation than whether their jobs became more pleasant and more under their operative control. Blauner's view of alienation was subjective and entirely linked to workers' feelings, whereas Marx regarded alienation as an objective state in the relations of production, and though perhaps linked with workers' feelings, was not intrinsically governed by them.

Critiquing Blauner

Blauner's work has been criticised by radical and perhaps less optimistic theorists on two main counts. First there is the detail of his analysis: his picture of people walking around in white coats measuring and checking instruments may have been true of technicians in process industries, but it was certainly not true of all workers, nor likely to be in the foreseeable future. Even in the process industries there were jobs to be done that were less skilled, more routine and involving hard physical labour, such as humping sacks of coal to run the machines that were being checked by technicians. Outside the process industries, there were still many jobs equalling the situation at the top of Blauner's curve, such as people still working on moving assembly lines. While much of this work may have been taken over by robots in the motor industry, it is certainly prevalent in many other types of production.

The computer chip industry, where many women are employed, particularly in South-East Asia, is one example. Computer technology itself has enabled many of the controls that were characteristic of moving assembly lines to be imposed on white-collar workers. The speed at which people work can be monitored by computers, and people are often rewarded or punished according to how quickly they do work. Breaks from the computer are also monitored, and there have been notorious examples in recent years of people working in call centres being humiliated for taking breaks considered too long when going to the lavatory. Clegg and Dunkerley (1980) point out that it is not necessarily the type of technology alone that will determine the way work is organised. They argue that the extent of routinisation and standardisation of work is more of a political decision consciously taken by senior management. Quoting Braverman (1974), they claim that there has been more standardisation even in high-status and high-skilled professions such as law and accountancy, the latter largely through computers.

Blauner has been criticised from a more theoretical basis for his functionalist approach. Similar criticisms have been made as those already mentioned with regard to human relations, motivation and other 'managerialist' theories. Blauner shares the same assumptions with them: that there can be a basis for consensus and true satisfaction in the current economic, social and political context. He does not take into account what is central to critical theorists – that one has to look at the context in which work is organised, or what labour process theorists, taking Marx's concepts and terminology, have called the relations of production. They argue that because these are unequal, in that owners and shareholders, often represented by managers, have much more power than do workers, this cannot make for a true consensus. Not only do workers not have any say in what is produced, how it is produced and how it is sold (which is the basis of Marx's concept of alienation), but they have very little say in their pay and conditions of work and in decisions as to whether they keep their jobs or not. This of course also depends to an extent on the legislation in force. Currently, in the UK, under Tony Blair's Labour government, workers have far fewer protective rights than do their counterparts in Europe, and lower pay than in many European countries.

Critical theorists would argue that Blauner's idea of alienation, dependent on how workers feel, is misleading, as it ignores the basis inequalities and opportunities for exploitation in society. Israel (cited in Scott 2003, p328) has forcefully argued that alienation is essentially an objective condition of the social structure, and not a subjective feeling. He uses Marx's argument of false consciousness, which can include psychological manipulation, as an explanation for why workers may feel 'happy' in their work situation and not alienated. Critical theorists such as Gramsci, Lukes and Habermas have taken a great interest in the ideological power of persuasion, and have analysed how it is that people on the wrong end of the power, wealth and status continuum are on the whole accepting of their condition, and in Western democracies keep voting governments in that (in the view of these theorists) do not operate in the interests of the general workforce and population. They would argue that if workers feel happy, this is mainly because they have been 'told' in various ways and with varying degrees of subtlety that they are in a good situation. Lukács has called this the 'universalisation' of managerial interests, which are really to the benefit of managers and those they represent rather than being in the interests of workers (Alvesson and Deetz 1996, p200).

KERR, DUNLOP, HARBISON AND MYERS

Clark Kerr and his co-authors (1960, 1964, 1973) also painted a bright picture of the future of work and society generally. Their analysis extended beyond Western society to include what was then the communist bloc in Eastern Europe and also the Third World, or what have been called 'developing' countries. Because they argued that all societies eventually would become similar to each other, their ideas have been known as the convergence theory. This book was a counterargument to Marxist portrayals of the likelihood of increasing inequality, exploitation and conflict in capitalist societies. The title of their book was *Industrialism and Industrial Man*, and the basis of their ideas was that the process of industrialisation, which would involve the whole world, would necessarily have certain consequences for work and for society in general, consequences that would lead to better lives, with less inequality and more consensus or solidarity – to use Durkheim's phrase.

Their arguments ran as follows: as societies industrialised, they would need more skilled staff to handle technological developments if the industrialisation process was to succeed. In order to have more skilled staff, governments would need to expand the education system to educate sufficient people so that they would be prepared to learn the new skills required. As people became more educated and skilled, they would be able to command higher pay and also to move up the social and economic ladder. As more people took advantage of those opportunities, those in unskilled positions would also be able to earn more as they became scarcer and therefore more sought after.

They took the argument further to include society as a whole. As more and more people became involved in the industrialisation process, which was bound to expand and become the major player in the economy, so the proportion of inherited wealth to earned income would decrease. All this together would serve to change the social structure from a pyramidal shape, where a small minority owned most of the wealth, with a small middle sector and the vast majority at the bottom of the economic heap, to a shorter, diamond-shaped figure, with the majority in the middle of the socio-economic ladder and also with the distance between the richest and the poorest smaller than previously. As industrial societies developed with occupational change and the increasing scale of the society, there would develop a consensus that scientific and technological expertise were crucial for industrial progress, and that social, geographical and occupational mobility were 'high-value' goals for the society (Clegg and Dunkerley 1980, p250).

This process would extend to other societies, no matter what their political system or stage of development. There is a substantial role for government because of the need to plan and co-ordinate the large range and scale of activities. This, Kerr *et al* argued, would be fully consistent with larger freedoms for individuals, who would be able to enjoy a larger variety of occupations and the goods and services produced because of their larger incomes. Certain freedoms would also be guaranteed in the workplace through a 'web of rules' determined by the technology and the scale of operations (Kerr *et al* 1964, p24). This web of rules would determine internal employment rules and conditions as well as norms of performance and output.

This web of rules depended to some extent on the technology, the markets and budgetary constraints of the enterprise. These, according to Kerr *et al*, would override cultural and national characteristics the more the pace of industrialisation increased. They therefore predicted that there would be similar changes in the Soviet Union, not because the government and party would suddenly see reason and become more democratic, but because of this logic of industrialism. To have a successful industrial society, one had to have skilled and willing workers who would participate in the establishment and operation of the rules. A totalitarian system would be unlikely to be able to produce workers who would contribute wholeheartedly and efficiently to this process, nor was it likely to have efficient procedures. So in order to become an effective industrial society and keep abreast of the other industrial societies, the authors argued, the communist countries would have to become more democratic as well as provide workers with education and skills, thus converging with Western societies. Developing, Third World societies, through the example of the First and Second Worlds, would eventually also industrialise and their path would follow that predicted for Western and communist countries.

Critique of the convergence thesis

In the foreward to the later (1973) edition of *Industrialism and Industrial Man*, Haddon referred to its optimism as a 'brief interregnum' in Western social thought (1973, p1), though one reads and hears similar ideas today (which is why these ideas have been included in this book). Haddon agrees with the convergence theorists in their criticism of Marx with regard to the insurgence of the working class in Western capitalist society. The working class was not about to make revolution and capitalism seemed secure for the foreseeable future. Where Haddon takes issue with the convergent theorists' ideas is in their confidence in the likelihood of decreasing inequality, redistribution of wealth and the elimination of poverty. He pleads ignorance by many of conditions of poverty in Western industrial societies, and quotes Engels's comments in the 1840s about the layout of towns, which Haddon considers still applicable, by way of explanation:

> The town itself is peculiarly built, so that a person may live in it for years and go in and out daily without coming into contact with a working-people's quarter or even with workers ... The members of this money aristocracy can take the shortest road through the middle of all the labouring districts to their places of business without ever seeing ... the grimy misery that lurks to the right and the left.
>
> (Engels, cited in Kerr *et al* 1973, p2)

Clegg and Dunkerley argue (as they do regarding Blauner's deterministic view of technology) that many problems of organisation are problems of structural inequalities, and cannot be solved simply by people acquiring more skills. The unequal relations of production which give rise to inequality, exploitation and alienation have not been considered as one of the factors likely to determine what happens, not only with regard to workers' satisfaction and feelings of well-being, but also with regard to the notion that inequality would decrease overall and that there would be more social mobility in society. They also make the point that many white-collar jobs are deliberately designed not to provide higher skill levels and more responsibility:

> a great deal of white-collar work is purposively designed to prevent the individual exercising discretion or judgment.
>
> (Clegg and Dunkerley 1980, p357)

There has certainly not been a reduction in income differentials. In a recent report in the *Guardian* (31 July 2003), it was stated that boardroom pay rose seven times as much as average earnings in 2002, and that the average pay for a FTSE-100 chief executive was now £1,677,685. The number of directors receiving more than £1 million during 2002 broke the record at 190 – 60 more than in the previous year. If these figures are compared to the national minimum wage, which many people get paid, the difference is enormous. If one then compares this difference to that of, say, 30 years ago, it is clear that pay differentials are far greater.

As regards the Soviet Union, while the communist party had control, its pace and type of industrialisation was, it has been argued by many, largely determined and distorted by the United States of America's defence spending. The amount of US defence spending during the Cold War put pressure on the Soviet Union to spend more on its defence, to the detriment of all other social and economic needs, except perhaps the development of space technology. There was no attempt at democratisation while the regime lasted, and its demise resulted from a number of factors both internal and external, though not because of the imperative of industrialisation.

COLONIALISM AND THE THIRD WORLD

Third World countries, particularly those in Africa and Latin America, have conspicuously not lived up to the predictions of the convergence theory. These countries are getting poorer, rather than benefiting from the example and experience of Western countries. It has been estimated that in 2001 there were more than 1.3 billion people living in absolute poverty, and that the number was increasing, partly because more people in the rich, First World were also becoming impoverished (Hoogvelt 2001). According to the UN *Human Development Report 1999* (cited in Hoogvelt 2001), the income gap between the 20 per cent of the population living in the richest societies and the 20 per cent in the poorest widened from 30:1 in 1960 to 74:1 in 1997. In the postscript to the 1973 edition of their book, Kerr *et al* recognise that their predictions for Third World countries fell short when it came to the development of rural areas (p288):

> In many African and Latin American countries industrialization has increased the disparities between ... the urban and rural areas. It has meant a new and challenging life for a smaller minority but it has largely bypassed the rural masses.

However, their arguments do not seek to explain further the difficulties in developing countries or look to see if there are links between the rapid and successful industrialising processes of Western countries and the lack of rapid progress in Third World countries. Many development theorists have, in fact, argued that the growth in the First World and its opportunities for industrialisation and further growth have been achieved at the expense of the rest of the world:

> the historical development of the capitalist system ... [has] generated underdevelopment in the peripheral satellites whose economic surplus was expropriated, while generating economic development in the metropolitan centres which appropriate that surplus – and, further, that this process still continues.   (Frank 1971, p27)

Initially, during what Hoogvelt has termed the *mercantilist* phase (1500–1800), European merchants acquired gold, spices, slaves and control of existing trade routes (which in Baran's *The Political Economy of Growth* was referred to as looting and plundering [Baran 1976]), enabling the economic surplus of these activities to pay for the industrialisation process in Europe. Conversely, this loss of wealth by the rest of the world removed the opportunity for it likewise to industrialise, and furthermore led to backwardness in its societal and economic development (Hoogvelt 2001). The estimate of 17 million people being removed from the African continent as slaves is indication enough of the harmful effects that such ravages are likely to have achieved.

The *colonial* period (1800–1950) saw massive investment in the infrastructure of colonies in the interests of trade for the metropolitan countries, ownership of mineral production and the export of cash crops. It also led to the internationalisaton of the division of labour (making the colonial areas producers and exporters of primary produce, traded at unfavourable rates for manufactured goods from metropolitan countries) and, according to Hoogvelt, the cultural Westernisation of local elites, which lapsed after the anti-colonial independence struggles, in the words of the radical Algerian writer, Fanon (cited in Hoogvelt 2001, 32):

> into extreme political lethargy, motivated only by private greed and vanity.

All these would allow the continuation of the domination of resources in postindependence former colonies by the metropolitan powers in the *neo-colonial* period (1950–1970), enabling the further development of international capitalism at the continued expense of Third World countries (Hoogvelt 2001).

There developed at this time what became known as dependency theory, which, in a sentence, located the causes of backwardness in Third World countries in the growth of the world capitalist system. The structures established under colonialism or before colonialism would continue the economic distortion, resulting in further economic stagnation and the pauperisation of the majority in Third World countries. One of the foremost writers in this area, Frank, concentrated his analysis on Latin American countries in particular. Using Chile as an example, he argued that there was an exploitation chain from the capitalist metropolis to national, to regional and then to local centres:

> At each step ... the relatively few capitalists above exercise monopoly power over the many below, expropriating some or all of their economic surplus and, to the extent that they are not expropriated in turn by the still fewer above them, appropriating it for their own use. Thus at each point, the international, national, and local capitalist system generates economic development for the few and underdevelopment for the many.   (Frank 1971, p32)

During the present or, in Hoogvelt's terminology, *postimperialist* period (1970 onwards), the First World has developed a new pattern of extraction of wealth from 'developing' societies – that of debt. The separation of contractual obligations to repay debt from the management of enterprises led to disregard by the foreign company as to whether the local enterprise was being run profitably, as it was guaranteed debt repayment by the state financial institutions. This has led to 'gross inefficiencies and deepening indebtedness' (Hoogvelt 2001, p49). By the end of the 1980s, Third World debt stood at $1 trillion. Not all countries were equally so affected, and a division has been developing between Third World countries, namely between the newly industrialising economies (NIEs) in South-East Asia beginning to participate in the more intensively integrated global capitalist production which transcends national boundaries and the other countries, such as those in Africa, which are becoming increasingly marginalised.

BELL

Bell (1962) had ideas that were similar to those of the convergence theorists. He decried, *inter alia*, the application of European theories of class to the United States, which, he claimed, were not applicable to that society. The Cold War, for one thing, with the need for Soviet containment:

> has set in its wake a whole consequent of political and social changes ... all of which have reworked the map of American society.   (Bell 1962, p14)

Examples of alternate forms of organisation which would weaken residual class ties in the USA included voluntary organisations which acted as pressure or ethnic groups, the cultural *embourgeoisement*, or what Bell calls the growth of a 'middlebrow' society (1962, p33). This was due to increasing levels of education, a healthy non-conformity because of the rise to prominence of many from diverse ethnic minorities, accompanied by the acceptance of Beatnik bohemianism by mainstream society. Because of the pioneering nature of US society, with no tradition of feudalism and with the normalcy of change and innovation, raising productivity and standards of living were not the obstacles they were in Europe, with its 'ingrained' resistance to increasing worker mobility and to broadening markets, or in underdeveloped countries, with their unwillingness to industrialise (Bell 1962, p37). Workers, whose grievances were once the stimulus to social change, were now more satisfied, with many expectations fulfilled because of the expansion of white-collar work.

Like the convergence theorists, Bell also argued that inherited property was losing its power in an industrial world where:

> technical skill becomes more important than inheritance as a determinant of occupation, and political power takes precedence over economic.   (Bell 1962, p398)

Because things were getting better for everyone in the West, with the modification of capitalism, the rise of the welfare state, the consensus among Western intellectuals for decentralisation, political pluralism and a mixed economy rather than untempered capitalism, class would lose its meaning. This claim was strengthened by the atrocities committed by the Soviet government: the Moscow trials, the pact with Nazi Germany in the l930s, the labour camps and the suppression of the Hungarian uprising (Bell 1962).

Unlike the convergence theorists, Bell did not foresee an increasing isomorphism between societies in different parts of the world. Rather, he saw the 'end of ideology' – the old nineteenth-century universal ideals and ideologies of humanism and democracy would be displaced in the newly independent countries in Asia and Africa by economic development, national power, and the rise of new and on occasion coercive elites, who would take their examples instead from Russia and China. What was even more alarming was the tacit support these repressive attitudes had from the 'new Left' intellectuals in the West, who trumpeted freedom and 'revolution' but who themselves were out of touch with those former ideals of democracy and civil rights, and were prepared to support the sacrifice of current lives as a means to a future utopian or revolutionary end (Bell 1962, p405).

Critique of Bell

Very similar comments apply to Bell as to Kerr *et al.* There was an ignoring of political and social inequality and poverty in the West; an over-optimism about the benefits for employees of white-collar and even professional work (Clegg and Dunkerley 1980); a denial of the possible conflicts of interest between workers' and management's interests; and no serious argument against writers who claimed that underlying economic and political structures would in the end perpetuate inequality and expoitation (Scott 2003). Perhaps Bell was more prescient in his analysis of the then communist and fascist dictatorships and the new elites' repression of people in newly independent countries.

FUKUYAMA

Fukuyama (1992) would be included by most people as a member of the optimistic school: his arguments seem similar to Bell's and to those of the convergence theorists. He espoused the German philosophers Hegel's and Marx's concepts of the end of history, by which they (and he) meant not the cessation of great events, but the end of an evolutionary process. Different types of human societies such as 'primitive'/'advanced' or 'traditional'/'modern' were part of an evolutionary development that would ultimately end:

> when mankind had achieved a form of society that satisfied its deepest and most fundamental longings.
>
> (Fukuyama 1992, pxii)

This would be the 'end of history' – a liberal state for Hegel, a communist society for Marx. Fukuyama's 'end of history' was the triumph of liberal democracy, which he saw as a system of government emerging all over the world, with the demise of hereditary monarchies, fascism and communism. He saw liberal democracy, while not without serious social problems and injustices, as free of the weaknesses and internal contradictions that had characterised those other systems. The basic principles of liberty and equality, which, according to Fukuyama, were ideals that could not be improved upon, he saw as fundamental to modern democracies, even if incompletely implemented. The 'end of history' had arrived, as in his view:

there would be no further progress in the development of underlying principles and institutions, because all of the really big questions had been settled.　　　　　　　　　　　　　　　　　　　　　　　　(Fukuyama 1992, pxii)

Fukuyama was optimistic that liberal democracy would be achieved not only in the West, but for the 'greater part of humanity' (1992, pxii). Despite the terrible regimes of Hitler, Stalin, Pol Pot and others, Fukuyama's arguments rested on the fact of their defeat. Liberal democracy appeared to be the only coherent political ideology spanning different areas of the world, coupled with the spread of free market economic principles, which he saw as 'producing unprecedented levels of material prosperity, both in industrially developed countries and in countries that had been, at the close of World War II, part of the impoverished Third World' (1992, pxiii). Fukuyama saw a close connection often between the free market and political freedom:

A liberal revolution in economic thinking has sometimes preceded, sometimes followed, the move toward political freedom around the globe.　　　　　　　　　　　　　　　　　　　　　　(Fukuyama 1992, ppxiii–xiv)

Critique of Fukuyama

The critiques of Blauner, Kerr *et al* and Bell in large part also apply to Fukuyama – the optimism about the West and disregard for its persistent poverty and increasing inequality, and his faith in free market principles not only for Western development but also for that of the Third World. A further criticism, which Fukuyama himself acknowledged, was his teleological approach to history – that there was evolutionary development towards a better, and ultimately, the best future possible. This has been one of the major criticisms of modernism (see below) in the last two or three decades.

Most people think that Fukuyama was celebrating this end of history, whereas in fact he was merely recording its inevitability. For him the 'last man' referred to in the title of his book meant 'men without chests' – a term he used to lament the lack of challenge arising from competing philosophies in a world in which liberal democracy was unchallenged. For him, as the quotation above illustrates, progress was dependent upon competing ideologies, and a world without this was a world full of these 'men without chests'. Most people are unaware of this aspect of his work and would therefore categorise him as optimistic, and we have placed him here for that reason. He was actually critical of this optimism and has since abandoned his end of history argument – presumably because it has been widely misunderstood and misquoted – to be more openly critical.

One of the major spurs to reject a teleological and social engineering approach to human progress was precisely the catastrophies, ie those already mentioned that occurred in the last century, such as fascism and communism, and those of earlier centuries wrought largely through the European quest for raw materials and markets: the spice and slave trades and some of the more disruptive effects of colonialism. Events in the USA in the 1960s, principally the civil rights disturbances and the anti-Vietnam protests, confirmed many in their opposition to the certainty and universal benefits of what Fukuyama called liberal democracy.

Unlike Fukuyama's arguments regarding the survival and spread of liberal democracy, many theorists have argued against 'modernist' 'meta-theorising', given these disasters, and have adopted a much more local and humble approach to the study of societies. There is a strong recognition that there are different interpretations of the same structures and events, so that not all may have the same positive attitude to liberal democracy and its potential. Similarly the attitude of the researcher is changed from certainty to a more reflexive one, with respondents given more respect for their opinions and with the allowance that the same situations can be given different meanings by different subjects or stakeholders, these too changing at different times and in different circumstances (Bauman 1992). Thus the consensus and certainty of all the above theories have been contested strongly also on these grounds.

FLEXIBLE MANUFACTURING

Flexibility has encompassed a number of factors. One of the most important has been to do with making manufacturing systems flexible. What this meant was using subcontractors for manufacturing operations. Benetton, for instance, subcontracted standard operations such as drilling, turning and milling, which obviated their having to invest in up-to-date machinery (Lorenz, cited in Clegg 1990, p124). This was part of a general change from the 1970s in centre-periphery relations in organisations, with work that had previously been part of the industrialised centre exported to various peripheral locations, the centre concentrating on managerial and financial functions. Piore and Sabel (1984) called the development of flexible manufacturing systems a 'second industrial divide', which they saw in a positive light (Clegg 1990, p180). In order for people to be able to adapt to the new changes in technology and in manufacturing systems, flexibility in work practices and in skills and re-skilling was thought to be helpful. There were different views about flexible systems. Some thought, like Blauner, that it would lead to a more skilled workforce and increased participation by it in those changing conditions. Work would become more 'flexible' and employees would be able to organise their work according to their particular needs, rather than be compelled to work at times more convenient to their employers. Clegg (1990) has identified three approaches to flexible manufacturing systems: neo-romanticism, neo-managerialism and neo-Marxian critiques.

Neo-romanticism

Piore and Sabel's (1984) claims constituted a new capitalist ideology (Swedberg 2003). One could regain the romantic or utopian aspects of the pre-industrial craft industry, with high-technology cottage industries where employees would be more generalist, and not subject to mechanisation and tight managerial control. They would also be living in a community and in solidarity, as opposed to the alienation of Fordist mechanisation, which Blauner put at the top of his U-curve of alienation. All this would happen because of the changes in patterns of consumption, which were becoming more differentiated and specialist, and unsuited to high levels of specialisation and rigid production processes (Scott 2003). Flexible organisations, with craftsmen working in a type of cottage industry based on new technology, would best succeed in this type of market, as did Benetton in the Emilia-Romagna area of Italy. Because flexible organisations and workshops were often embedded in broader institutional bases – kinship ties or local political structures – this would encourage co-operation and long-term social ties (Scott 2003). Piore and Sabel then extended the idea of community and solidarity to large-scale manufacturing plants such as Boeing, which would also have to include flexible, responsive manufacturing in order to withstand Japanese competition (Clegg 1990).

Neo-managerialism

Cross (1985) and the National Economic Development Office (NEDO) Report (1986) emphasised consumption in similar fashion to Piore and Sabel, and also looked at the system of production. Employers had to encourage a core of committed, flexible, well-trained and well-looked-after core employees in order to respond successfully to changing market conditions. The other side of this privileged workforce was the peripheralisation of other workers who were casualised, untrained and without the benefits enjoyed by the primary workers. This was explained on the grounds of the rational organisation of production in response to the market (Clegg 1990).

Neo-Marxian critiques

Neo-Marxian critiques focused on the welfare of the worker, and his or her autonomy and opportunity for skilled and responsible work and for a degree of independence and trust by management. As often is the case, they saw in these new systems of work not a great divide for the better, as did Piore and Sabel, but novel ways of managers exerting control over the workforce. Flexible specialisation, then, was seen as yet another means of exploiting workers through the intensification of work and through the division of the workforce into core and peripheral workers, the latter receiving none of the benefits and privileges of the core workers. This in addition served to split the political strength of the trade union movement between representing the privileged core workforce or attempting to fight for the casualised workers, who were in a very weak and declining position (Clegg 1990).

It is interesting that Piore and Sabel themselves were able to recognise an agenda of control when specialised machinery replaced the old, more generalised tools:

> Power in the market, not efficiency ..., decided the contest.
>
> (1984, p40, cited in Scott 2003, p247)

Coriat (1980) argued that workgroup autonomy was an internal means of surveillance replacing former external surveillance. New technology was a means of intensifying work, coupled with new types of participation by the workforce in the organisation, as was done in Japan (see Chapter 5). Some writers such as Pollert (1988) argued that some of the new technology, under the guise of flexibility, served to de-skill workers rather than the opposite. Microprocessor technology was cited as an example.

CONCLUSION

These arguments are still continuing, and optimistic as well as more radical or cynical approaches are present in the area of organisation studies, extending from questions of employee autonomy and discretion versus routinisation and standardisation, to issues of gender equality and diversity. Wider and more local approaches are also both current. Functionalist and many postmodern theorists have tended to avoid broad societal analyses in favour of more local and organisation-based analyses, while radical and critical theorists have tended to start their analysis from what they see as the underlying social, economic and political structures and how this affects organisational processes and people at the workplace. In subsequent chapters less optimistic approaches will be considered further, based largely on the theories of Karl Marx.

SUMMARY

- Writers optimistic about society, organisations and their workforces based their ideas on interpretations of Durkheim's theories of organic solidarity.

- Blauner: industrial process now more skilled and less alienating.

- Critique: not true for all workers; radical theorists argue alienation is objective (eg class), not subjective; implication of unitarist goals.

- Kerr *et al*: societies would 'converge' internally, providing more mobility and less inequality as they industrialised, and this convergence would spread throughout the world through industrialisation.

- Critique: no convergence for many poorest in the West and especially not for most in Third World societies; radical theorists argue that structural change is needed to reduce inequality; much of wealth in the West has been at the expense of Third World countries.

- Bell: class weak in USA because of weak traditions; cultural and material 'middlebrowness', education and technological skills.

- Critique: similar to Kerr *et al*.

- Fukuyama: 'end of history' because triumph of liberal democracy eventually the world over.

- Critique: similar to above regarding optimistic views of Western and Third World societies, confirmed by civil unrest in the USA in 1960s and 1970s.

FURTHER READING

BLAUNER, R. (1964) *Alienation and freedom: the factory worker and his industry*. Chicago: University of Chicago Press.

CLEGG, S. and DUNKERLEY, D. (1980) *Organization, class and control*. London: Routledge & Kegan Paul.

HOOGVELT, A. (2001) *Globalization and the postcolonial world: the new political economy of development*. 2nd ed. Basingstoke: Palgrave.

KERR, C., DUNLOP, J.T., HARBISON, F.T. and MYERS, C.A. (1964) *Industrialism and industrial man: the problems of labor and management in economic growth*. 2nd ed. New York: Oxford University Press.

REFERENCES

ALVESSON, M. and DEETZ, S. (1996) Critical theory and postmodernism approaches to organizational studies. In S.R. Clegg, C. Hardy and W.R. Nord (eds) *Handbook of organization studies*. London: Sage.

BARAN, P. (1976) *The political economy of growth*. Harmondsworth: Penguin.

BAUMAN, Z. (1992) *Intimations of postmodernity*. London: Routledge.

BELL, D. (1962) *The end of ideology: on the exhaustion of political ideas in the fifties*. New York: Free Press.

BLAUNER, R. (1964) *Alienation and freedom: the factory worker and his industry*. Chicago: University of Chicago Press.

BRAVERMAN, H. (1974) *Labour and monopoly capital: the degradation of work in the twentieth century*. New York: Monthly Review Press.

CLEGG, S. (1990) *Modern organizations: organization studies in the postmodern world*. London: Sage.

CLEGG, S. and DUNKERLEY, D. (1980) *Organization, class and control*. London: Routledge & Kegan Paul.

CORIAT, B. (1980) The restructuring of the assembly line: a new economy of time and control. *Capital and Class*, Vol. 11, 34–43.

CROSS, M. (1985) *Towards the flexible craftsman*. London: Hamilton.

ELDRIDGE, J.E.T. and CROMBIE, A.D. (1974) *A sociology of organisations*. London: Allen & Unwin.

FRANK, A.G. (1971) *Capitalism and underdevelopment in Latin America*. Harmondsworth: Penguin Books.

FUKUYAMA, F. (1992) *The end of history and the last man*. London: Penguin Books.

HOOGVELT, A. (2001) *Globalization and the postcolonial world: the new political economy of development*. 2nd ed. Basingstoke: Palgrave.

KERR, C., DUNLOP, J.T., HARBISON, F.T. and MYERS, C.A. (1960) *Industrialism and industrial man: the problems of labor and management in economic growth*. 1st ed. Harmondsworth: Penguin Books.

KERR, C., DUNLOP, J.T., HARBISON, F.T. and MYERS, C.A. (1964) *Industrialism and industrial man: the problems of labor and management in economic growth*. 2nd ed. New York: Oxford University Press.

KERR, C., DUNLOP, J.T., HARBISON, F.T. and MYERS, C.A. (1973) *Industrialism and industrial man: the problems of labor and management in economic growth*. 3rd ed. Harmondsworth: Penguin Books.

LOUNSBURY, M. and VENTRESCA, M. (2003) The new structuralism in organization theory. *Organization*, Vol. 10, No. 3, 457–480.

NEDO (NATIONAL ECONOMIC DEVELOPMENT OFFICE). (1986) *Changing working patterns*. London: Author.

PIORE, M.J. and SABEL, C.R. (1984) *The second industrial divide: possibilities for prosperity*. New York: Basic Books.

POLLERT, A. (1988) The flexible firm: fixation or fact? *Work, Employment and Society*, Vol. 2, 281–316.

SCOTT, W.R. (2003) *Organizations: rational, natural, and open systems*. 5th ed. New Jersey: Pearson Education Inc.

SWEDBERG, R. (2003) Economic versus sociological approaches to organization theory. In H. Tsoukas and C. Knudsen (eds) *The Oxford handbook of organization theory*. Oxford: Oxford University Press.

The community-based approach

INTRODUCTION

Most organisational theory takes the view, as far as an organisation is concerned, that the only activities with which the organisation should be concerned are those which take place within the organisation, or between the organisation and its direct stakeholders – employees, suppliers or customers. This view places the organisation at the centre of its world and the only interfaces with the external world take place at the beginning and end of its value chain. These interfaces comprise of, at the commencement of the organisational processing cycle, resources acquisition (raw materials, labour capital etc) and, at the end of the cycle, selling its wares (goods or services) and distributing a share of the value created through its transformational process to its owners (ie shareholders). This view is essentially concerned with the transformational process within the organisation, and the management of that transformational process.

It is apparent however that any actions an organisation undertakes will have an effect not just upon itself but also upon the external environment within which that organisation resides. In considering the effect of the organisation upon its external environment it must be recognised that this environment includes both the business environment in which the firm is operating, the local societal environment in which the organisation is located and the wider global environment. This effect of the organisation can take many forms, such as:

- the utilisation of natural resources as a part of its production processes
- the effects of competition between itself and other organisations in the same market
- the enrichment of a local community through the creation of employment opportunities
- transformation of the landscape due to raw material extraction or waste product storage
- the distribution of wealth created within the firm to the owners of that firm (via dividends) and the workers of that firm (through wages) and the effect of this upon the welfare of individuals.

ORGANISATIONS AND THEIR ENVIRONMENTS

It can be seen from these examples that an organisation can have a very significant effect upon its external environment and can actually change that environment through its activities. It can also be seen that these different effects can in some circumstances be viewed as beneficial and in other circumstances be viewed as detrimental to the environment. Indeed the same actions can be viewed as beneficial by some people and detrimental by others.[1] This is why planning enquiries or tribunals, which are considering the possible effects of the proposed actions by a firm, will find people who are in favour and people who are opposed.

---

1 See Child (1984) and Crowther (1996) regarding the different dimensions of performance.

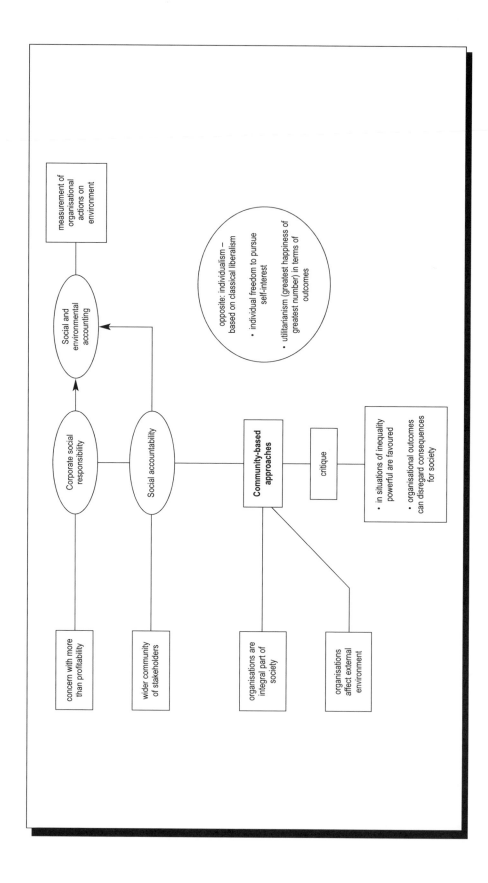

This is of course because the evaluation of the effects of the actions of an organisation upon its environment are viewed and evaluated differently by different people.

A growing number of writers, however, have recognised that the activities of an organisation affect the external environment. Such a suggestion first arose in the 1970s, and a wider view of company performance is taken by some writers who evince concern with the social performance of a business as a member of society at large. This view was stated by Ackerman (1975) who argued that big business was recognising the need to adapt to a new social climate of community accountability but that the orientation of business to financial results was inhibiting social responsiveness. McDonald and Puxty (1979) on the other hand maintain that companies are no longer the instruments of shareholders alone but exist within society and so therefore have responsibilities to that society, and that there is therefore a shift towards the greater accountability of companies to all participants.

Recognition of the rights of all stakeholders and the duty of a business to be accountable in this wider context therefore has been largely a relatively recent phenomenon.[2] The economic view of accountability only to owners has only recently been subject to debate to any considerable extent.

THE DEVELOPMENT OF SOCIAL ACCOUNTABILITY

Implicit in this concern with the effects of the actions of an organisation on its external environment is the recognition that it is not just the owners of the organisation who have a concern with the activities of that organisation. Additionally a wide variety of other stakeholders justifiably have a concern with those activities, and are affected by those activities. Those other stakeholders have not just an interest in the activities of the firm but also a degree of influence over the shaping of those activities. This influence is so significant that it can be argued that the power and influence of these stakeholders is such that it amounts to quasi-ownership of the organisation. Indeed Gray et al (1987) argue for a stakeholder approach to organisational management, recognising the wider stakeholder community.

Thus the performance of businesses in a wider arena than the stock market and its value to shareholders has become of increasing concern. Fetyko (1975) considers social accounting as an approach to reporting a firm's activities and stresses the need for identification of socially relevant behaviour, the determination of those to whom the company is accountable for its social performance and the development of appropriate measures and reporting techniques. Klein (1977) also considers social accounting and recognises that different aspects of performance are of interest to different stakeholder groupings, distinguishing for example between investors, community relations and philanthropy as areas of concern for accounting. While these writers consider, by implication, that measuring social performance is important without giving reasons for believing so, Solomons (1974) considers the reasons for measuring objectively the social performance of a business. He suggests that while one reason is to aid rational decision-making, another reason is of a defensive nature.

Unlike other writers, Solomons not only argues for the need to account for the activities of an organisation in term of its social performance but also suggests a model for doing this, in

---

2 Mathews (1997) traces its origins to the 1970s, although arguments show that such concerns can be traced back to the industrial revolution.

terms of a statement of social income. His model for the analysis of social performance is given in Figure 7.1.

From social accountability to corporate social responsibility

In recent years the concept of corporate social responsibility (CSR) has gained prominence to such an extent that the concept seems ubiquitous in popular media and is gaining increasing attention among academics from a wide range of disciplines. There are probably many reasons for the attention given to this phenomenon, not least of which is that of the corporate excesses of recent times. For many people, particularly in the Western world, the year 2002 will be remembered as the one in which corporate misbehaviour was exposed by the collapse of some large corporations. In particular the spectacular collapse of Enron and the subsequent fallout among the financial world – including the firm that Arthur Andersen himself founded in 1913 – will have left an indelible impression among people that all is not well with the corporate world and that there are problems needing to be addressed (Crowther and Rayman-Bacchus 2004a). This will be particularly the case amongst those adversely affected by this collapse, not least of whom are the former employees of the company who have lost their jobs, their life savings and their future pensions. Equally remembered, however, in other parts of the world is that 2002 was the tenth anniversary of the Union Carbide incident in Bhopal, India – the worst pollution incident in the history of the world. This incident killed thousands, left thousands permanently injured and an even greater number in the area surrounding the former plant living a life of misery. To date not one penny has been paid in compensation to those whose lives have been blighted by an incident caused by a lack of safety precautions that would have been required in the Western world and that any socially responsible organisation would implement as a matter of course.

Issues of socially responsible behaviour are not of course new and examples can be found from throughout the world, at least from the earliest days of the industrial revolution and the concomitant founding of large business entities (Crowther 2002a) and the divorce between ownership and management – or the divorcing of risk from rewards (Crowther 2004). However, corporate social responsibility is back on the agendas of corporations, governments and individual citizens throughout the world.

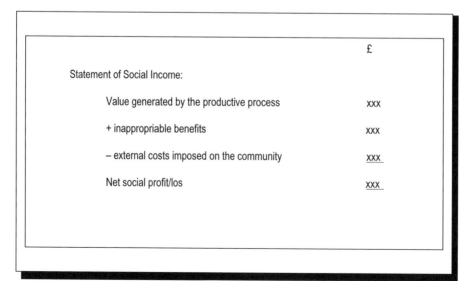

	£
Statement of Social Income:	
Value generated by the productive process	xxx
+ inappropriable benefits	xxx
– external costs imposed on the community	xxx
Net social profit/los	xxx

Figure 7.1 *Analysis of social performance*

This raises the question as to what exactly can be considered to be corporate social responsibility. According to the EU Commission (2002, p347):

> CSR is a concept whereby companies integrate social and environmental concerns in their business operations and in their interaction with their stakeholders on a voluntary basis.

A concern for stakeholders

All definitions seem to be based upon a concern with more than profitability and returns to shareholders. Indeed involving other stakeholders, and considering them in decision-making, is a central platform of CSR. Stakeholder management is based upon a consideration of all stakeholders. Numerous definitions of a stakeholder have been provided within the literature, and Sternberg (1997), who demonstrates that Freeman (1984)[3] has used multiple definitions, cites the following two as examples:

> those groups without whose support the organization would cease to exist   (Sternberg 1997, p31)

> any group or individual who can affect or is affected by the achievement of the organization's objectives.
> (Sternberg 1997, p46)

A stakeholder-managed organisation therefore attempts to consider the diverse and conflicting interests of its stakeholders and balance these interests equitably. The motivations for organisations to use stakeholder management may be in order to improve financial performance or social or ethical performance, howsoever these may be measured. In order to be able to adequately manage stakeholder interests it is necessary to measure the organisation's performance to these stakeholders, and this can prove complicated and time-consuming. Recently the Centre for Business Performance at Cranfield University set up a 'catalogue of measures' related to their Performance Prism that contains measures of each of the 'dimensions of performance' – stakeholder satisfaction, strategies, processes, capabilities and stakeholder contributions. The stakeholders identified were customer, employee, investor, regulator and community, and suppliers; in total the catalogue includes over 200 relevant measures. This shows the vast number of stakeholder measures that could be used in any organisation, although it is not expected that all of these will be relevant for any individual organisation. This again highlights the potential complexity of measuring performance for stakeholders, as these numerous measures will provide conflicting evidence on performance that somehow must be reconciled.

A number of themes arise from this concern. The first theme is the extent to which we can assess the accountability of organisations to a broader constituency by reference to an implicit or hypothetical *social contract*. In the process it is attempted to show how social contract theory also helps bind the relationship between corporate social responsibility and ethical behaviour. This raises questions about the scope and depth of commitment among corporate leaders to *social responsibility*. Assessing this commitment is made difficult, given what appears to be a runaway free market ideology, a belief system that seems to be elevating the corporation above the nation state and is being transmitted through corporate global expansion and USA-led government sponsorship. This can be developed in the context of the globalising process by considering the extent to which corporate and social exploitation of Internet technology is helping corporate bodies, consumers and citizens transform our world into *a global village* and can then be broadened to consider the wider relationship between *technological innovation and social change*. In examining this

---

3 This work is very often referred to as the seminal work in the area of stakeholder management.

relationship it can be shown that technological development is underpinned by a utilitarian perspective, and at the same time technological change is unavoidably bound up with making moral choices. Lastly, the wider debate about corporate social responsibility could be understood by drawing in a consideration of the extent to which there is, or should be, an underlying utilitarian assumption, and how our rights might be affected.

The broadest definition of corporate social responsibility is concerned with what is – or should be – the relationship between the global corporations, governments of countries and individual citizens. More locally the definition is concerned with the relationship between a corporation and the local society in which it resides or operates. Another definition is concerned with the relationship between a corporation and its stakeholders. For us, all of these definitions are pertinent and represent a dimension of the issue. A parallel debate is taking place in the arena of ethics – should corporations be controlled through increased regulation or has the ethical base of citizenship been lost, and does it need replacing before socially responsible behaviour will ensue? In the UK at present the government seems to believe that citizenship needs teaching to our schoolchildren, presumably in the belief that this will manifest itself in the behaviour of corporations in the future. However this debate is represented, it seems that it is concerned with some sort of social contract between corporations and society.

THE SOCIAL CONTRACT

This social contract implies some form of altruistic behaviour – the converse of selfishness. Self-interest connotes selfishness, and since the Middle Ages has informed a number of important philosophical, political and economic propositions. Among these is Hobbes's world where unfettered self-interest is expected to lead to social devastation. A high degree of regulation is prescribed in order to avoid such a disastrous outcome, but in the process we sacrifice our rights. Self-interest again raises its head in the utilitarian perspective as championed by Bentham (1789), Locke (1690a, 1690b) and J.S. Mill (1848a, 1848b). The latter, for example, advocated as morally right the pursuit of the greatest happiness for the greatest number. Similarly Adam Smith's free-market economics is predicated on competing self-interest. These influential ideas put the interest of the individual above the interest of the collective. Indeed, from this perspective, collective interests are best served through self-interest. At the same time this corporate self-interest has come to draw disapproval in modern times, as reflected in many of the arguments within this book. The moral value of individualism has all but vanished.

Has the pendulum swung too far toward encouraging corporate self-interest at the expense of the public interest? Indeed the continuing conversion of public-service provision to market testing by many governments suggests a strengthening belief that the two interests are not in conflict. Self-interest and altruism (promoting the welfare of others over self) need not be in conflict. There is ample evidence that encouraging corporate self-interest (and risk-taking) does benefit society (albeit unequally from a Marxist perspective). Some of that evidence is contested, as in the case of genetically modified foods. However, as this book shows, there is also abundant evidence to the contrary: that the pursuit of corporate self-interest continues to burden society with hitherto unimaginable costs. Nevertheless, since the 1980s most of the world's nations have set about creating anew, or refining, (capitalist) economic and political institutions that encourage corporate self-interest.

While governments and consumers alike look to business to continue delivering economic and social benefits, many observers remain concerned about corporate self-interest, a self-interest that is synonymous with those of the managers. Managerial self-interest is unavoidably driven by a combination of shareholder interests (backed up by markets for corporate control and managerial talent), and occupational rewards and career opportunity. The public interest is easily sacrificed on the altar of these managerial motivators (or constraints). Moreover, public interest is not homogeneous and therefore cannot be simply represented. Public interest has become factionalised into constituencies and stakeholder groupings, each concerned with their particular interests. Consider for example the 'not-in-my-back-yard' (NIMBY) protests over the building of recycling plants and mobile telephone masts, yet opinion polls support the former and sales of mobile phones demand more of the latter.

CORPORATE ALTRUISM

As has often been noted, from a global perspective corporate self-interest seems to be associated with an unequal distribution of economic and social benefits. However, it seems unfair to lay the responsibility for such inequality solely at the door of the corporation. National and regional politics, religious conviction and differentiated moral values all play an immeasurable role in shaping a nation's life chances.

There are many examples of corporations behaving altruistically, from the paternalism of nineteenth- and twentieth-century industrialists, to modern-day donations to charities and the *ad hoc* secondment of managers to community projects. However, the perceived value of such giving is tainted by suspicions that many such acts seem self-serving. For example, there is room to ask whether Microsoft is giving away computers out of altruism or as part of an aim to reinforce its brand name. Many modern projects of altruism are tied to the purchase of products from the giving corporation. Other initiatives are clearly pushing at the boundaries of acceptable corporate behaviour, such as donations to political parties. These examples show that corporate altruism covers a wide range of socially acceptable behaviour, from selfless giving to self-interested giving.

Perhaps one reason for corporate self-interest being such a mixed blessing is that we are overly reliant on evaluating the *consequences* (a notion discussed in our introduction) of corporate action, especially our fixation with the bottom line. Nothing concentrates the managerial mind like performance targets and outcomes. However, as Wilbur (1992) argues, self-interest encompasses not just consequences and results, but also requires freedom of choice and consistency. From this perspective the pursuit of corporate (self-interested) activity should be guided by structured alternatives and consistency, in order to ensure that the self-interest of others is not undermined by selfish action. Sensing that we cannot rely on corporate altruism we the public are demanding our governments initiate more legislation and tighter regulation. However, even this move has shown important weaknesses. Many of the politicians and policy-makers are in the pockets of business. Self-interest is even here, and it is not acceptable to us. These arguments cast doubt on the extent to which we are able to arrange our economic and political institutions in order to harness self-interest for the benefit of society. The functioning of a civilised society includes putting the interests of others before self-interest. As Baron *et al* (1992) and Mansbridge (1990) observed, altruism is part of social, political and economic life. However, the exploitative nature of capitalism sits uncomfortably with Kant's (1959) ideal of mutual respect for the interests of others, and even less with Rawls's (1971) desire to see a strong form of egalitarian liberalism. These tensions (between capitalism and liberalism, and between meeting unconditional social obligations and the pursuit of economic value) drive the need for constant vigilance of corporate activity. Since we are unlikely to abandon capitalism or escape from the fixation on performance measurement managerial commitment to upholding the interests of others could straightforwardly be included in the managerial performance appraisal (Crowther and Rayman-Bacchus 2004b).

Crowther and Rayman-Bacchus (2004a) have argued that the corporate excesses, which are starting to become disclosed and which are affecting large numbers of people, have raised an awareness of the asocial behaviours of corporations. This is one reason the issue of corporate social responsibility has become a much more prominent feature of the corporate landscape. Other factors have helped raise this issue to prominence, and Topal and Crowther (2004) argue that the effects of bioengineering and genetic modifications of nature are also giving rise to general concern. At a different level of analysis Crowther (2000, 2002b, 2002c) has argued that the availability of the World Wide Web has facilitated the dissemination of information and has enabled more pressure to be brought upon corporations by their various stakeholders.

SOCIAL AND ENVIRONMENTAL ACCOUNTING

Alongside this recognition that corporations are accountable to their stakeholders has come a development of the principles upon which this demonstration of accountability should be based. Inevitably this is predicated in accounting as a mechanism by which such action can be measured and reported. In generic terms this has come to be called either social or environmental accounting. The objective of environmental accounting is to measure the effects of the actions of the organisation upon the environment and to report upon those effects. In other words the objective is to incorporate the effect of the activities of the firm upon externalities and to view the firm as a network extending beyond just the internal environment to include the whole environment (see Crowther 2000, 2002a). In this view of the organisation the accounting for the firm does not stop at the organisational boundary but extends beyond to include not just the business environment in which it operates but also the whole social environment. Environmental accounting therefore adds a new dimension to the role of accounting for an organisation because of its emphasis upon accounting for external effects of the organisation's activities. In doing so this provides a recognition that the organisation is an integral part of society, rather than a self-contained entity with only an indirect relationship with society at large. This self-containment has been the traditional view taken by an organisation as far as their relationship with society at large is concerned, with interaction being only by means of resource acquisition and sales of finished products or services. Recognition of this closely intertwined relationship of mutual interdependency between the organisation and society at large, when reflected in the accounting of the organisation, can help bring about a closer, and possibly more harmonious, relationship between the organisation and society. Given that the managers and workers of an organisation are also stakeholders in that society in other capacities, such as consumers, citizens and inhabitants, this reinforces the mutual interdependency.

OPPOSING INDIVIDUALISM

The increasing concern being given to social responsibility (to which we will return in Chapter 12) is a reaction to the individualistic ethos of the 1980s. Individualism, which led to the greed of this era, is based upon the philosophy of classical liberalism. Classical liberal theory started to be developed in the seventeenth century by such writers as John Locke as a means of explaining how society operated, and should operate, in an era in which the divine right of kings to rule and to run society for their own benefit had been challenged and was generally considered to be inappropriate for the society which then existed. Classical liberalism is founded upon the two principles of reason and rationality: reason in that everything had a logic which could be understood and agreed with by all, and rationality in that every decision made was made by a person in the light of what their evaluation had shown them to be for their greatest benefit. Classical liberalism therefore is centred upon the individual, who is assumed to be rational and would make rational decisions, and is based upon the need to give freedom to every individual to pursue his or her own ends. It is therefore a philosophy of the pursuance of self-interest. Society, insofar as it existed and was considered to be needed, was therefore merely an aggregation of these individual self-interests. This aggregation was considered to be a sufficient explanation for the need for society. Indeed Locke argued that the whole purpose of society was to protect the rights of each individual and to safeguard those private rights.

There is, however, a problem with allowing every individual the complete freedom to follow his or her own ends and to maximise his or her own welfare. The problem is that in some circumstances this welfare can only be created at the expense of other individuals. It is through this conflict between the rights and freedoms of individuals that problems occur in society. It is for this reason therefore that de Tocqueville (1840) argued that there was a necessary function for government within society. He argued that the function of government therefore was the regulation of individual transactions so as to safeguard the rights of all individuals as far as possible.

Although this philosophy of individual freedom was developed as the philosophy of liberalism, it can be seen that it has been adopted by the 'New Right' governments throughout the world, for example by the UK government in the 1980s. This philosophy has led increasingly to the reduction of state involvement in society and the giving of freedom to individuals to pursue their own ends, with regulation providing a mediating mechanism where deemed necessary. It will be apparent, however, that there is a further problem with liberalism: the mediation of rights between different individuals only works satisfactorily when the power of individuals is roughly equal. Plainly this situation never arises between all individuals and this is the cause of one of the problems with society.

LIBERALISM AND INDIVIDUALISM

While this philosophy of liberalism was developed to explain the position of individuals in society and the need for government and regulation of that society, the philosophy applies equally to organisations. Indeed liberalism considers that organisations arise within society as a mechanism whereby individuals can pursue their individual self-interests more effectively than they can alone. Thus firms exist because it is a more efficient means of individuals maximising their self-interests through collaboration than is possible through each individual acting alone. This argument provides the basis for the theory of the firm (Coase 1937), which argues that through this combination of individuals the costs of individual transactions are reduced and efficiency increased. The doctrine of the free market is based upon the notion that this efficiency in combinations will be increased and businesses will thereby benefit. The notion that this will benefit all individuals is of greater concern, however, because the doctrine ignores the inequalities in power relations between individuals, which led to the corporate greed discussed above, which caused a renewed concern with social responsibility.

The concept of utilitarianism was developed as an extension of liberalism in order to account for the need to regulate society in terms of each individual pursuing, independently, his or her own ends. It was developed by people such as Bentham and John Stuart Mill, who defined the optimal position for society as being the greatest good of the greatest number. They argued that it was government's role to mediate between individuals to ensure this societal end. In utilitarianism it is not actions that are deemed to be good or bad but merely outcomes. Thus any means of securing a desired outcome was deemed to be acceptable, and if the same outcomes ensued then there was no difference, in value terms, between different means of securing those outcomes. Thus actions are value-neutral, and only outcomes matter. This is of course problematical when the actions of firms are concerned, because firms only consider outcomes from the point of view of the firm itself. Indeed accounting (as we know) only captures the actions of a firm insofar as they affect the firm itself and ignores other consequences of the actions of a firm. Under utilitarianism, however, if the outcomes for the firm were considered to be desirable then any means of achieving these outcomes was considered acceptable. In the nineteenth and early twentieth centuries this was the way in which firms were managed, and it is only in more recent times that it has become accepted that all the outcomes from the actions of the firm are important and need to be taken into account. The development of utilitarianism led to the development of economic theory as a means of explaining the actions of firms. Indeed the concept of perfect competition is predicated in the assumptions of classical liberal theory. From economic theory, of course, accounting developed as a tool for analysis to aid the rational decision-making assumed in that very theory.

COMMUNITARIANISM

During the era of individualism in the 1980s, however, a theoretical alternative was developed in the USA, which became known as communitarianism, although the concept goes back to the earlier work of such people as Tonnies (1957) and Plant (1974). Communitarianism is based upon the argument that it is not the individual, or even the state, which should be the basis of our value system. Thus the social nature of life is emphasised alongside public goods and services. The argument is that all individuals, including corporations, have an obligation to contribute towards the public nature of life rather than pursue their own interests. Underpinning the theories of communitarianism is the assumption that ethical behaviour must proceed from an understanding of a community's traditions and cultural understanding. Exponents argue that the exclusive pursuit of private interest erodes the network of social environments on which we all depend, and is destructive of our shared experiment in democratic self-government. A communitarian perspective recognises both individual human dignity and the social dimension of human existence, and that the preservation of individual liberty depends on the active maintenance of the institutions of civil society where citizens learn respect for others as well as self-respect, and where we acquire a lively sense of our personal and civic responsibilities, along with an appreciation of our own rights and the rights of others.

Thus the ideas of communitarianism seem to resonate with the ideas of corporate social responsibility. The theory has, however, received a bad press because many of the ideas have been usurped by neo-conservatives and used as a platform for recommending the subjugation of women and ethnic minorities, using the argument that the maintenance of community is dependent upon each person knowing his or her place in that community – basically a reinvention of the medieval view of society. In the work of such people as Etzioni (1994, 1997) and Bellah (1985) it has also acquired a quasi-religious tone. As such its relevance to organisational theory has become much less.

THE THIRD WAY

Although it has become the butt of many jokes in the present, the idea of the third way was originally developed as an alternative to the untrammelled individualism of free market economics without returning to a controlled economy. It was a term introduced by the incoming Prime Minister Tony Blair in 1997 and based upon the ideas of his adviser, Anthony Giddens (1998). It was intended to address the problems of social exclusion brought about through the previous 20 years of individualism. Unfortunately it failed to be supported by any obvious policy ideas and has been extensively challenged as failing to address many of the problems of society. Indeed many have stated that the problem of social exclusion cannot be addressed without also addressing the issue of wealth redistribution. The basic problem with this approach is that there is little in the way of theory to support it. As such the third way seems to have fallen from fashion and to have been little more than political rhetoric of its time. Implications for organisational theory are certainly not apparent.

CONCLUSIONS

The various theories addressed in this chapter have shown that there is a strong body of opinion placing organisations firmly within society as an integral part of that society. Thus the arguments here suggest that organisational theory cannot be considered in isolation from social and political theory, which themselves vary over time. Some of these theories have had their time and have been superseded as the fashion of the time has moved on. Others, such as the idea of corporate social responsibility, are very much in vogue.

Underpinning all of the approaches in this chapter is a concern for ethics, and this is a subject we will return to later in the book. Equally, however, there is a recognition in these approaches that problems of organisations cannot be addressed by an approach that treats organisations as self-contained entities.

SUMMARY

- Organisations interrelate with and affect external society as well as affecting their direct shareholders.
- This has led to concerns about the social performance of business.
- Development of the concept of social accountability for organisations.
- Development of the concept of corporate social responsibility (CSR), particularly in the light of the collapse of some large financial firms.
- Concern with all stakeholders' interests.
- Relationship between global corporations and local societies.
- Social contracts between corporations and the public interest.
- Social and environmental accounting.
- Liberalism, utilitarianism, communitarianism as different approaches.

FURTHER READING

CROWTHER, D. (2002) *A social critique of corporate reporting*. Aldershot: Ashgate.

CROWTHER, D. and RAYMAN-BACCHUS, L. (eds). (2004) *Perspectives on corporate social responsibility*. Aldershot: Ashgate.

GIDDENS, A. (1998) *The third way: the renewal of social democracy*. London: Polity Press.

REFERENCES

ACKERMAN, R.W. (1975) *The social challenge to business*. Cambridge, Mass: Harvard University Press.

BARON, L., BLUM, L., KREBS, D., OLINER, P., OLINER, S. and SMOLENSKA, M.Z. (1992) *Embracing the other: philosophical, psychological, and historical perspectives on altruism*. New York: New York University Press.

BELLAH, R. (1985) *Habits of the heart*. Los Angeles: University of California Press.

BENTHAM, J. (1789) An introduction to the principles of morals and legislation.

CHILD, J. (1984) *Organisation: a guide to problems and practice*. London: Harper & Row.

COASE, R.H. (1937) The nature of the firm. *Economica*, iv, November, 386–405.

CROWTHER, D. (1996) Corporate performance operates in three dimensions. *Managerial Auditing Journal*, Vol. 11, No. 8, 4–13.

CROWTHER, D. (2000) Corporate reporting, stakeholders and the internet: mapping the new corporate landscape. *Urban Studies*, Vol. 37, No. 10, 1837–1848.

CROWTHER, D. (2002a) *A social critique of corporate reporting*. Aldershot: Ashgate.

CROWTHER, D. (2002b) Psychoanalysis and auditing. In S. Clegg (ed) *Paradoxical new directions in management and organization theory* (pp227–246). Amsterdam: J. Benjamins.

CROWTHER, D. (2002c) The psychoanalysis of on-line reporting. In L. Holmes, M. Grieco and D. Hosking (eds) *Distributed technology, distributed leadership, distributed identity, distributed discourse: organising in an information age* (pp130–148). Aldershot: Ashgate.

CROWTHER, D. (2004) Limited liability or limited responsibility. In D. Crowther and L. Rayman-Bacchus (eds) *Perspectives on corporate social responsibility* (pp42–58). Aldershot: Ashgate.

CROWTHER, D. and RAYMAN-BACCHUS, L. (2004a). Introduction: Perspectives on corporate social responsibility. In D. Crowther and L. Rayman-Bacchus (eds) *Perspectives on corporate social responsibility* (pp1–18). Aldershot: Ashgate.

CROWTHER, D. and RAYMAN-BACCHUS, L. (2004b) The future of corporate social responsibility. In D. Crowther and L. Rayman-Bacchus (eds) *Perspectives on corporate social responsibility* (pp229–249). Aldershot: Ashgate.

DE TOCQUEVILLE, A. (1840) *Democracy in America*.

ETZIONI, A. (1994) *The spirit of community: the reinvention of American society*. New York: Pocket Books.

ETZIONI, A. (1997) *The new golden rule: community and morality in a democratic society*. New York: Basic Books.

EU COMMISSION. (2002) *Corporate social responsibility: a business contribution to sustainable development*.

FETYKO, D.F. (1975) The company social audit. *Management Accounting*, Vol. 56, No. 10, 645–647.

FREEMAN, R.E. (1984) *Strategic management: a stakeholder approach*. Boston: Pitman.

GIDDENS, A. (1998) *The third way: the renewal of social democracy*. London: Polity Press.

GRAY, R., OWEN, D. and MAUNDERS, K. (1987) *Corporate social reporting: accounting and accountability*. London: Prentice-Hall.

KANT, I. (1959) *Foundations of the metaphysics of morals* (trans. L.W. Beck). New York: Liberal Arts Press.

KLEIN, T.A. (1977) *Social costs and benefits of business*. Englewood Cliffs, NJ: Prentice-Hall.

LOCKE, J. (1690a) *An essay concerning human understanding.* many editions.

LOCKE, J. (1690b) *Two treatises of civil government.* many editions.

MANSBRIDGE, J. (1990) *Beyond self-interest*. Chicago: University of Chicago Press.

MATHEWS, M.R. (1997, March) *Twenty-five years of social and environmental accounting: is there a silver jubilee to celebrate?* Paper presented at the British Accounting Association National Conference, Birmingham.

McDONALD, D. and PUXTY, A.G. (1979) An inducement–contribution approach to corporate financial reporting. *Accounting, Organizations and Society*, Vol. 4, No. 1/2, 53–65.

MILL, J.S. (1848a) *On liberty.* many editions.

MILL, J.S. (1848b) *Principles of political economy.* many editions.

PLANT, R. (1974) *Community and ideology*. London: Routledge & Kegan Paul.

RAWLS, J. (1971) *A theory of justice*. Cambridge, Mass: Harvard University Press.

SOLOMONS, D. (1974) Corporate social performance: a new dimension in accounting reports? In H. Edey and B.S. Yamey (eds) *Debits, credits, finance and profits* (pp131–141). London: Sweet & Maxwell.

STERNBERG, E. (1997) The defects of stakeholder theory. *Corporate Governance: An International Review*, Vol. 5, No. 1, 3–10.

TONNIES, F. (1957) *Community and society* (trans. C.P. Loomis). New York: Harper & Row.

TOPAL, R.S. and CROWTHER, D. (2004) Bioengineering and corporate social responsibility. In D. Crowther and L. Rayman-Bacchus (eds) *Perspectives on corporate social responsibility* (pp186–202). Aldershot: Ashgate.

WILBUR, J.B. (1992) *The moral foundations of business practice*. Lanham: University Press.

Marx and his influence

CHAPTER 8

INTRODUCTION

One of the best-known political theorists in the world is Karl Marx. Marx has also had an enormous influence on organisation theory and on what became popular subjects for investigation and theorising. Marx himself wrote about wider societal issues and processes and did not address his analyses to organisations specifically. However, his ideas have relevance for organisations, and later theorists and writers have used them or argued with them, as we have already seen. In this chapter we will discuss some of Marx's major ideas that have been important for the development of organisation theory and research into organisations.

The importance of social class and its influence on society is one of Marx's distinguishing theories. Marx examined the productive forces in different societies, at different stages of development. He argued that in societies where the means of production or the source of income or produce and wealth were equally owned there would be a large measure of equality. However, in societies where the means of production were owned by one section of the population, this meant that there were different relationships to the means of production among the people – for example, factory owners and shareholders on the one hand, and workers or employees on the other. Marx called such societies class societies, with the owners of the means of production belonging to one class, and those who had only their labour power to sell, to a different class. These two classes – capital and labour – are central to all the analysis Marx undertook.

CLASS AND SOCIETY

Class was significant because it affected the structure and workings of society and people's lives and life chances. Those who owned the means of production – land, capital or technology – were in a position to accumulate wealth from rents or profits, and were therefore more powerful than those who did not own the means of production. This position of power and privilege could then be passed on to their children in terms of quality of education, employment opportunities, income, wealth, status and power.

Many writers have undertaken studies to show what has happened intergenerationally in terms of people's life chances. There have been variations in the degree of upward social mobility from (for example) 'working class' to 'middle class' occupations and life style. In 1980 Goldthorpe *et al* carried out an extensive social mobility survey of males in England and Wales, to check to what extent they had remained in the same social class as their fathers or had moved 'up' or 'down'. What they found was that there was very little downward movement, but that about a third of all the men ended up in a different and higher class than their fathers (Goldthorpe *et al* 1980). This was a consequence of more jobs being available in the professional and service class, rather than a loosening up of the social structure to make it more meritocratic (Grint 1998). Later studies, as job opportunities decreased, showed less social mobility (see for example Goldthorpe and Payne 1986). Even in the USA – supposedly

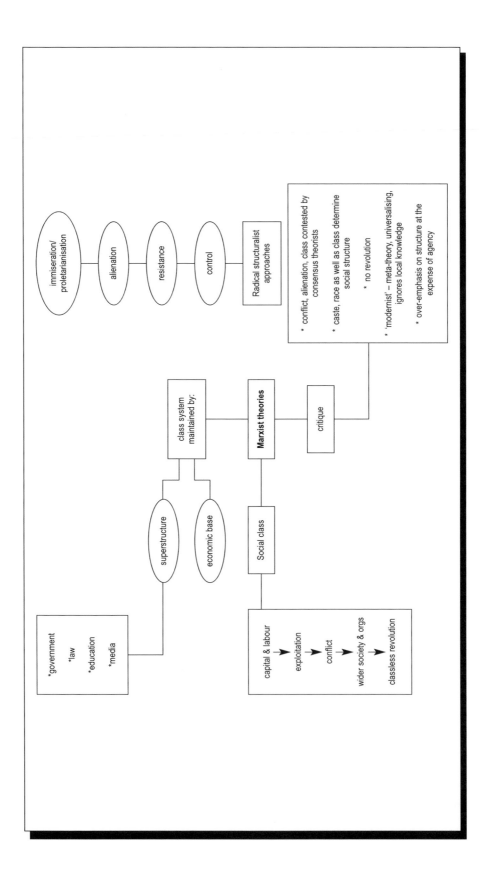

a class-free society – it has been shown that these classes exist and that mobility between the classes is becoming more difficult (see for example Hertsgaard 2002). For many this can currently be explained in terms of globalisation, but the work of Marx provides a powerful explanation of this phenomenon.

Marx took the argument further, and this is where his ideas are important for the study of organisations. He claimed that in class-based societies there could not be real, open social mobility. Those who owned the means of production or capital, whom he called the 'bourgeoisie' (along with senior managers acting in their interests and themselves often highly paid, highly privileged and powerful), achieved their wealth essentially at the expense of the subordinate class, which Marx called the 'proletariat'. If they owned land and buildings, the bourgeoisie accumulated their wealth through rents, and in the workplace they increased their wealth through the surplus profits made from their workers' labour – from the difference between the value of what they produced and what they were paid. Marxist theorists assume therefore that the workplace is an exploitative situation where employees' wages and conditions of work are continually depressed as much as possible in order to reap richer rewards for owners, shareholders and, increasingly, senior managers. This is significant for the conceptualisation and study of organisation culture and processes and is a very different perspective from that of the consensus theorists discussed in earlier chapters.

ECONOMIC BASE AND SUPERSTRUCTURE

Marx saw capitalist society as the highest form of class society because everything and everyone was increasingly subject to the imperatives of class and the relations of production. He divided up the maintenance and furtherance of the class system into two major aspects: (1) the economic base, which was the way productive forces were owned and organised, including the relationships between owners and workers or managers and subordinates, and (2) all the other institutions in society that served to maintain and strengthen the economic base, including the government, the civil service, the legal system, the police, the media and even the education system. This second aspect will be discussed in Chapter 9.

Burrell and Morgan (1979), in an influential book, called theorists who were interested in the economic base 'radical structuralists', and those interested in the superstructure 'radical humanists'. Radical structuralists are interested in questions of power relationships, control, levels of skill, workers' autonomy and general working conditions. They have focused on structural relationships in society and have sought to explore and explain relationships in the workplace in this broader context. Unlike the functionalist theories mentioned earlier, their analysis is based on a premise of conflictual rather than consensual relationships because of what they see as a system of domination and exploitation. They also believe in studying society as a whole and analysing organisations within this total context, including wider societal crises and their effects on organisations. Conflict is positive, as it is seen as a means to emancipation from existing oppressive structures.

Conventional social theories are rejected on the grounds of portraying a static reality in which consensus, equilibrium and an organic unity are assumed. This static approach is particularly visible in analyses of organisations, where disparate, data-packed, problem-centred studies are undertaken. They are largely descriptive and avoid causal analysis, ongoing dynamic processes and making links with the past and with the environmental context of the organisation (Allen, cited in Burrell and Morgan 1979). Mainstream theorists are also criticised for ignoring the notion of contradiction, another important concept in Marxist sociology, which could serve as an important explanation for factors leading to change in society and also in organisations.

CONTROL

Radical scholars have investigated techniques of control, which are seen potentially as methods of exploitation. With the development of monopoly capitalism, radical theorists see processes of production as becoming more rationalised and subject to increasingly tighter controls (Burrell and Morgan 1979). Control has been identified in various organisational processes and technologies. Edwards (1979) categorised three types of control in the US workplace: direct control by a foreman or supervisor, and the less direct and less visible methods of technical and bureaucratic control.

Technical control included the assembly line, which determined what work a person did. The moving assembly line controlled the pace and the manner in which the work was done. More recently, computer technology has been used as a control mechanism to monitor the amount, speed and accuracy at which people work and the breaks they take. It has had the effect of pressuring people to work faster, as has the reduction in the size of the workforce (Braverman 1998). Lastly bureaucracy – people are controlled through 'impersonal' rules and procedures, particularly in large and public-sector organisations. Weber has ideas similar to Marx in that he also claimed that workers were exploited and alienated under capitalism and that bureaucracy, which he is famous for studying and theorising, constituted an 'iron cage' for its employees, despite its advantages of impersonality and therefore fairness in terms of their conditions of work and opportunities for promotion (Burrell and Morgan 1979, p350).

Labour process theorists have been particularly interested in questions of control and its corollary, resistance. They are keen to explore control by management over the workforce, and also the extent to which workers have been given, or have themselves taken control over, their jobs and work situation generally. Technological control is something that interested Beynon (1975), who carried out a study of workers at Ford in relation to how they felt about working on a moving assembly line. He published some of the conversations he had with them, and a picture emerges of very hard work carried out at a gruelling pace for long periods.

Some of the concerns of labour process theorists have been more with strategies of resistance by workers, and sometimes by managers too. Noon and Blyton (2002), for example, have been interested in what they call survival strategies, which include bargaining or 'cheating' over time, quantity of work, routines and pilfering – goods, money or, as in the case of one secretary who felt badly treated by her boss, avoiding work outside her immediate remit even when it meant doing unnecessary work and then shredding it at the end of the day. Burawoy (1979) has also researched the way managers obtain consent from workers to increase productivity and the way workers manage to manipulate management. Managers too have resorted to survival strategies. Noon and Blyton (2002) cite the example of one manager in a supermarket branch who solved the problem of a short balance sheet by asking the cashiers to run the cost of a packet of tea through each customer's shopping bill!

Organisation theorists interested in exploring these ideas have taken more than one direction. Some have been interested in seeing to what extent people have been separated from any skill, autonomy or responsibility over their work and what the trends are. Other writers have applied their analyses of control to other aspects of organisations. New organisational structures of decentralisation combined with managerial ideologies of 'empowerment' mentioned in earlier chapters have been regarded by radical writers as further and tighter ways of controlling subordinates, but disguised in rhetorics of empowerment (Alvesson and Willmott 2003). Ogden and Anderson's study of the water industry (see also Chapter 5) cited a senior manager who described the empowerment policies for district managers as in effect:

> *signing in blood* to say that [they] will deliver all these specific outputs to specific standards in return for quantified resources of money and people and things.
>
> (interview, emphasis in original, cited in Ogden and Anderson 1999, p109)

Subtler ways of control have been suggested by writers over recent decades. One of the most insidious, according to radical writers, has been attempts at domination through cultural control. This has taken many forms, all having in common the exertion of pressure on employees, either from their managers or from their peers, to give a high degree of commitment to their organisation, even if this includes working long hours in their own time, and ignoring consciously or subconsciously those aspects of the organisation showing an uncaring face, such as firing employees who may have shown loyalty over many years. Hephaestus, the company Casey studied that is mentioned in Chapter 5, is one such example. Another example is the informal, first-name, Friday night pub social culture at organisations like Tandem (see Chapter 5), where employees were expected to show a high degree of commitment. The quality movement (such as quality circles, total quality management and the other versions mentioned in Chapter 5) and the prescriptions offered by writers such as Peters and Waterman to achieve 'excellent companies' have also been interpreted as methods of control.

ALIENATION

Marx's theory of class division, control and exploitation leads to his concept of alienation. We have already seen that his definition of alienation differed from Blauner's (Chapter 6) in that Marx regarded alienation as an objective condition rather than being solely dependent on how people felt. In Marx's view, workers in a capitalist system might feel happy, but they were still alienated because of their objective class position. They were removed from making any decisions about the work they were doing, because it was owned and controlled by others. As Braverman put it:

> Having been forced to sell their labor power to another, the workers also surrender their interest in the labor process, which has now been 'alienated'. *The labor process has become the responsibility of the capitalist.*
>
> (Braverman 1998, p39, original italics)

In his later writings Marx developed the concept to relate to the treatment of employees as commodities to be bought and sold on the labour market (Burrell and Morgan 1979).

If one compares craftsmen in pre-industrial Europe one can see the difference between their situation and that of the factory worker in industrial societies. Craftsmen, once they had ceased their apprenticeships, which ranged between three and seven years, had a high level of traditional knowledge regarding their particular trade and complete discretion over how the work would be carried out (Braverman 1998). In the earlier stages of industrialisation too, before scientific management job design was introduced, some factory workers had a high degree of skill and jobs ranging over a wide variety of processes. Braverman pointed out that in Taylor's day machinists:

> started with the shop drawing, and turned, milled, bored, drilled, planed, shaped, ground, filed and otherwise machine- and hand-processed the proper stock to the desired shape as specified in the drawing. The range of decisions to be made in the course of the process is ... by its very nature enormous.   (Braverman 1998, p76)

A contemporary factory worker can make none of these decisions and, as we have seen, might be enormously constrained in the manner and pace of working as well. Taylor's aims, as we have seen from Chapter 2, which are still largely applicable to many workers both in manual and increasingly in non-manual jobs, included the 'dissociation of the labor process from the skills of the workers'; the removal of 'all possible brain work' from the shop floor and increasingly from the office; and management's monopoly over knowledge to enable it to 'control each step of the labor process and its mode of execution' (Braverman 1998, pp78–82). The only decision probably open to many workers is whether to accept a job or leave it – if they can find a better job or withstand the economic loss.

Others, particularly those with hermeneutic (interpretive) or postmodern perspectives, have studied how people perceive their work situations and what their feelings are about them. This can also serve to explain some of their actions, otherwise not easily understood. Gouldner (1955), for example, wrote about a wildcat strike at a gypsum mine in Pennsylvania, which was represented differently when interviewing the strikers themselves from what was portrayed in the official management–union negotiations and in official documents. The miners had, under a previous manager, enjoyed a system of 'indulgences' whereby there was a 'give and take' approach to working practices and, for example, the lending of company machinery for the personal use of the miners. With the appointment of a new manager who was concerned with upholding rules and regulations, the miners were denied these indulgences. As they had been essentially illegal in any case, the miners could not demand their reinstatement. Instead, they went on strike for higher wages.

Interesting research has been done, if not always in 'orthodox' ways. Postmodern theorists, following on from social action or hermeneutic approaches, have opened up the field of what counts as knowledge from the narrower positivist criteria of observable, quantifiable data. This has included allowing people's stories to be considered as constituting important knowledge, and their representations of these stories as valid, publishable research. One story appearing in an early volume of the journal *Organization* contained a powerful depiction of alienation, showing a racial rather than class-based origin. Two black women managers were invited to a US Fortune 500 company that prided itself on its progressive outreach policies. The women were subjected to conscious or unconscious racism, starting with the women's cloakroom, where white employees removed the toiletries they normally left lying around, and proceeding to the boardroom, where the women were escorted from a meeting held in their honour after having presumed to ask a question about the ethnic composition of the board (Lane 1996).

IMMISERATION AND THE SOCIAL AND OCCUPATIONAL STRUCTURE

Immiseration is connected with Marx's interpretation of alienation. Marx predicted that social classes, instead of becoming more mobile with less inequality and improvement in their conditions, as 'optimistic' theorists held, would instead become increasingly polarised. At the time that Marx was writing, and right up to the present, there have been people with occupations and situations that have not fitted neatly into either the bourgeoisie or the proletariat. Between the bourgeoisie and the proletariat there were small businesspeople such as shopkeepers, people in trades, and independent craftsmen like motor mechanics and plumbers. Marx called them the 'petit-bourgeoisie' and predicted that as capital became more concentrated these small, independent entrepreneurs would be swallowed up by larger corporations, and that people would either succeed in developing their business into larger firms or, more probably, be pushed down into the proletariat and become paid employees.

Others who did not fit into this dualistic structure were people in a large number of categories that also lay between the bourgeoisie and the proletariat, but who were not self-employed. They differed from manual workers in that they did more skilled or less physically difficult work, ranging from white-collar office workers, through teachers, nurses and technicians, to the higher-level professional, administrative and technical occupations – surgeons, university professors, judges, senior civil servants, higher-level managers, top scientists and so on. Marx argued that the more senior people worked in the interests of the bourgeoisie and could be classified as such; others commanded high salaries that could be turned into capital. Intermediate and lower-level cadres would eventually be 'immiserated' – ie become subject to poorer wages and conditions of work and so become part of the proletariat.

Braverman (1998) took up Marx's argument with regard to white-collar work in an influential book, *Labor and Monopoly Capital*. Braverman's thesis was that not only were manual workers being de-skilled, but that those in white-collar work were being similarly de-skilled through routinisation and technology, and their jobs were being 'degraded' to the quality and status of manual work. White-collar workers would lose their power and ability to have higher salaries, as their skills would no longer be needed and they could easily be replaced. Citing Lockwood (1958), Braverman pointed out that in the middle of the nineteenth century, clerks in Britain earned wages that could only be met by about 10–15 per cent of manual workers, and that in the USA clerical work earned twice as much as manual labour. In those days clerks were akin to craftsmen, in that they were engaged in a total labour process over which they had full control.

However, following the incursions of management control into clerical work, the labour process was reorganised into a system where work was standardised and divided up so that each clerk dealt with only one small part. The mechanisation of offices took the de-skilling process further, and computers were able precisely to measure the output of office workers. One extreme example of routinisation was an attempt by Leffingwell to implement scientific management principles to office work and save costs by reducing the movements of office workers. He recommended that water fountains be placed near the clerks so that they would not have to walk far, as this was a waste of employers' time, and therefore of their money. He worked out that a few hundred yards of walking time per day of a thousand clerks would amount to fifty thousand miles each year (Braverman 1998).

With this 'proletarianisation' process came the feminisation of work (ie the employment mainly of women) and a drastic lowering of wages. The US 1970 census showed that the median earnings of 'service' occupations, which included three million clerical workers as well as craftsmen, operatives and professional and technical employees, were lower than in any other occupational group except for farm workers (Braverman 1998). Statistical analyses have shown an expansion of jobs where workers have relatively little control over the labour process, and a corresponding decline in work offering high autonomy. 'Lean production' in the 1980s and 1990s has further accelerated this tendency (Wright and Singleman, cited in Braverman 1998).

There were those not in employment at all – at the top this would include people who owned capital and did not need to work, as they could live off rents or profits. At the bottom end were people who could not or would not find work, whom Marx called the 'reserve army' of the working class (Burrell and Morgan 1979, p381). He saw them having an important position in the capitalist system. In *Capital* he wrote that the mass of unemployed people, created because of the mechanisation of industry, constituted 'for the changing need of the self-expansion of capital, a mass of human material always ready for exploitation' (Braverman 1998, p265). This reserve army also served to hold down wages in these newly mechanised industries and organisations, being a constant reminder to the employed that they could easily be replaced. Marx saw immiseration and the polarisation between the classes worsening as capital became more concentrated and more powerful. As capital accumulated so there was also an 'accumulation of misery' (Marx op.cit., p604, cited in Braverman 1998, p269).

REVOLUTION

Perhaps Marx's most controversial claim was that as capitalism developed in the most industrialised societies, the proletariat would become more aware of its class position through improved communications because of increased contact in urban areas and more advanced technology. Because of increasing exploitation and misery, and their clearer awareness of their collective class position, workers would organise against the system and ultimately overthrow it to create a classless society. Thus for Marx a revolution to achieve this overthrow was inevitable. Indeed many of his followers (eg Kautsky) parted company with others (eg Lenin) over this question of the inevitability of revolution.

CRITIQUE
Positive

Some of Marx's claims appear to be valid. Although there are still many independent businesses, one can argue that many others have had to close in the face of competition from larger corporations. This is most visible in the UK on the 'High Street', where food shops in particular have been unable to withstand competition from mega-supermarkets established out of town and, increasingly, in suburban centres, with smaller outlets in urban centres. Similarly while there are certain independent tradesmen and craftsmen, some occupations, such as tailoring and carpentry, have largely been absorbed into larger firms.

Many radical writers have taken these ideas further and applied them to administrative, professional and technical occupations at higher levels, particularly in the public sector. They have supported Marx's ideas regarding the eventual downgrading of higher-qualified employees by examining how their work has developed and by looking at the quality of their working life – their autonomy, pay, conditions and status. Studies have been done on various public-sector organisations, including the NHS, educational institutions, local government and the Royal Mail. Much research has been done to show how attempts were made to gain managerial control over professional work processes in the context of the cultural change undertaken in many of these services, following the Conservative Thatcher government's push to introduce private-sector market values into the public sector (Pollit 1990; Farnham and Horton 1993; Kirkpatrick and Martinez Lucio 1995). The present Labour government under Tony Blair seems determined to continue and extend this policy.

Research has also been done on former public services such as the utilities,[1] which in the last few decades have been privatised. One of the intended changes from public-sector management was to make it principally cost- and profit-conscious, instead of putting care and service first. The reasoning was that, ultimately, better care and service would be provided if there was more awareness of costs and more careful spending. This led to the appointment

1 Utilites are the industries that provide services to all – gas, electricity, water, telecommunications etc.

of a new category of personnel managers – who now had decision-making authority and control of the purse-strings, unlike the administrators before them, who did not have these powers.

What this has meant for professionals previously in positions of authority was a definite move towards their de-professionalisation. Generally knowledgeable and respected expert professionals have had their judgements overridden and their decision-making powers reduced in the interests of a different set of values from those they would normally consider fundamental to their work and, in some cases, their vocation. Carter and Crowther (2000) analysed the processes in a newly privatised electricity industry that divested the expert senior engineers of their power and authority. Their knowledge was 'codified' and made into rules, which were then considered to be useable by people without expert knowledge. Power was then transferred to managers. The system worked well enough until technical problems arose that could not be solved by the rule-book, but needed people with an in-depth knowledge of the electricity industry.

In some cases professional judgement was overridden by the setting of national standards. This has happened in schools, with increased national testing, and in universities, with the imposition of highly contested measures for teaching and assessment, such as learning outcomes. In the case of many public servants there has been a strong push to change pay and conditions to the disadvantage of employees in order to achieve more 'productivity', often at the expense of public standards, as claimed in the fire-fighters' dispute of 2002–3.

Negative

Criticisms of Marx have been of two kinds: first, regarding the content, such as his analysis of how society worked and his predictions for the future; and second, his and other radical theorists' theoretical perspectives – what their fundamental assumptions were about the way the world worked (ontology), what counted for them as valid and relevant knowledge (epistemology), and how they did their research (methodology).

Content

- *Conflict and alienation.* There has been much criticism of Marx's ideas, some of which we have already seen. Many of the theorists mentioned earlier – particularly those who were prescriptive regarding issues such as organisation structure, management style and technology to achieve the most efficient or profitable organisation – assumed a consensus, as opposed to Marx's idea of conflict in organisations. Without a consensus, the bases of their theories would have been seriously weakened. We have seen in Chapter 6 how theorists in the 1960s (mostly from the USA) wanted to show how society at large and organisations in particular were much better and happier places for the workforce than previously, and that this trend was likely to continue. The convergence theorists in particular argued for an increasing consensus brought about by increasing social mobility, more opportunities for the lower occupational strata and a closing of the gap between the wealthiest and poorest – in Western industrial societies and eventually world-wide.

Where Marx saw exploitation, many of these theorists argued for a commonality of interest. Unitarist theorists, like the classical management and human relations theorists and those advocating strong, managerially led corporate culture, assume that organisations work like traditional football teams – all with the same aim, pointing in the same direction with different roles being upheld by all: the managers leading and the workers willingly following. Pluralist theorists, such as Fox (1966), while admitting that different sectors in organisations (different levels, different departments, workers v managers) may have different interests and that there is a situation of potential conflict, argue that in a democratic society it can all be sorted out to achieve harmony and consensus. Just as in the wider democratic society, different views, ideas and wishes are taken into account by the government through various influences such as pressure groups, so in organisations managers are there to negotiate with trade unions to achieve a compromise that will be acceptable to the different interests and thus achieve a meaningful consensus.

Following on from this, Marx's concept of alienation is unacceptable to theorists who, firstly, do not accept that there was a situation of conflict and exploitation in the first place and, secondly, are of the firm belief, as was Blauner, that the development of technology will ease life for workers and provide them with more interesting and responsible work. This would do away with the alienation, ie worker unhappiness in its various manifestations, caused by forms of technology in the earlier stages of the industrial revolution.

Theorists who agreed with the fact of conflict and alienation did not always attribute this wholly to class relations. Weberians, such as Dahrendorf, believed conflict arose from any situation where there were unequal power and authority relations, and the reason for such conflict stemmed from these unequal relations of authority rather than from relations of class. If people in common positions in the authority structure recognised their common interests, they became a true conflict group with the potential to instigate social change (Burrell and Morgan 1979). Weber himself saw conflict and restrictions on people's freedoms arising from industrial societies as they became more bureaucratic and regulatory. He included in this the burgeoning communist state in Russia in the early 1920s (Weber 1970a).

- *The social and occupational structure.* There has been a great deal of controversy over what shape the occupational structure would take. Many theorists have disagreed with Marx's pessimistic view of how the social structure would polarise into two increasingly unequal groups[2] – the bourgeoisie and the proletariat. Weber, the third 'father' of sociology, was one of the early theorists who, while agreeing with Marx about the economic base being the most important determinant of societies and the stratification of their peoples, nevertheless suggested an alternative source of wealth, power and status to that of relationships to the productive forces – namely occupation. Weber saw the proliferation of occupations that were neither manual nor related to ownership of capital as one of the important developments of the twentieth century. He foresaw that more and more people would obtain the education and skills to be employed in administrative, technical and professional work at different levels. Unlike Marx, Weber argued that these occupations would not fall victim to the immiseration predicted by Marx. They would become increasingly relevant to technologically developing societies, and increasing numbers of people would be located in a social and occupational structure in positions that were neither proletarian nor bourgeois. In this sense Weber shares the optimism about the future of work and workers with the optimistic theorists.

Weber also differed from Marx in that he suggested other factors causing social stratification that were not primarily based on economic relations. Weber's additional categories for social

---

2 This argument has, however, been resurrected recently by the opponents of globalisation, who argue and produce evidence of this polarisation.

'closure' included caste and race, which showed that Marx's class divisions were not enough to explain social stratification in all societies. Studying different types of society in different parts of the world, Weber argued that there were other factors which opened opportunities to certain sections of the population while closing them to others (Weber 1970b). The caste system in India was one such example; societies based on racial discrimination were another. Until 1994, South Africa was an example of a society where the majority of the population was denied opportunities in housing, education, employment and other freedoms and services simply because of the colour of its skin. The example given earlier of the alienation of the two black women managers in a US Fortune 500 company is another example based on racial rather than economic distinctions.

Braverman's analysis of what would happen to white-collar work and the continued de-skilling and disempowerment of the workforce has also been criticised by other radical writers as being over-pessimistic, because many jobs have not in fact been de-skilled, and there are alternatives to Taylorism in capitalist systems (Grint 1998). The role of the potential resistance of the workforce has also been underestimated, as has the degree of participation by the workforce (Wood 1989). Braverman, incidentally, in response to these criticisms, denied pessimism and expressed 'every confidence in the revolutionary potential of the working classes of the so-called developed capitalist countries'. He affirmed his opinion that as pressures on the working class intensified, workers would have forced upon them 'the fulfillment of the task which they alone can perform [ie bringing about revolution]' (Braverman 1976, cited in Braverman 1998, p315).

- *Proletarian revolution.* The optimism about the coming of a classless society brought about by a proletarian revolution in the most advanced capitalist societies was perhaps Marx's (as well as Braverman's) greatest failure of imagination. Attempts to implement revolutions in Marx's name happened in largely agrarian, technologically backward societies, and then usually took very different directions from Marx's theories and ideals. Many have used what now seem to be his utopian ideas as a way of denying credibility to all Marx's ideas. There are however radical explanations for this failure by Western working classes to engage in revolutionary activity, and for the apparent consensus of many in the workplace with their organisation's ethos and policies and with their pay and conditions. It may be to do with the cushioning effect that radical development theorists have argued are enjoyed by workers in the industrialised West at the expense of the much greater exploitation of worker surplus in many Third World societies (see Chapter 6).

Any prospect of a proletarian revolution is much more remote now as the manual working class has decreased in size due to the decline of many traditional industries. New industries, particularly those involved with information technology, often have non-union agreements with their workforce, which further decreases any possibility for militant action by this 'new working class'.

Theoretical perspectives

- *Modernism.* Like functionalism, Marxism has been grouped under modernism, and the weaknesses associated with it. There is 'meta-theorising' or providing theories about how society is structured and how it works, generalised to all societies. Functionalist theories such as convergence theory also engaged in generalised theorising, and the weaknesses of attempting to provide the same analysis for very different societies were highlighted in Chapter 6. Many postmodern theorists have emphasised the importance of localised, small-scale studies in which 'meta-theorising', or the putting forward of ideas that are assumed to be universally applicable, is avoided.

Some have also argued that researchers, even radical ones, have not always allowed everyone's voice to be heard. The voices usually heard are those of the powerful people in the organisation – senior management. Other voices heard lower down the hierarchy still do not usually include all voices but, again, those who are the strongest from among the weak – usually white, male voices. Voices of women, ethnic minorities and the disabled have generally been unresearched and unheard. Since the 1980s more work has however been done in this area. Writers such as Calas and Smircich (1992) have written extensively about women in organisatons, and Nkomo and Cox (1996) have written on race and gender issues in organisations. Postmodern theorists have insisted that the researcher should also be reflexive, in order to allow space for people's perceptions of their own experience, check their findings against those of their respondents, and be aware that their own power in such situations might influence their research findings.

- *Structuralism.* Again, similar to functionalist explanations, Marxists' ontological position (ie questioning what is reality) have emphasised structure as being concrete and independently 'out there' in 'reality', rather than being dependent on people's constructions or affirmations, as interpretive theorists would argue (Burrell and Morgan 1979). And, as mentioned, structures for Marxists are the most important determinant of social and organisational processes and outcomes – in their case the underlying economic structures stemming from the means and relations of production. An over-emphasis on structure in organisations (as in the wider society) can ignore other factors determining events, processes and outcomes. One of the opposites to structure in the organisation literature has been 'agency', or the action of groups or individuals. There have been many case studies showing that employees at comparatively low levels in the organisation have acted successfully against senior management's policies either through misunderstanding, more expert knowledge or to serve their own political agendas – which Marxist writers may not have paid enough attention to, grounds on which Braverman also has been criticised.

One example showing successful active agency on the part of junior managers occurred in the plastics containers division of a divisionalised company in England. Preston (1986) initially intended to research how a new computerised production information system was introduced to factory managers. When he started his investigations Preston found that the managers had already familiarised themselves with the new system without having had any official documentation about it. This was an interesting situation, as there was obviously a difference of understanding of what was happening in the company between senior and lower levels of management.

Preston was able to carry out research in the company as an observer for a year, during which he attended meetings and spoke with various 'actors' in the organisation informally. What he found was an alternative, informal system of communication and support to the formal hierarchical organisation chart. This was instituted for political and survival reasons. If these managers' immediate superiors were slow with, or provided inaccurate, information, they sought faster, more reliable sources, be it sideways from their colleagues in other departments or from other superiors who had better information. This helped them take a more proactive role in the organisation for their own political interests. A support network was thus developed that bore little relation to the formal lines of communication and hierarchy, and which senior management was obviously unaware of.

■ *Local knowledge and researcher reflexivity.* These criticisms are made from a postmodern perspective and link with the former points made. The criticisms may be unfair in that they have often been made with hindsight, and comment negatively on research done at a time when no one was being reflexive and considering local knowledge much. Marxist writers, like those writing from the functionalist perspective, have often been content to do broad research without necessarily finding out from the people 'on the shop floor' how they have understood and perceived the events and processes being researched, when the research has been about them. Bougen (1989), for example, produced an interesting analysis showing how accounting information was used to manipulate workers into going along with management at a time of high revolutionary feeling after the First World War, and that later, when things were quieter and because workers began to demand the bonuses they had been promised, access to these accounts was withdrawn. Evidence was drawn mainly from archival records of management–employee meetings, historical records and the writings of the organisation founder's son. In this case, of course, most of the workers would probably not have been alive when Bougen was doing his research.

Similarly, postmodern theorists have been very aware of the power of the researcher in their representation of a situation. They have argued strongly for 'reflexivity' on the part of the researcher – checking and rechecking their analysis through as much awareness of their own assumptions as possible, and also against the understandings and perceptions of those the research is about. These criticisms have also been levelled at many functionalist researchers who have used 'positivist' methods for their research. One method postmodernists are particularly critical of is the survey or questionnaire, which some have argued reveals more about the researcher who has determined what questions to ask than about the organisation or the employees being researched. Those with the intention of being helpful will answer the questions as best they understand them and to the best of their knowledge about what is being asked; this does not guarantee that they are the most pertinent questions for the study in hand, or that everyone will understand the questions in the same way. Then there are those who will answer not according to their knowledge, but perhaps according to what they think the researcher wants to hear or what their bosses, if informed of their answers, will want to hear, or for some other political agenda of their own. Such research, when completed, has been criticised particularly for its lack of reflexivity regarding the respondents' own understanding of the situation.

CONCLUSIONS

Marxist theory has had alternating spells of popularity and spells of unpopularity for organisational theorists ever since Marx developed the theory. Despite Marx's failure of analysis about the possibility of a proletarian revolution in industrialised societies, many of his ideas are still very relevant to organisational structures and processes, to management strategies and to possible employee reactions, enactments and acts of resistance or survival. Job design and questions of de-skilling and upskilling are still analysed by radical theorists and argued about with theorists using alternative perspectives. Trends in organisations and in the quality of working life, and the concerns of labour process theorists in particular, are still very relevant to current company policies, management strategies and the cultures of organisations.

SUMMARY

- Marx had a profound influence on various aspects of organisation theory:
    - social class, social mobility and workplace relationships
    - economic base and power relationships, levels of skill and autonomy in the workplace
    - control – technological, bureaucratic and psychological
    - alienation from the labour process
    - future of social and occupational structures.
- Critique: the weakening of small, independent entrepreneurs and the managerialisation of public services support Marx and neo-Marxist theorists such as Braverman; conflict and alienation in society are contested by optimistic theorists; social and economic structures can be determined by other than economic factors; revolution by the working classes has not materialised.

FURTHER READING

ALVESSON, M. and WILLMOTT, H. (2003) Introduction. In M. Alvesson and H. Willmott (eds) *Studying management critically*. London: Sage.

GRINT, K. (1998) *The sociology of work: an introduction*. 2nd ed. Cambridge: Polity Press.

NOON, M. and BLYTON, P. (2002) *The realities of work*. Basingstoke: Palgrave.

REFERENCES

ALVESSON, M. and WILLMOTT, H. (2003) Introduction. In M. Alvesson and H. Willmott (eds) *Studying management critically*. London: Sage.

BEYNON, H. (1975) *Working for Ford*. Wakefield: E.P. Publishing.

BOUGEN, P.D. (1989) The emergence, roles and consequences of an accounting–industrial relations interaction. *Accounting, Organizations and Society*, Vol. 14, No. 3, 203–234.

BRAVERMAN, H. (1976) Technology, the labor process, and the working class. *Monthly Review*, Vol. 28, No. 3, July–August.

BRAVERMAN, H. (1998) *Labor and monopoly capital: the degradation of work in the twentieth century*. 25th anniversary ed. New York: Monthly Review Press.

BURAWOY, M. (1979) *Manufacturing consent*. Chicago: University of Chicago Press.

BURRELL, G. and MORGAN, G. (1979) *Sociological paradigms and organisational analysis*. Aldershot: Ashgate.

CALAS, M. and SMIRCICH, L. (1992) Re-writing gender into organizational theorizing: directions from feminist perspectives. In M. Reed and M. Hughes (eds) *Rethinking organisation: new directions in organisation and analysis*. London: Sage.

CARTER, C. and CROWTHER, D. (2000) Unravelling a profession: the case of engineers in a British regional electricity company. *Critical Perspectives on Accounting*, Vol. 11, 23–49.

EDWARDS, R. (1979) *Contested terrain*. USA: Basic Books.

FARNHAM, D. and HORTON, S. (eds). (1993) *Managing the new public services*. Basingstoke: Macmillan.

FOX, A. (1966) *Industrial sociology and industrial relations* (Royal Commission Research Paper No.3). London: HMSO.

GOLDTHORPE, J.H., LLEWELLYN, C. and PAYNE, C. (1980) *Social mobility and class structure in modern Britain*. Oxford: Clarendon.

GOLDTHORPE, J.H. and PAYNE, C. (1986) Trends in intergenerational class mobility in England and Wales 1972–1983. *Sociology*, Vol. 20, No. 1, 1–24.

GOULDNER, A. (1955) *Wildcat strike*. London: Routledge & Kegan Paul.

GRINT, K. (1998) *The sociology of work: an introduction*. 2nd ed. Cambridge: Polity Press.

HERTSGAARD, M. (2002) *Why America fascinates and infuriates the world*. London: Bloomsbury.

KIRKPATRICK, I. and MARTINEZ LUCIO, M. (1995) *The politics of quality in the public sector: the management of change*. London: Routledge.

LANE, P.M.P. (1996) You can't walk a straight line with a crooked shoe. *Organization*, Vol. 3, No. 4, 462–467.

LOCKWOOD, D. (1958) *The blackcoated worker: a study in class consciousness*. London: Allen and Unwin.

NKOMO, S. and COX, T., Jr. (1996) Diverse identities in organizations. In S. Clegg, C. Hardy and W.R. Nord (eds) *Handbook of organization studies*. London: Sage.

NOON, M. and BLYTON, P (2002) *The realities of work*. Basingstoke: Palgrave.

OGDEN, S.G. and ANDERSON, R. (1999) The role of accounting in organisational change: promoting performance improvements in the privatised UK water industry. *Critical Perspectives on Accounting*, Vol. 10, 91–124.

PETERS, T.J. and WATERMAN, R.H. (1982) *In search of excellence: lessons from America's best-run companies*. New York: Harper & Row.

POLLIT, C. (1990) *Managerialism and the public services: cuts or cultural change in the 1990s?* 2nd ed. Oxford: Blackwell.

PRESTON, A. (1986) Interactions and arrangements in the process of informing. *Accounting, Organizations and Society*, Vol. 11, No. 6, 521–540.

WEBER, M. (1970a) Bureaucracy (Wirtschaft und Gesellschaft, part III, chap. 6, pp650–678). In H.H. Gerth and C. Wright Mills (eds) *From Max Weber: essays in sociology*. London: Routledge & Kegan Paul.

WEBER, M. (1970b) Class, status, party (Wirtschaft und Gesellschaft, part III, chap. 4, pp631–640). In H.H. Gerth, and C. Wright Mills (eds) *From Max Weber: essays in sociology*. London: Routledge & Kegan Paul.

WOOD, S. (1989) The transformation of work? In S. Wood (ed) *The transformation of work? Skill, flexibility and the labour process*. London: Unwin Hyman.

Critical approaches

CHAPTER 9

INTRODUCTION

Two approaches to analysing and understanding organisations have the label of 'critical' attached to them; although different, they share some ideas in common. We will look at both of these in this chapter. The first is what is known generally as a critical perspective. This label has been used in a broad sense to mean being 'critical' about ideas, theories, research methodologies and so on. This does not mean being 'negative'; rather it means not accepting at face value or taking for granted any scholarship in the field of organisation studies and also in other disciplines in the social sciences, such as those concerned with education, prisons and hospitals (Alvesson and Deetz 2000). Critical approaches are also present in many contemporary social movements such as feminism, environmentalism, consumer issues and postcolonialism (Alvesson and Willmott 2003).

The main point of difference for theorists with a critical perspective (these being different from critical theorists, whom we will consider later in the chapter) has been with scholars using scientific methods, with their world view (ontology) and with what is considered to count as true knowledge (epistemology). As mentioned previously, traditional organisation and management research start from the premise of being able to create objective knowledge based on finding out more 'real' or 'observable' facts about a 'real' world that exists 'out there'. The same confidence about finding objective truth is there when exploring people's experiences and the meanings they give to them (Alvesson and Skoldberg 2000). There is also the assumption of autonomous 'actors' with fixed personalities and identities 'progressively emancipated by knowledge acquired through scientific methods' (Alvesson and Deetz 2000, p13).

CRITICAL PERSPECTIVES

Over the last few decades these views have been contested on several counts. Firstly the existence of a 'real' world is disputed on the grounds that people, because of their different backgrounds, different experiences both past and present, different organisational contexts in which they find themselves or their different relationships within the same context, will see the world differently. This does not mean that they will have radically different views about the existence of external objects such as rooms, walls or bridges. Rather, they may have different feelings and perceptions about such objects, which may have different meanings for them. For example, crossing a bridge on the way to work will have very different connotations depending on whether individuals making that journey are happy or unhappy with their jobs.

How much more pertinent when considering organisations and organisation processes, and the experiences and attitudes different employees might have regarding them and what constitutes reality in them? Preston's (1986) research is an example of how, for many managers in the plastics production firm he researched, the formal organisation structure did not constitute 'reality' as an effective communication system; instead they developed their own informal structures that did (see Chapter 8). The argument thus continues to postulate a

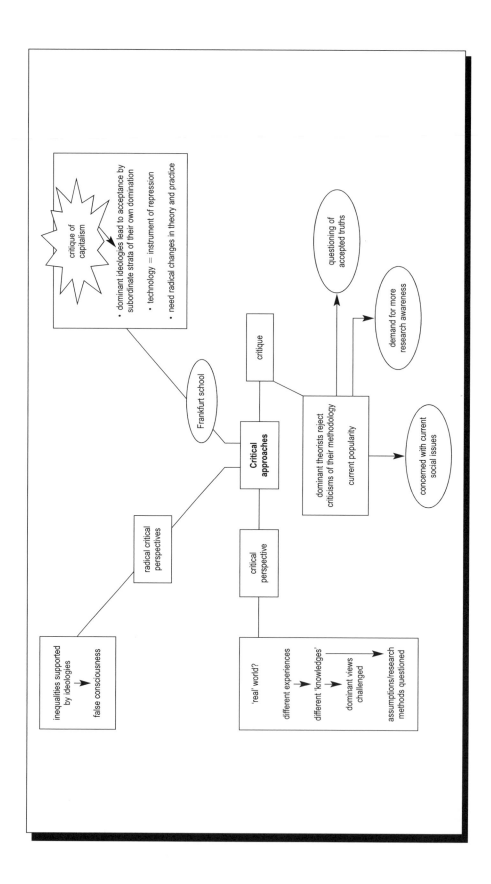

close relationship between the 'knower' (or respondent to the researcher) and the knowledge produced. The implications therefore are that the researcher cannot take for granted what is real or that the research has portrayed objective truths. Rather, the data or facts being dealt with are the constructions or interpretations of people; and not only can these constructions be quite different, but they can also change.

People in organisations are therefore not regarded as independent, self-determining and unchanging. They dispute the central functionalist notion that 'the individual creates the world in which he lives' (Willmott 2003, p89). Thus people's achievements may not necessarily be because of their independently achieved superior merit or successes, but may also be because of the context they are in, and the social processes and relationships with which they are interacting. So opportunities may have come more or less easily because of factors in addition to their own individual efforts and talents (Alvesson and Willmott 1996). They are also not regarded as passive subjects of managerial strategies, but as 'active sense makers like the researcher' interrelating with their perceptions, experiences and relationships they have both within organisations and in the wider world (Alvesson and Deetz 2000, p33). Although people differ, they are regarded by critical theorists also as products of cultural processes, such as those of their family, school and, not least, their organisations.

A critical approach in this broad sense will also be concerned with 'identifying and challenging assumptions behind ordinary ways of perceiving, conceiving and acting' (Alvesson and Deetz 2000, p8). In the field of organisation studies, dominant assumptions about the way organisations 'work', organisational goals, ideas and ideologies, and the way the workforce operates are challenged by critical writers. Alvesson and Skoldberg (2000) give an example of a researcher not conforming to dominant opinions, but asking questions that go against 'common sense' notions or taken-for-granted norms and values. Burawoy (1979), rather than asking the conventional question 'Why don't the workers work harder than they do?', instead wanted to know 'Why do they work as hard as they do?' (quoted in Alvesson and Skoldberg 2000, p132). Alvesson and Willmott (1996) argue that interactions between people in organisations are unstable and unpredictable and not easily subject to organisational theorists' prescriptions or managerial strategies. This breaking open of assumptions can be arrived at also through considering alternatives. Rorty (1982, p163) suggested that in order to go beyond common assumptions, there should be a rephrasing of questions to: 'What would it be like to believe that? What would happen if we did? What would we be committing myself to?' (quoted in Alvesson and Deetz 2000, p45).

There are also different 'ways of doing knowledge' (Calas and Smircich 1992, p240, quoted in Alvesson and Skoldberg 2000, p5.) This includes the language used, as this determines what is considered valid and important, and the social, political and theoretical framework(s) and assumptions used to interpret the empirical material. This leads to an important premise in critical research – the concept of 'reflexivity', which involves careful consideration of the research process and findings, starting from the assumption that it is a complex process. Not only must reality be considered in terms of people's theoretical assumptions and the contextual determinants mentioned, the research produced must also involve researchers reflecting about their relationship between themselves as 'knower' and how they construct their own reality in terms of their research and the knowledge produced. This knowledge must also be considered more widely in terms of the tradition from which the particular research springs, deepening the level of reflection about it (Alvesson and Deetz 2000).

Thus instead of having the confidence that there is an objective, real world, more critical approaches would take into account the fact that there are different, shifting, complex and more ambiguous 'realities' and that the interpretation of these is also subject to the context in which the researcher is working. What this does is shift the focus of attention from the empirical findings of the research to questions of how interpretations of the data were arrived at, giving consideration to the theoretical and linguistic framework and the perceptual, political and cultural circumstances that influence such interpretations (Alvesson and Skoldberg 2000).

RADICAL CRITICAL PERSPECTIVES

Another approach to being critical is based upon ideas taken from Marx, principally from his ideas on the superstructure and how it supports dominant/subordinate economic and power relationships. As mentioned earlier, Marx saw all the institutions of society working to support and strengthen the economic base in the interests of the dominant class. These would include political parties, government, the media and many other major institutions in society. The legal system, for example, protects private property, even if homes lie empty and homeless people live on the streets. (This used to be mitigated and there was some legal allowance for squatters to occupy vacant properties.) It has been argued that the education system too promotes the class-based status quo in various ways. Different types and quality of education, the streaming of students into different academic levels and the awarding of different marks and grades according to the academic quality of the work can all serve to promote the idea that people have different academic worth and can be graded accordingly. Difference in quality of work in terms of interest of the job and the degree of responsibility, challenge and personal and career development can therefore be justified, as can different rewards, opportunities for promotion and other life chances. As Bowles and Gintis put it (1976, p114):

Education reproduces inequality by justifying privilege and attributing poverty to personal failure.

The notion of the promotion of ideas and ideologies congruent with dominant strategies by institutions, conscious or not, to protect and strengthen their class position in society was an important part of Marx's theory. He respected the strength of these ideas, and a famous phrase from his book *The German Ideology* echoes this:

The ruling ideas are nothing more than the ideal expression of the dominant material relationships ... hence of the relationships which make the one class the ruling one, therefore the ideas of their dominance.

(Marx and Engels 1970, cited in Felluga 2003)

From this Marx developed the argument that the strength of these ideas had seeped into the consciousness of the population at large and had weakened perceptions of their own class interests. This he called 'false consciousness' (Burrell and Morgan 1979). This has been taken up particularly by critical theorists, many of whom were in a group called the 'Frankfurt school' (see below).

The idea that the society is basically working well and that people belong to a 'nation' that provides them with a unifying interest is one often assumed and fostered by the national press and the media, which radical theorists would, of course, disagree with, as they assume a class interest over any national interest. In organisational terms this can be translated into the promotion of views of management as the experts and decision-makers, supported by theorists who develop ideas designed to help them manage more effectively and to foster consensus and loyalty. Critical theorists would substitute functionalist theories about knowledge for management with knowledge of management, including in this knowledge alternative perspectives and voices hitherto marginalised and silenced (Alvesson and Willmott 2003). As summed up by Parker, critical theorists have shifted the image of management and the theoretical agenda 'from saviour to problem' (cited in Alvesson and Willmott 2003, p2).

CRITICAL THEORY – THE FRANKFURT SCHOOL

Marx, as we saw in the previous chapter, believed that the root cause of exploitation was the opposing forces of capital and labour. For Marx this was to be resolved through revolution, which he described as emancipation. This notion of change through revolution was adapted by later Marxists, such as Kautsky, to resolution by political change without revolution. In this respect the work of Kautsky is similar to that of English Christian socialists such as Tawney. The problem with Marxist theory, which gave rise to considerable criticism, is that it is a bourgeois interpretation that implicitly gives validity to the dialectic and privileges the idea of consciousness-raising. This objection led to various theorists using Marx's work to define a new set of theory from first principles – this became known as critical theory or the Frankfurt school.

The Frankfurt school was founded in 1923 within Frankfurt University (hence its name), and its most important early leader was Max Horkheimer, who coined the term critical theory. The work of the school was instigated because of the perceived problems of the extensive and pervasive use of technology within society. This was viewed as one of the root causes of the ills of society. Critical theorists considered that only radical change in theory and practice would cure such problems. The school closed in Frankfurt during the 1930s; most of its members emigrated to the USA, where they continued their work before returning to Frankfurt in the early 1950s.

The theory of the school therefore was concerned with developing critiques of advanced capitalist societies. Its main influences, apart from Marxism, were existentialism, to oppose dehumanisation because of the pervasiveness of technology, and psychoanalysis, and its theory of human instincts.

The premises of the school can be described as follows:

- Science and positivism embody value judgements, such as the desirability of technological domination of nature.
- The postulate of value-freedom is so entrenched in the scientific and technological paradigm that any criticism is disqualified.
- Only radical change in theory and practice can cure the ills of modern society, especially that of unbridled technology.
- Every one-sided doctrine should be subject to criticism – including Marxism.
- An emancipating proletarian revolution is not inevitable.
- Theory should be independent of social and economic forces – but theory is a product of social processes, so critical theory should trace their origins, rather than simply accept them and thereby implicitly endorse the processes themselves.

Implicit within the school's theoretical position is the notion that by providing a critique of capitalism it is possible to escape the dominant Western paradigm. This idea has itself been criticised by Jacques Derrida, who disputes this base for developing theory. In order to understand the work of the school and its influence upon subsequent theory we need to consider the work of some of the key members of the school.

Horkheimer

Horkheimer was concerned with an examination of the concept of reason within society. He argued that reasoning had narrowed with society to such an extent that behaving reasonably implied the acceptance of a rigid set of behaviours and beliefs designed to fit the instrumental requirements of society. This he considered to be the cause of fascist ideology. One of the causes of this was that science had become a tool of the bourgeoisie and had reconstructed itself as value-free. Additionally, the culture industry had had the effect of sacrificing human autonomy and imagination to serve the needs of mass society.

Adorno

Adorno was also concerned with these issues and regarded bourgeois culture as a narcotic that seduced people into a false sense of tranquillity. This was part of a process of eliminating autonomy to force people to fit the needs of society rather than society being shaped to fit the needs of people.

Marcuse

Marcuse also argued that consumerism was becoming increasingly pervasive in society. This, in his view, was leading to the creation of the 'one-dimensional man', a theme he explores in his book of the same name (1968). More than the other members of the school he made extensive use of the psychoanalysis of Freud to critique society. He argued that human instincts are repressed because of capitalism, but could be liberated to create a life of beauty and peace. In doing so he developed his ideas of a utopian postcapitalist society.

Lukács

Lukács emphasised the importance of the superstructure in influencing consciousness, such as ideology and art. He wrote about the 'universalisation' of managerial interests, by which he meant that managers' goals and agendas were made to look as if they were for the good of the whole of society and for everyone in organisations. Even though certain policies, procedures and actions might be more favourable to managers and particularly shareholders because of the overriding importance given to capital as against other contributions, they are presented in such a way as to seem neutral or for the common good (Alvesson and Deetz 1996, p200).

As already mentioned, some of the criticism against the more functional theories, such as classical and scientific management, have been on the grounds of their appearing to be neutral, although in effect they recommend a system of control, with employees being de-skilled and/or controlled in ways which are not necessarily in their best interests. For Lukács, the way out of this mental prison was through the proletariat – if and when it threw off this false consciousness and became cognisant of the true implications of capitalism and of its ability to change and overthrow it (Burrell and Morgan 1979).

Gramsci

Gramsci too believed in the importance of the superstructure. Not only was power maintained by the dominant classes through economic coercion and oppression, but also through a belief system of 'ideological hegemony'. Current power structures were legitimated through emphasising the need for order, discipline and stability, and through decrying protest and the possibility of revolutionary change. Such ideas were fostered in schools (as mentioned earlier), and in families and the workplace. Hegemonic structures in society generally left people with little power to fight against strongly established structures and processes, underpinned by a strong and pervasive ideology. Gramsci, however, was optimistic about the possibility of revolutionary change in the future, for he believed that people were ultimately their own theorists and sources of consciousness, and like Lukács argued that workers would develop a consciousness of their true class interests and would resist the hegemonic status quo (Burrell and Morgan 1979).

Habermas

Habermas (1971), a later theorist of the Frankfurt school, shared with other critical theorists the emphasis on superstructural factors. Moving away from orthodox Marxism, he believed that advanced capitalist societies could iron out economic crises, and that what was crucial to the maintenance of power relations of dominance and subordination was the 'legitimation' of the status quo through factors such as science, ideology, technology and language (Burrell and Morgan 1979). Habermas effectively inherited the aims of the Frankfurt school and has become the most influential of its followers. His aim has been to reclaim the project of enlightenment critiques of the school, which he named the philosophical discourse of modernity. He explicitly rejected the Marxist theory of value and has argued that science has become the slave of instrumental rationality. For him science and rationality have been turned against human beings and this has led to an impoverished cultural life for people in modern society. He has been concerned with an exploration of the structures of the 'life world', particularly those concerning language and communicative actions. For him the 'life world' is the same as the horizon of consciousness, and this embodies both the private and the public spheres of human interaction. In doing so he has extensively critiqued other philosophers, changes in modern society and some of the major political events of the post-Second World War decades. One of his major concerns is with the sources of legitimation in modern society and the way that these have changed as power balances within society have changed.

He gave two important explanations for why it was that society in general and employees in particular accepted the continuation of inequity in supposedly democratic societies. He developed a theory about 'cognitive interests', which he viewed as knowledge originating from people's universal, transcendent, human condition, which involved openness and liberation. Three cognitive interests underpinned the production of different forms of knowledge – 'technical reason', 'practical reason' and 'emancipatory reason'. Habermas's vision was that cognitive interests, which would include different types of knowledge as well as the different cognitive interests, would be harmonised to achieve his emancipatory project, in which 'rational' social relations and institutions would be developed.

Technical reason

The value given to science and technology, and hence to technical rationality, has taken precedence over other, human and ethical, issues. There is an aura of neutrality over the type of knowledge produced, but Habermas has argued that scientific knowledge is a one-sided, instrumental view of reason, and the way research has been carried out discloses a reality subject to certain interests. It is about control, with ends taking precedence over means. Moreover, although scientific knowledge has been liberatory, in that it displaced earlier myth and superstition, it has in itself engendered and continued certain blind ways of thinking that are just as, if not more, harmful than the previous ideas from which the Enlightenment sought to liberate people. An example of this is the:

> relentless and mechanized effort to dominate nature and the widespread environmental destruction and pollution associated with the ruthless exploitation of scarce natural resources.   (Willmott 2003, p92)

Translated into an organisational context, technical reason involved decisions being taken in order to improve effectiveness and/or efficiency to achieve certain ends. These can become part of a 'system' in which prediction and control are key, but in which other considerations such as 'human interests', to use part of the title of one of Habermas's books, are ignored. Such decisions are made and recommended to be made by people, usually managers, who are senior in organisations, without consulting employees or people in the wider community. Examples of theories based on such considerations include, as already mentioned, scientific management, Peters and Waterman's (1982) ideas on excellence, and the flexibility theorists (see Chapter 5). Contingency theories – where organisation structure should fit with the product, and technological and/or organisational environment in order to achieve effectiveness – also fall into this category (see for example, Burns and Stalker 1966).

This has meant that the goals of senior management in organisations are all-important, and employees are expected to fulfil the goals of all management strategies. Even those aimed at motivating or empowering employees are primarily instituted to achieve certain objectives, and not necessarily for the intrinsic benefit of employees. Such 'human' aspects of organisations are transformed from ends in themselves to means to be brought under technical control for the benefit of dominant interests (Alvesson and Deetz 1996).

Practical reason

Practical reason, on the other hand, is concerned with achieving mutual understanding between people. Instead of prediction and control, what becomes important is communication, so that people can reach mutual understanding. Habermas considers that if people can make sense of the world in the same way they can then go on to take social action. This is true even in terms of the decisions made on the basis of technical reason, as people need to agree on processes in order to be able to predict and control them (Willmott 2003). The type of inquiry undertaken would disclose a reality that would preserve and expand 'the intersubjectivity of possible action-oriented mutual understanding' (Habermas 1971, p310). Here not only the goal but the means are important. In the organisational context, it is about how employees make sense of their work and how these are embedded in and influenced by current and historic systems and social practices. Employees' wishes and their interests could then be better understood and taken into account, as could those of customers. Habermas (1971) argued for reciprocity in the workplace, where there would be shared expectations about behaviour, and where violations on either side would command widely based sanctions.

Emancipatory reason

This led to Habermas's third type of reason – emancipatory reason, which would be achieved when communication was truly consensual and conducted free of domination. There would then be equality of participation, with knowledge used to clarify relations of dependence in order to transform consciousness to become more reflective and critical. Habermas (1971) regarded 'self-reflection' as a way of releasing people from dominant ways of thinking. He considered it to be determined by an 'emancipatory cognitive interest'.

In organisations, relations of domination are often hidden or made ambiguous rather than clarified. Managerial strategies of 'empowerment', for instance, often obfuscate what is really happening, such as an intensification of work without extra pay or promotion (Willmott 2003). Habermas regarded critical science as a means to assert more autonomy and responsibility in the face of embedded institutional processes and practices that were repressive. Thus it would not be enough to recommend employee participation without dismantling repressive structures for such participation to be meaningful. Otherwise employees might understandably be indifferent or hostile to such moves, attitudes that some industrial relations theorists have not understood or recognised as rational responses.

Systematically distorted communication

Linked to these ideas is Habermas's theory about the nature of communication. He claimed that one of the ways in which true interests were suppressed was through the lack of disclosure of true information because of the way the system worked. Habermas coined the phrase 'systematically distorted communication', which he claimed resulted from this type of communication. An 'ideal speech situation' was one where people were equally positioned and a genuine consensus was arrived at without the distortions resulting from the influence of unequal power relationships (Burrell and Morgan 1979, p295). Instead of achieving understanding from the restrictions of the system and organisational structures, Habermas recommended free discussion based on good-will and argument, which would achieve comunicative understanding that was undistorted and based on consensus in the community (Alvesson and Deetz 1996). Many economists, including John Maynard Keynes and some Nobel prize-winners – Richard Stone and Joseph Stiglitz – have emphasised the importance of disclosure as an essential underpinning of a democratic society where the common good was paramount (Medawar 1976; Stiglitz 2002).

According to Habermas's analysis, contemporary Western societies are far from democratic, in that information necessary for the common good is withheld and distorted, in society at large and in organisations. Habermas himself did not see this changing by the last part of the twentieth century when he wrote some of his work.

Deetz

Deetz is a critical theorist who also uses postmodern approaches in his interest in the embeddedness in organisational processes to maintain existing power relationships. He writes about how meaning in organisations is engineered so as to maintain dominant interests, through what he sees as the creation and 'reproduction' of employee identities. Citing Laclau and Mouffe (Deetz 2003, p24), he agrees with them that however much it may seem that way, people are not rational and transparent subjects; that their work situation is not one of democratic and consensual decision-making; and that the individual is not a free agent in their interpretation and enactment of relationships with others. Such misconceptions help maintain and reproduce dominant structures and processes. Deetz argues that the identities of 'constructed-as-presumed free' subjects are vulnerable to systems of domination, and the construction of their identities as free and independent give advantage to managers and the dominant interests they represent. He has looked more closely, as do many postmodern theorists, at how actual organisational processes reproduce ideologies to maintain dominant power relationships, and how through identity constructions employees themselves connive at maintaining this domination.

He goes on to argue that identities are created and reproduced in various ways: through the language or 'discourse' used, which distinguishes people and events in particular ways;

through who determines the type of discourse or 'code' used; and through who has opportunities to speak. Other factors include the organisational culture – what becomes 'normalised' as organisational knowledge and practice, which can marginalise people, put economic cost above other interests and concerns, and suppress conflict, all under the guise of legitimate consensual processes. So, for example, there may be procedures which result in the surveillance of employees or in their self-surveillance introduced under the guise of 'expert' advice on supposedly 'neutral' criteria (Deetz 2003).

THE SIGNIFICANCE OF CRITICAL THEORY

Critical theory provides a different way of interpreting our findings from our research and is particularly important in questioning the notion of value freedom with research and with seeking out power relationships. It must be remembered however that the political agenda of the school has permeated all its work and still remains prominent in the work of Habermas. Nevertheless, the ideas of the school have had considerable influence, and even if we do not have the same agenda, their critiques and interpretations can significantly affect our interpretations of our own research projects.

The primary question critical theorists have addressed is why, if Western capitalist democratic societies are run primarily in the interests of those who own capital and their higher-level servants, are governments voted in time and again that continue to side, as they see it, with the dominant class at the expense of everyone else. Like radical theorists they would argue that workers generally are exploited in terms of their pay and conditions and controlled in ways which deny their autonomy and creativity, and that despite that they normally accept their lot and do not show much resistance (Alvesson and Deetz 1996).

Various answers have been given to these questions, mostly based on Marx's original concept of the force of the ideas of the dominant class. Critical theorists are opposed to the mainstream assumption that knowledge is 'unified, authoritative and value-free' (Willmott 2003, p90). Critical theorists argue (as do postmodernists) that all knowledge, including scientific knowledge, is unavoidably influenced by dominant sources of power in society from its production through to its transmission and legitimation. Apparently universal, law-like regularities in people's behaviour and organisational processes are 'discovered' in the context of specific historical, social and political contexts. Scientific and classical management theories are an example of the kind of knowledge sought and found by theorists anxious to help managers become professional and efficient and control their newly recruited workers, unused in many cases to the discipline of factory and, later, office life. This then became organisational 'knowledge', fixing in advance what should be studied: what was important and what was 'real' in organisations.

Critical theory translated into examples of organisational practice

Critical theorists saw their main task as demystifying and clarifying how the system worked by providing a critique of the status quo, emphasising types of domination, deprivation and the possibility of radical change and emancipation (Burrell and Morgan 1979). One example of research in this area is by Hassard (1988), who wrote an article where he showed how people writing from different perspectives or theoretical paradigms might approach a particular situation. He took the example of a firefighters' unit, and suggested that what would interest a critical theorist would be studying a situation where someone from the ranks was being promoted to a supervisory post, where they would now have authority over their former 'mates'. What would be of interest would be how their new job might result in an altered consciousness in terms of themselves and their new role *vis-à-vis* their former colleagues. Hassard detailed the instructions given to the newly promoted person which included the new ideological position they should take: they were one of 'us' (the managers) and no longer one of 'them'; their loyalties accordingly were to lie with the former in all dealings with those now subordinate to them.

CRITIQUE

Functionalist or positivist theorists have always asserted that their work can be objective, particularly in the light of the stringent efforts being made continuously to improve and refine their research methods to ensure the elimination of bias. They have taken exception to critical assumptions about the lack (or indeed impossibility) of work being objective because of the relationship between power and knowledge and the promotion of false consciousness. Critical reposts to this include the idea that the very methods used to detect and reduce bias are themselves the subject of certain values and interests (Willmott 2003). An example of this might be the refining of questionnaires and the statistical techniques used to analyse the findings. Critical, interpretive and postmodern theorists might well question the use of questionnaires in the first place as a valid method of inquiry for finding out about what actually happens regarding, for instance, the control systems of organisations, and how people interpret and enact those.

Habermas himself has been criticised by some postmodern and critical theorists for his optimism about the possibility of free communication. Foucault, who was generally sympathetic to the ideas of the Frankfurt school, argued that:

> The thought there could be a state of communication which would be such that the games of truth could circulate freely, without ... constraint and without coercive effects, seems to me to be Utopia.
>
> (Foucault, quoted in Alvesson and Willmott 2003, p3)

Willmott (2003) also argued against the notion that 'ideal speech situations' could overcome relations of domination. Like many other critical theorists, he has been unable to accept that free discussion alone could lead to an escape from power relations that are so pervasive in Western societies and organisations.

CONCLUSIONS

Critical approaches are currently very popular. This could be because their mission is to question accepted truths and assumptions about how organisations and people within them operate; and also to question more widely held beliefs. The position on research is also attractive, as it demands more awareness by the researcher and promises the potential of more rigour in arriving at conclusions from the research. This would be achieved by requirements for reflexivity by researchers about their research methodologies, by the need to be sensitive to researchers' influencing their data and findings, and by the need to take into account the social and cultural context in which the research is embedded. Critical theory also has affinities with current postmodern approaches, as shown in Deetz's analysis; it can be applied to a variety of current issues regarding organisations such as culture and discourse; and it is used in analyses of contemporary social movements, as mentioned earlier.

SUMMARY

- Critical perspectives argue against mainstream organisation theory and research methodologies.

- They challenge assumptions about how organisations, employees and researchers 'work', and what is accepted knowledge.

- Radical critical theory is based partly on Marx's ideas and is concerned with domination through ideology.

- The Frankfurt school was principally concerned with the technological dehumanisation of society and consumerism, as well as ideological domination.

- Habermas identified three types of rationality: technical – promoting science and technology over human and ethical considerations; practical reason – promoting mutual understanding through communication; and emancipatory reason – equality in participation and decision-making.

- Critique: questioning of claims to objectivity and about the validity of certain research methods led to counter-claims by functionalist theorists; Habermas has been criticised by other radical theorists for allowing for the possibility of free communication in capitalist societies where there are relations of domination and subordination.

FURTHER READING

ALVESSON, M. and WILLMOTT, H. (1996) *Making sense of management: a critical introduction.* London: Sage.

ALVESSON, M. and WILLMOTT, H. (2003) Introduction. In M. Alvesson and H. Willmott (eds) *Studying management critically.* London: Sage.

DEETZ, S. (2003) Disciplinary power, conflict suppression and human resources management. In M. Alvesson and H. Willmott (eds) *Studying management critically.* London: Sage.

REFERENCES

ALVESSON, M. and DEETZ, S. (1996) Critical theory and postmodernism approaches to organizational studies. In S.R. Clegg, C. Hardy and W.R. Nord (eds) *Handbook of organization studies*. London: Sage.

ALVESSON, M. and DEETZ, S. (2000) *Doing critical management research*. London: Sage.

ALVESSON, M. and SKOLDBERG, K. (2000) *Reflexive methodology: new vistas for qualitative research*. London: Sage.

ALVESSON, M. and WILLMOTT, H. (1996) *Making sense of management: a critical introduction*. London: Sage.

ALVESSON, M. and WILLMOTT, H. (2003) Introduction. In M. Alvesson and H. Willmott (eds) *Studying management critically*. London: Sage.

BOWLES, S. and GINTIS, H. (1976) *Schooling in capitalist America*. London: Routledge & Kegan Paul.

BURAWOY, M. (1979) *Manufacturing consent*. Chicago: University of Chicago Press.

BURNS, T. and STALKER, G.M. (1966) *The management of innovation*. 2nd ed. London: Tavistock Publications.

BURRELL, G. and MORGAN, G. (1979) *Sociological paradigms and organisational analysis*. Aldershot: Ashgate.

CALAS, M. and SMIRCICH, L. (1992) Re-writing gender into organizational theorizing: Directions from feminist perspectives. In M. Reed and M. Hughes (eds) *Rethinking organisation: new directions in organisation and analysis*. London: Sage.

DEETZ, S. (2003) Disciplinary power, conflict suppression and human resources management. In M. Alvesson and H. Willmott (eds) *Studying management critically*. London: Sage.

FELLUGA, D. (2003) Modules on Marx: on ideology. *Introductory guide to critical theory*. Available from http://www.purdue.edu/guidetotheory/marxism/modules/marxideology.html [accessed 15 June 2004].

HABERMAS, J. (1971 [1968]) *Knowledge and human interests*. 2nd ed. Boston: Beacon Press.

HASSARD, J. (1988) *Sociology and organisation theory: positivism, paradigms and postmodernity*. Cambridge: Cambridge University Press.

MARCUSE, H. (1968) *One dimensional man*. London: Sphere Books.

MARX, K. and ENGELS, F. (1970 [1888]) *The German ideology*. London: Lawrence & Wishart.

MEDAWAR, C. (1976) The social audit: a political view. *Accounting, Organizations and Society*, Vol. 1, No. 4, 389–394.

PETERS, T.J. and WATERMAN, R.H. (1982) *In search of excellence: lessons from America's best-run companies*. New York: Harper & Row.

PRESTON, A. (1986) Interactions and arrangements in the process of informing. *Accounting, Organizations and Society*, Vol. 11, No. 6, 521–540.

STIGLITZ, J. (2002) *Globalization and its discontents*. London: Penguin Books.

WILLMOTT, H. (2003) Organization theory as a critical science? Forms of analysis and organizational forms. In H. Tsoukas and C. Knudsen (eds) *Organization theory*. Oxford: Oxford University Press.

The postmodern approach

INTRODUCTION

Much of the theory we have considered so far is based upon the ideas of modernity (see below) and in particular upon the concept of structuralism. Structuralism is a distinctive yet diffuse body of research conducted across a range of disciplines between the 1950s and 1970s. Although principally adopted in France, it nevertheless had a substantial effect on sociology, anthropology, philosophy, political theory and literary criticism, as well as upon organisation theory.

Structuralism represents an attempt to uncover the general structures that underpin human activity; it is also characterised by the search for the general laws that serve to define these structures. The perspective emphasises a notion of 'depth'; this posits that structure is seldom found to be immediately perceptible, but rather is an underlying reality beneath the surface of observable phenomena. Of primary concern to postmodernists are linguistic structures, as opposed to social structures. This shift of emphasis from social structures to language, or more generally 'signs', is often referred to as the 'linguistic turn'.

Structuralism accepts the idea of 'the grand narrative' or 'meta-theory' and is based upon the notion of simplification in order to identify commonalities. Once these commonalities are established as knowledge, then structuralism accepts the view that the summation of these ideas leads to larger theories for explanation. This is all predicated in the ideas of modernity. For structuralists, modernity equates to the ideas of the Enlightenment (ie the eighteenth-century explosion of new thinking in philosophy, politics, economics, literature and art etc, where man rather than God was seen to be the prime 'mover and shaker' in society). This in turn is based upon the rejection of the religious imperative of premodernity. Structuralism was developed to combat the then dominant paradigm of 'historicism' – the idea that things only make sense in a process of historical change. This was developed by Sartre in his *Critique of Dialectical Reason*, with its concern with evolutionism.

LEVI-STRAUSS AND STRUCTURALISM

Although Claude Lévi-Strauss, the French anthropologist, is generally acknowledged as the founder of structuralism, the work of Ferdinand de Saussure during the early twentieth century is seen as providing the key organising principles of the perspective. Thus, in discussing the origins of structuralism, it is important to outline the work of both these Frenchmen. Saussure is widely regarded as the founder of modern linguistics and is also the originator of what has become known as 'semiotics' or 'semiology' (ie the study of signs). His seminal work is represented by the *Course on General Linguistics* (1916). Arguing against the prevailing approaches to linguistics, Saussure produced a 'scientific' model of language. This model can be understood as a closed system of elements and rules that account for the production and the social communication of meaning. The implication of this approach, often referred to as 'structural linguistics', was that language could be studied regardless of its social context, and that agency (action) was an effect of structure. In this respect,

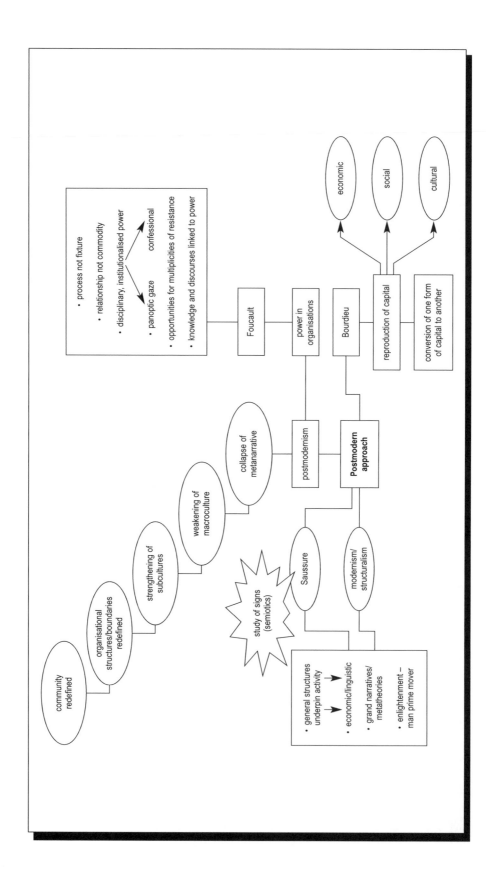

structuralism shares the anti-humanism that characterises post-structuralism. Furthermore, the approach tends to be far less preoccupied with considerations such as history in its treatment of meaningful discourse.

SAUSSURE AND LANGUAGE

Saussure viewed language as a repository of shared signs within a given community. He distinguished between two elements of language: 'langue' (the structure of language) and 'parole' (the actual speech); 'parole' is seen as dependent upon 'langue', because a structure is required for meaning to be produced. Saussure further saw langue as made up of a system of 'signs', where a 'sign' is the unity of the 'signifier' (eg a sound or a graphical symbol) and the 'signified' (eg what the sound or graphical symbol indicates). It is important to note that the 'signified' and the 'signifier' are not naturalistically linked, that is, their relationship is arbitrary. Furthermore, a distinction needs to be made between the 'referent' and the 'signified'; the 'referent' equates to what the 'signified' is referring to, but the 'signified' is not actually the 'referent' itself, but simply creates the mental image of the referent. Thus the relationship between the 'signifier', the 'signified' and the 'referent' may vary between communities, and within a community over time.

Saussure argued that identity and meaning within a society emerge out of the interplay between signs, and that differences in the interplay between signs creates a 'system of differences'; he believed that these differences ultimately shape the social world. The subsequent extension of linguistic structuralism to incorporate other sign and symbol systems, such as pictures and facial expressions, is termed 'semiotics'. Furthermore, the notion that language has only an arbitrary relation to reality, and even constructs that reality, creates a further link to the development of post-structuralism.

Although Saussure played a major role in laying the foundations for structuralism, it is Claude Lévi-Strauss who is acknowledged as the founder of structuralism. His extensive social anthropological studies, beginning with *Elementary Structures of Kinship* (1949), advanced the perspective dramatically from the 1950s. His approach is often referred to as 'structural anthropology'. Lévi-Strauss argued that 'primitive societies' have monolithic, mythological systems of thought, which are based on logical structures common to all societies. He saw these 'deep' structures as primarily linguistic and based on binary opposites (eg good/bad, god/man), and argued that these structures ensured consensus in values and therefore allowed for the development of social classification and stratification. Furthermore, Levi-Strauss believed that these binary structures were seen as fixed and enacted in all societies. Thus, modern and primitive societies are simply based on different combinations of these binary codes. As with Saussure, Lévi-Strauss contended that agency can be seen as a product of these structures.

POST-STRUCTURALISM

The term post-structuralism implies both that this body of theory came after structuralism and that it has superseded structuralism. While it is true that the body of theory was developed later than structuralist theory it is less certain that it has superseded it. Some proponents of this kind of theory would argue that it has indeed superseded structuralism, while others would argue that it is merely an alternative perspective upon the interpretation of data and phenomena. We take the latter view and suggest that some of the perspectives of post-structuralism can assist us in formulating our research question and in analysing and interpreting the data we gather in our research. First, however, we need to decide just what post-structuralism actually is. Delanty (1997, p98) argues that:

> post-structuralism can be seen as a radicalisation of the Saussurean idea that language constructs reality and that our language is only arbitrarily related to reality ... Post-structuralists, while being critical of structuralists, were clearly influenced by structuralist ideas in their rejection of Marxist and existentialist methodologies, which rested too much on the primacy of agency.

Indeed, the emergence of post-structuralism is often seen as an expression of cynicism following the crisis of Marxism among French intellectuals after 1968, as well as a rejection of existentialism that had been very influential in France during the 1950s and 1960s.

There are so many diverse strands to post-structuralism that it is impossible to come up with a single definition. Indeed many theorists who are classified as post-structuralist by others would reject the term, while other writers are classified as structuralists by some people and as post-structuralists by others. Identifying what we mean by post-structuralism is therefore difficult, and the easiest way to explain the idea is in terms of what it is not. This is simple – it is not structuralism!

THE POSTMODERN ORGANISATIONAL FORM

One aspect of post-structuralism that has entered popular discourse is postmodernism. Postmodernism has a relatively long history and draws upon a variety of strands (Anderson 1998). It has been defined in a number of different manners: for example as being epochal in replacing modernity as the current time frame; or epistemological (Newton 1996), in its relativity to other interpretations of social structures; or as a negation of modernity itself (Featherstone 1988). The concept of postmodernity was first mentioned by Olson in 1951 (cited in Anderson 1998), who defined it as post-industrial and post-West. The term was brought more into public awareness by Lyotard (1984), who questioned the use of modernist metanarratives which legitimate society as existing for the good of its members, with the consequent presumption that the whole unites the parts as an expression of the common good.

Thus the metanarrative of economic rationality legitimates both the existence of organisations and the liberal approach, which assumes that the free market provides a mediating mechanism that ensures the freedom of organisations to pursue their own ends will inevitably become synonymous with that freedom leading to optimal benefit for both the owners of that organisation and for the other stakeholders in that organisation. Jameson (1991, 1998), on the other hand, viewed the postmodern as epochally late capitalist, marking a break with previous social forms.

A multitude of aspects exists to postmodernism[1] but in this chapter it is the collapse of the metanarrative, as applied to organisations which is considered in detail. This collapse of the metanarrative[2] calls into question the existence of the organisation as discrete from its environment, and questions therefore the maintenance of the organisational boundary.

1 Indeed not only is the meaning of postmodernism debated but the very existence of the term is itself subject to dispute. It is not intended to enter this debate but merely to use some of the arguments to shed more light on the dynamics of organisations.
2 It is the contribution of Lyotard (1984) concerning the collapse of the unifying metanarrative that is of concern here. His argument concerning the unifying force of this metanarrative within society has been extended here to a consideration of organisations on the basis that they are micro-societies with the same arguments applying.

Furthermore it calls into question the definitions of internal and external aspects of the organisation, its operations, and its reporting. The reinstatement of this organisational discreteness through the reinstatement of its boundary is essential to managers in order to maintain both the internal v external dialectic and thereby to maintain their primacy. Our analysis here starts with a consideration of society and narrows to a consideration of organisations as micro-societies.

The collapse of the metanarrative and the consequent weakening of the macroculture of society is accompanied by the rise of an increasingly robust set of subcultures. These subcultures are operating both at a local level geographically and at a local level in terms of common interest and identity even when geographically disparate. One conclusion to be drawn from this is that, rather than universal politics, the dominance of local or regional politics becomes paramount. Thus the dominance of community as the agent of local need, as manifest by the place of people within that community and operating at a local level as an integral part of each community, assumes priority as the expression of societal organisation. This applies to organisations as micro-societies just as it does to society at large. Consequently organisational and societal structures are needed which recognise this change.

POSTMODERNISM AND SOCIETY

A postmodernist stance therefore leads to a redefinition of locality and divorces it from geographical proximity. Indeed Harvey (1990) argues that one of the significant features of the postmodern era is the compression of space and time, brought about through developments in the technological and informational architecture of society. This compression of space and time has the effect of removing territorial boundaries from an organisation, and this has the effect of providing an opportunity for the redefinition of the concept of organisation in terms of organising local societal structures for the provision of local goods and services. The implication of this is that organisational structures need no longer be dictated solely by the need for transaction-cost-minimising models of service provision, and the ability to define afresh organisations for the provision of individual goods and services becomes possible.

This redefinition of organisations contains within itself one of the inherent contradictions of a postmodernist view of the world, namely the contradiction between the borderlessness of any organisation within the communities within which it is seen to be operating and the extreme nationalistic inclusion/exclusion criterion adopted for any performance evaluation and reporting systems. This criterion has the effect of polarising organisations away from a national focus in their operating and reporting structures, as the nation state collapses in significance. It also expands the concept to inclusion in an expanded state for some purposes while at the same time shrinking the concept of locality of operations to a local level for other purposes (Radhakrishnan 1994).

Thus postmodernity suggests that different spaces are needed for different histories and purposes, and that a dominant model of society has no rational meaning. When considering the question of organisations and the identity of the constituents of such an organisation therefore, and their relationship with the macroculture and with societal structure, this suggests that the local structure has dominant importance for the individual and that his or her sense of community is defined circumstantially. Thus an individual considers him or herself to be a stakeholder in an organisation as a community for a particular purpose, and a stakeholder in different organisational communities for different purposes, this identity being defined in terms of commonality of interest for specific purposes rather than being an overriding part of a definition of self.

This redefinition of the relationship between self as an organisational stakeholder for a particular purpose and community is in perfect accord with the concept of liberal democratic pluralism, which requires a separation of social spheres in order to maximise individual welfare (du Gay 1994). The pluralistic view of liberal democracy is not however extant in the economic rationality paradigm of societal and organisational functioning, which is predicated entirely within a monistic view of society. This definition of the relationship is however in perfect accordance with the concept of communitarianism (Fox and Miller 1995), which regards the self as atomistic and aiming to maximise value (in the liberal sense of welfare) to the lonely self through acting in a community for any specific purpose.

POST-BUREAUCRATIC STRUCTURES

A postmodernist view of organisations and their behaviour is that they are sustained by the rules governing their existence and by the resource appropriation mechanisms that apply to them rather than by any real need among the people whom they purport to serve. Thus the legitimation of their very existence is not founded upon this redefinition of organisational identity and community need. Rather, this redefinition of community suggests that a very different type of organisational structure is needed, and indeed exists, in order to cater for the needs of the individual constituents of that organisation who aggregate for one common purpose while atomising (or aggregating with different individuals) for others.

Such a structure of organisations has been defined by Heckscher (1994) as a post-bureaucratic structure, with its rationale for continuing existence not being through self-referential normalising mechanisms but rather through the maintenance of an interactive dialogue, based upon consensus, with the individual members of the stakeholder community the organisation exists to serve. This view of organisation structure can be extended also to exclude a territorial basis for existence (Nohria and Berkeley 1994) whereby the organisation, through the use of information and communication technology, needs be little more than a virtual organisation existing in a virtual environment as the need arises. Thus the continuing existence, either temporally or geographically, of any organisation as a unit of service provision has no meaning in its own right, as the organisation has no purpose other than the provision of the functions mandated to it by the stakeholder community (Barnett and Crowther 1998), in its widest definition, which it serves.

Baudrillard (1998) claims that there is a need to break with all forms of enlightened conceptual critiques and that truth in the postmodern era is obsolete, while Fish (1985) claims that truth and belief are synonymous for all practical purposes. In terms of any measurement and evaluation of organisational performance this would suggest therefore that the meaning of any reported performance becomes whatever it is interpreted to mean. This interpretation will of course depend upon the perspective of the person performing that interpretation, and the purpose for which that interpretation is undertaken. This naturally places a heavy emphasis upon the interpretative ability of the receiver of the reported information as well as presupposing that this receiver understands the language of the reporting system sufficiently well to be able to extract meaning from this information.

For much of the last four decades that discussion, particularly within the realm of organisation studies, has been driven by one of the three perspectives of power – pluralist, reformist or radical. However, the last decade has been marked by a heightened interest in post-structural perspectives, which have become increasingly influential in the domain of organisation studies. In this section we will consider the central ideas of Michel Foucault, who is arguably the most influential post-structuralist theorist in terms of discussions on power, especially within the UK (see Clegg 1989; Burrell 1997).

A FOUCAULDIAN PERSPECTIVE ON POWER

Burrell (1997, p176) stated that Foucault's work has a 'direct though poorly recognized relevance for the study of organizations'; and his importance to organisation studies is not in doubt. This attention is well deserved in view of the insights from Foucault's work and their capacity to speak to some of the aspects of the present. The intention here is not to provide a comprehensive account of Foucauldian thought; rather it is to explore some of the insights that Foucault brings to the discussion of power and the implications for the management of change. An engagement with Foucauldian thought is a stimulating but at times frustrating experience, as his body of writings is ambiguous.

Power 'is the name one attributes to a complex strategic relationship in a particular society' (Foucault 1977, p92). The strategic relationship is always in the process of being achieved because of the resistance of those subjected to it. Thus power relations are never fixed, nor are they immutable. Power masquerades as a supposedly rationalist construction of modern institutions, a regime of truth that induces and extends the effects of power. No one, strictly speaking, has an official right to power; and yet it is always being exerted in a particular direction, with some people on one side and some on the other. It is often difficult to say who holds power in a precise sense, but it is easy to see who lacks power.

Foucault's view is shared by relational theorists (eg Clegg 1989; Grieco 1996; Jacques 1996) who argue that power is the property of a relationship rather than the commodity of an individual. Clegg (1989) has gone to great lengths to argue for power as a relationship, not a possession, yet he still is able to produce for the *Sunday Times* newspaper an annual power list of 'powerful' people. This demonstrates the pervasiveness of the 'possessional' nature of the linguistics of power. Mills (1995) in her account of discourse cites the example of a young, junior man talking to a senior colleague. In terms of positional power, 'a possessional perspective', the senior colleague would be more powerful. However, she notes that in a relationship power can shift: for instance as conversation moves to subjects in which the supposedly powerful person is relatively powerless. This is a point also made by Foucault.

Similarly, Grieco's (1996) account of the operation of power in working-class communities in the East End of London demonstrates the relational nature of power, and contributes the notion of 'moments' of power. Relational perspectives help to avoid what Bourdieu (2000) has described as the Manichaean view of power, that polarises between powerful and powerless. The corollary of Foucault's denial of power as a commodity was to ask different questions of power. Rather than puzzling over what power is and who has power, he turned to try to understand instead how power is exercised and by what means: '[I] want to describe how power is exercised rather than possessed' (Foucault, 1977, p26). Moreover, he regarded his approach as unique. This commitment to trying to understand how power was exercised led him to develop an interest in physical sites, such as the hospitals, the jail and the school, within a network.

It was this insight that leads to the second orthodox assumption that Foucault calls into question: that of the sovereign nature of power. In the opening pages of *Discipline and*

Punish (arguably Foucault's most widely read book), Foucault reproduces a historical description of the execution of Damiens, the infamous regicide. The passage is shocking in terms of its sheer brutality. It is used to set up an analytical distinction between the periods of modernity and premodernity. Rather than marking a development to a more 'humane' society, Foucault argues that the contrast between the exercise of power in the contemporary era with that of the past is that we are now living in a disciplinary society, whereby power is not exercised through physical force, the materiality of violence, but rather through a panoply of sites, technologies and techniques in which:

> power had to be able to gain access to the bodies of individuals, to their acts, attitudes, and modes of everyday behaviour
>
> (Foucault, 1973, p67)

Essentially Foucault is pointing out that in advanced industrialised societies, power operates in a different manner from the past; this is also resonant with the writings of Weber. The success of disciplinary power in this function can be attributed to its simplicity of techniques. The 'new power operates by universal surveillance' (Foucault, 1972, p74):

> Power as 'visible coercion' was supplanted by detailed disciplinary practices and sustained observation and monitoring of conduct:
>
> (Dandeker 1990, p25)

Thus far our survey of Foucauldian thought has highlighted how it can be considered to be contrary to the established mores on power. Foucault argues against power as a commodity; moreover, he also suggests that we are living in an age of disciplinary power. This leads us to his third argument: the positive effect of power. Conventionally, those on whom power is exercised are thought to have done something they would not normally do (remember our discussion of power in Chapter 5). The assumption is that the effects of the exercise of power will be negative for those objectified by and subjected to the exercise of power. Foucault traces the genesis of this assumption back to the Middle Ages, where there was a chasm between those exercising and those undergoing power.

Foucault's perspective flies in the face of conceptions of power that hold that power is dominatory and by implication oppressive. The work of Chris Grey is useful in this regard. In his studies of the socialisation of accountants undergoing their ICAEW training, he notes that the trainees are subject to a range of disciplinary techniques. They are evaluated, ranked and expected to behave in a particular way. In addition to this they have a challenging set of examinations to complete. This process, while undoubtedly difficult, has positive power effects in that the trainees are produced as accountants, a subject position that is inscribed with a certain social cache and the concomitant ability to enjoy relatively large material benefits associated with such a position. This understanding of power is somewhat more nuanced than the simple zero sum of 'power = oppression'.

TECHNOLOGIES OF POWER

The discussion above highlights the way in which a Foucauldian conception of power challenges many of the assumptions held by other traditions concerned with the issue of power. Foucault's position within the academy is that of 'consecrated heretic', through his challenge to many of the taken-for-granted epistemological positions immanent to conceptualisations of power. That said, it is now time to move the discussion from the abstract to the more practical in order to gain a more concrete sense of how Foucault's view of power may be fruitfully employed in studying organisations: what does his disciplinary sense of power look like in the reality of organisational life? The building block of a Foucauldian perspective is the notion of a discourse, which is a world view sustained by structures, embodied in people and circulated through talk, speech and the dispositional practices associated with behaviour. Therefore, one could talk about a discourse of engineering: a world view on engineering which has emerged and has been sustained through bodies such as the Institute of Electrical Engineers. The discourse produces engineers through training; the embodied engineers then practise the discourse of engineering in their working lives. A discourse possesses its own regime of truth, ie what counts as being true, what is seen as reasonable, what is seen as nonsensical, and what is taken to be 'normal' and what is taken to be 'abnormal' in organisations.

A regime of truth that is immanent to a discourse highlights the way in which both power and knowledge interrelate, for Foucault argues that it is impossible to distinguish knowledge from power. This discussion is of course very similar to the power of meaning introduced by Hardy and Phillips (1998) in reference to the work of Lukes and his followers. This demonstrates the (sometimes tenuous) fault line between structural and post-structural work. According to Foucault, therefore, knowledge is seen as being a product of power; therefore it cannot be understood without reference to power relations. This suggests that the notion of 'neutral' knowledge divorced from power does not exist.

Therefore the knowledge possessed by a psychiatrist is linked to power in the sense that a psychiatrist possesses an authority to speak, an authority to cast judgement on patients; a psychiatrist draws upon the psychiatric discourse to ascribe an interpretation to an event, something that will be framed through the categories within the discourse. At the same time the 'patient' is silenced and is the object of the exercise of power. This is absolutely fundamental to understanding power in organisations, as problems will be defined, categorised, and solutions proffered through the eyes of a particular discourse. Foucault illustrates this argument by studying deviance over time, and demonstrating that definitions of madness and sexuality have changed dramatically over time.

The suggestion is that discourses exist and are acted out in daily life. This of course means that individuals have to be constituted through a particular discourse, ie to be constituted through the discourse of accounting or through the discourse of engineering. Attached to such discourses are ways of doing things. It is possible to see that a particular repertoire is enmeshed within the relations of power in the organisation in the sense that certain things are done because they are deemed to be important. Therefore elements of a repertoire that may be deeply embedded within the organisation, having lain dormant for some time, will be ineluctably linked to the prevailing power/knowledge discourse.

In this sense a discourse perspective is not ethereal, far from it in fact; rather it is manifest in both the practice of people and the structuring of institutions. The primary vessel through which discourse functions is language, which in turn shapes practice; individual discourses will possess their own language code (see Bernstein 1961, 1975), which may be either elaborate or laconic. Such insights correspond closely with the insights of Bourdieu (1988), for whom there is a 'reproduction of the corps' by way of the transmission of social and cultural capital. One of Reed's (1989) criticisms of Foucault is that structure is dangerously downplayed, *pace* the death-of-the-author discussion. This is based on a misinterpretation as for discourse to exist it must inhabit structures which are preconfigured. Therefore the structures play an important part in the theorising of discourse and power.

THE PANOPTICON

Foucault has argued that discourses exist and people are constituted within discourses. This is of interest in itself but it is also important in terms of thinking about organisational change, as one of the central concerns of change programmes is to enact behavioural changes among employees. Townley (1994) provides a detailed account of how employees are both constituted or created through discourse and are objectified through the same discourse.

In the age of disciplinary power, discourses inscribe themselves on people through a vast array of different forms. Foucault provides us with a metaphor, the panopticon (see below), in order to understand the exercise of power in contemporary society. He also provides an analysis of the means through which the panopticon works, ie through the gaze, the normalising judgement, the exam and the confessional. These metaphors should be regarded as highly stylised conceptions of the means through which power operates. In the same way that classical conceptions of power express themselves through concepts such as possession and domination, so Foucauldians carry with them a highly stylised toolkit of well-defined notions of *how power works*.

Foucault, through his studies of various institutions (army barracks, the school and the hospital), claimed that power is exercised through observation. For instance, in examining a temporary military camp he interprets the camp as being the:

> diagram of a power that acts by means of general visibility.
>
> (Foucault, cited in Rabinow 1986, p189)

The implication is that to see is to be able to exercise power: it is the ability to render activity as transparent. Foucault draws attention to the importance of architecture in this exercise of power, which in addition to military establishments can be seen in 'working class housing estates, hospitals, asylums, prisons and schools' (Foucault, cited in Rabinow 1986, p189). It is at this point necessary to consider Foucault's most celebrated and most controversial metaphor – the panopticon. Foucault resurrected Jeremy Bentham's largely forgotten prison design (the panopticon), which was designed by Bentham with the aim of improving behaviour in prisons. The panopticon was a rotunda; within the prison there was a central observation point from which all prisoners could be observed. The ingenuity of the panopticon was however that prisoners did not know when they were being observed, yet they knew that observation could be taking place at any time.

Therefore, rather than the prisoners having to be disciplined, they would actually discipline themselves through the knowledge that they fell under the panoptic gaze. Perhaps a more vivid example can be found in Pat Barker's *Regeneration* trilogy, where she presents a historical fiction set in the First World War. In dealing with the experience of conscientious objectors, she chronicles the way in which on a prison door there was 'an eye in the wall', or 'Iris'. Prisoners from their bunk would gaze at the Iris, not knowing if they were being observed or not but, making the assumption that they were, would modify their behaviour accordingly. In this particular example, the prisoners would be self-disciplining themselves to remain naked, rather than don the military uniform placed at the end of their bed (Carter and Grieco 2000).

Numerous commentators (eg Sewell and Wilkinson, 1992; Zuboff, 1988) have pointed out that the surveillance techniques found in disciplinary power are relevant to the contemporary workplace. This is especially the case in the age of information technology and smart systems, techniques that afford the opportunity for panopticism through informational

architecture. Ball and Wilson (1998) look specifically at computer-based monitoring within call centres, and in particular they look at the extent to which employees discipline themselves to meet the expected performance criteria, but also how in this process they are constituted as work subjects. People within different institutions such as the workshop, school and army were argued to be subject to a 'whole micropenality' of 'time, activity, behaviour, speech, body and sexuality'.

Therefore a Foucauldian analysis assumes that there is 'a correct way of being', which is determined by the prevailing power/knowledge discourse. Deviation from the expectations of the discourse would result in some form of 'punishment'. The pressure is for people to normalise themselves to the expectations of the discourse. For instance, Hodgson (2000) demonstrates how male life assurance salesmen are expected to normalise to particular macho norms of behaviour; similarly, Grey (1998) portrays how trainee accountants are expected to work long hours in order to satisfy the 'client'. Foucault argues that this process of normalisation is one of the 'great instruments of power'. In contrast to its homogenising qualities, normalisation also serves to distinguish between individuals. Townley (1994) applies these ideas to contemporary human resource management (HRM). She presents HRM as a process of power/knowledge, looking at the production of knowledge and its effects. Townley (1994) cites the selection process as an example of differentiating between individuals.

PANOPTICISM AND POWER

The gaze of panopticism also operates through the examination: it 'is a whole type of power' (Foucault 1972) whereby individuals are both observed and differentiated. For example, the exam objectifies people or groups – an annual profit statement by an organisation is an examination of sorts. The exam also individualises in that it creates an archive – another opportunity for observation. An individual can be ranked against his or her peers, with comparisons being made. Thus Hodgson's life assurance salespeople could be judged on their commissions earned, Ball and Wilson's call centre workers could be compared on the number of calls a day that were answered and so on. It is through the panoptic gaze that normalises and examines that power operates in contemporary organisations. Thus, according to Foucault, the very features of penal life have come to pervade all elements of society – society has become 'carceral'.

The concept of a carceral society is a contentious one: Foucault is suggesting that the mechanisms of control that affect our lives resemble those of prisoners. For Habermas this is problematic and he argues that it is an absurdity to draw a comparison between social democratic France of the 1970s and the Soviet gulags of the 1950s. Giddens (1984) argues that it is inappropriate to use an extreme form of organisation as an example for other organisations. In his defence Foucault argues that it is important to look to the extremes in order to make sense of the commonplace. However, while it is useful to draw insights from one type of institution, it is problematic to elevate them as providing a template for society: Poster (1988) notes 'at times discipline and punishment regresses to a totalising logic in which the panopticon becomes the model for all forms of domination'.

Another forum in which self-discipline can be observed is, according to Foucault, the confessional; he takes the practices of the Catholic Church and extends them as a metaphor for the operation of power. The confessional denotes the subjection of a person to a discourse, ie a Catholic subjecting themselves to the teachings of the Catholic Church, being offered the opportunity to purge their sins and be granted forgiveness. We have previously considered Wilson's (1992) account of programmed change. He highlighted the way in which many such initiatives are aimed at individual managers – that is the manager is invited to reconstitute herself and discuss her practices in relation to a particular discourse. Such a process could be regarded as an act of confession. Townley explained that the use of Foucault is in terms of focusing our attention on seemingly innocuous techniques and opening them up to critical scrutiny.

For instance, Townley recounted that as part of her teaching at the University of Warwick she had to teach personnel management topics such as performance management. For many critical theorists, especially those for whom their analytical concerns were at the level of the state, such techniques were not worthy of consideration. Townley however engages with such techniques and demonstrates that they had important consequences in terms of constructing subjectivities. Thus, through a performance appraisal an employee is constructed as a 'successful' or 'unsuccessful' employee, which in turn is internalised. Similarly, Townley (1994) demonstrated how such technologies also serve to categorise and organise larger populations – an illustration would be in terms of selection and recruitment whereby a large field of applicants is organised into a population. This concentration on specific mechanisms deployed in organisations has proved a fruitful line of analysis, and has highlighted the fact that techniques in the workplace, however apparently innocuous, need to be problematised. It is this localised analysis of power that is one of the analytical strengths of a Foucauldian-inspired analysis.

DOUBTING FOUCAULT

Earlier we suggested that Foucault now holds one of the dominant conceptual positions in organisational theory. This is not to say that there is a broad consensus relating to the efficacy and status of Foucault's work. In fact, a number of critics have lined up to question Foucault. Reed (1989) argued that Foucault provides brilliant insights into the operation of power but that there are a large number of difficulties with his writings. Reed's concerns are also reflected in the writings of a number of other theorists. The totalising logic of the panopticon is deeply problematic. It has also caused readers of Foucault to question his notion of agency and of resistance. If we are 'docile bodies' constituted through discourse, are we capable of agency?

This is an important question and goes to the heart of the previous critique of the efficacy of employing the metaphor of an unbuilt prison to explain contemporary society. In *Discipline and Punish* there is a denial, or at any rate an obscuring of, agency, which incidentally is at odds with many accounts of carceral life. This is perhaps the corollary of Foucault studying the plans, and not praxis, of a total institution (see Goffman 1967). Instead we would suggest that people's subjectivities are constructed through a range of discourses and biographical experiences that are not capable of being reduced to one totalising discourse. Thus in liberal society there are limits to Foucault's position; moreover, for individuals there is a zone of manoeuvre, a space for agency. The corollary of this position is that we may well be able to generalise about how, for instance, an accountant, as compared with a marketer, may approach a particular problem, but it is not to deny that people can change or be constituted through different and contradictory discourses.

Similarly, there has been a great deal of controversy as to whether Foucault provides room for resistance within his conception of power. As Knights (1997) notes, for those whose reading of Foucault is restricted to *Discipline and Punish* there is little evidence of resistance, but in his later works there is more attention paid to the possibility of resistance. Where there is power there is also the potential for resistance; rather than Foucault closing down the possibility of resistance, Knights argues, he opens up a multiplicity of sites for resistance. Edward Said, however, argues the opposite, stating that Foucault aligns himself with power rather than with resistance, conceiving power as being 'irresistable and unopposable' (1978, p158), his position coming from the 'actual realisation of power, not of opposition to it'.

Related to this point are the insights from contemporary theorists such as Bauman (1989) or Clegg (1989), who have highlighted the fact that the panopticon has become inverted: figures of power, of institutions of power, have themselves become subject to the gaze, but the gaze of the 'other', be it the patient, the client or the student. This has been referred to as 'reverse panopticism', while Bauman (1989) describes it as synopticism. An example of this would be, for instance, patients with a particular medical problem looking on the Internet, and hence learning about their own condition, and then going to a General Practitioner in order to have particular drugs prescribed. This is a radical departure from the idea of the doctor as omnipotent, a Herculean character with the power of science in (usually) his hands. For instance, people of previous generations would routinely address a doctor as 'sir' and follow his (never a woman's) prescriptions closely, without asking any questions, for it was not their place to do so. Now the situation is quite the reverse: a harassed General Practitioner may well be confronted by an 'empowered' patient who, through accessing websites, may well be far better informed than the General Practitioner (Grieco 1996).

Foucault's sense of exploring institutions, and in particular looking at the extremes or margins of society, resulted in a silence over the role of the state. At one level, this can be read as his escaping an intense attachment to the state, as a rejection of his Communist Party affiliations of both his Marxist past and his French ethnicity. The localised conception of power problematised Marxist notions of freedom, for it emphasised the fact that power relations are an ever-present part of social life, be they in the family, the office or at the level of the nation state. A disinterest or an analytical blindness to the role of the state seems problematic and perhaps explains why some of his interlocutors, at least within the British business school academy, have tended to concentrate on finely grained analyses. These analyses are remarkable for their silence on the state. Instead, organisational action is seen as reducible to discourse within a particular organisation or department.

There are other reservations about Foucault and his work that are too detailed for this book. The main critiques levelled at him are his lack of agency and an aggrandisement of the disciplinary society, which at times lapses into a transcendental essentialism that he abhorred. Undoubtedly his work was ethnocentric, and his approach to history transgressed the verisimilitude demanded by the subject. The inherent disagreements over interpretation that seem to bedevil Foucault's work would no doubt have provided a great deal of amusement to the writer himself. It is mistaken to debate endlessly what he *really* meant, as if such an exercise would produce some sort of definitive theory of power. In this sense what is important is to take insights from his work rather than to attempt to be a Foucault purist.

SYMBOLIC VIOLENCE

Foucault's account of disciplinary society describes the technologies and techniques through which populations are ordered, categorised and controlled. Equally, he illustrates the way in which a particular discourse affects the shaping of individual subjectivities. These are quite clearly important contributions. *Discipline and Punish* commences with a description of the execution of Damiens, and the argument follows that sovereign power, as exemplified for instance by Louis XIV of France declaring '*l'état c'est moi*', gives way to disciplinary power. The lacuna in his work is that while he brilliantly describes the symbolism of sovereign power and of the architecture of disciplinary power, there is silence on the symbolism of the exercise of power in contemporary society. Populations are not managed silently, but rather there are hugely important symbolic demonstrations. Bourdieu (1988) introduces the term symbolic violence, whereby one group, through an action, is violated by another. Similarly, Castells (2000) is alert to the particular importance of symbolism in contemporary society. Thus protests against the World Bank, fox-hunting or the British government, while having limited substantive *effects*, are important symbolically. Equally the representation of a group in a particular way, eg one that demeans them or silences them, can be considered to be an act of symbolic violence. For instance, during his long spell of incarceration, Nelson Mandela (and other ANC prisoners) was compelled to wear shorts.

A REGIME OF POWER

We can now attempt an inclusive, exploratory conception of power. Quite clearly, the individual guile of managers or workers in particular positions may well constitute acts demonstrating the skilful use of power. In that sense, we should not fully follow Foucault's lead in terms of cutting off the king's head, and announcing the end of sovereign power. Rather we should acknowledge that individual agency takes place within the constraints of preconfigured institutional structures and discourses. We can consider that Foucault's insights into the functioning of power offer great insights into how a system of technologies emerges to legitimate a particular world view. In this sense, there are interstices between meaning and system. Furthermore, Foucault demonstrates the way in which, far from being a seamless teleology, history is actually a series of ruptures and discontinuities, which, as Orwell observed, are then rewritten by the winners! Accepting this and a Foucauldian notion of discourse, sustained through texts, institutions and dispositional practice, that is resonant with the notion of recursiveness, we can construct an argument about the way in which we can make sense of the role for people endogenous to a discourse and the notion of a competition or at any rate a contestation between discourses.

Turning to the issue of the role for people within a discourse, in the sections above the way in which people exist through a discourse, through archives, performance scores etc has been documented. In short, people are subjectified and objectified by the technologies – the power of the system – of a particular discourse. Being constituted through a particular discourse will give a person access to the resources and linguistic tropes of a particular discourse. This is something recognised by Foucault in his descriptions of the hospital. Someone (for instance, a doctor) has, by virtue of their position, an authority to speak, an authority to delimit. Foucault's account is, however, limited and gives little idea of the relative mastery of a particular discourse, although this is helpfully filled by the work of Bourdieu (1977, 1988, 2000). A fully detailed account of Bourdieu's work is outside the scope of this chapter, but to illustrate the point about positions within an endogenous discourse I want to draw on that part of his work that relates to the concept of cultural capital.

BOURDIEU AND THE REPRODUCTION OF CAPITAL

One of Bourdieu's broader concerns is to demonstrate the means through which capital reproduces itself. Bourdieu delineates between types of capital: in particular he argues that there are 'three fundamental guises' of capital, namely the distinct categories of economic capital, social capital and cultural capital, which are not reducible one to another but are capable of being converted. While economic capital needs little elaboration, social capital refers to the social networks that an agent is positioned within. In more common parlance, it is the 'who you know' of social action (see Grieco 1987, 1996). Thus to be rich in social capital is to be well positioned in relevant social networks. For Bourdieu, social capital is tied to familial relations or positions within a particular institution (eg a profession). The third form of capital, and the one which will form the focus of this section, is that of cultural capital. Cultural capital refers to the knowledge of a particular domain – it is the 'what you know', ie skills, knowledge and competences. For Bourdieu, cultural capital has three core manifestations: *embodied*, whereby a person is the embodiment of particular knowledge; *objectified*, where cultural capital is inscribed in artefacts such as books, paintings, reports etc; *institutionalised*, where cultural capital is conferred or consecrated upon an individual by virtue of their association with an institution, such as through holding a particular appointment or holding a particular credential, such as a degree from an elite institution. Bourdieu (1988) holds that education institutions such as the (business) school or the French Grand Ecole are important sites for conferring credentials or consecrating cultural capital, and arguably Bourdieu's work has had greatest impact upon the sociology of education (Bourdieu 1988).

It does not follow that to be rich in one form of capital equates with an overall richness in capital. For instance, Bourdieu draws a distinction between those who are rich in cultural capital and poor in economic capital and vice versa. Bourdieu studied the dynamics of capital over two generations and discovered that those rich in a particular form of capital – especially economic – were able to convert richness in one form of capital to that of another, thus perpetuating an elite. It is the conversion mechanisms between the different forms of capital that are of particular interest to Bourdieu. Relating this to corporations, it may be that a managerial elite will be able to use its economic capital in order to be able to purchase cultural capital.

The above account is necessarily a brief sketch of Bourdieu's work, but his analysis can be summarised in terms of the implications of differentials in individuals' mastery of a particular management discourse. In Bourdieu's metaphorical usage, such mastery means being 'richer' in cultural capital. The acquisition of a richness in cultural capital affords, among other things, a capacity to speak and cast pronouncements on a particular domain. For instance, if we are to focus on managerial cultural capital, there are a number of routes to acquisition. These range widely, from reading pop management books to graduation from a prestigious business school. A further important but implicit route to the acquisition of cultural capital is those processes of knowledge exchange which Abbott, in a study of professional groups, termed 'workplace assimilation'. Abbott (1988) highlights the way in which less-qualified workers are able to assimilate the practices and language of those that are relatively more qualified. It is especially relevant here, because management consultancy praxis is based in organisations, increasing the possibility that managers exposed to the consultants will assimilate some of the 'language and practice' of the consultants by virtue of their 'legitimate peripheral participation' (Lave and Wenger 1991).

A regime of power is constituted by a central meaning and is supported by a system that legitimates and perpetuates that system of meaning. The regime of power is ineluctably connected with knowledge: the knowledge created by the technologies of power and the knowledge worked with by members of a particular discourse (ie dispositional cultural capital). Such discourses may well be complementary, for instance that of the New Right and New Managerialism. In this sense they can be considered to be intertextual: there is enough overlap and resonance to allow for co-existence. Conversely, some discourses may well be considered the antithesis of each other, and may well 'confront' each other as competing ideologies. This raises the spectre of binarism, with the concomitant notion of a context between good–bad, right–wrong etc.

In interpreting such relations, Foucault and others argue that such are a consequence of power relations in society – that is how power operates in a particular society – and that some groups are relatively powerful in their ability to define 'realities' of situations. Thus for Foucault some discourses are elevated above others, are allowed a voice at the expense of other discourses. Derrida (1978) has worked on this problem, arguing that in the contestation between discourses there is the tendency for a discourse to lock another into a violent hierarchy, whereby one knowledge is subjugated and rendered relatively powerless. For instance, Crowther *et al* (2001) have argued that 'all binary opposition seeks to polarise the text in terms of two opposite poles but this normally is undertaken in the context of portraying one pole as good and the other as bad'. Similarly, Laclan (1990, p33) has argued:

Derrida has shown how an identity's constitution is always based on excluding something and establishing a violent hierarchy between the two resultant poles.

These insights are important for they are suggestive that there may not be room for a pluralist co-existence between two discourses, but rather that there may instead be a confrontation. The relevance of these insights for the study of organisations is through the way in which new discourses may emerge and problematise the status quo; the means through which the status quo may be challenged is through a panoptic gaze or a dividing practice.

POWER IN ORGANISATIONS

In this chapter we have addressed the issue of power in organisations and taken a postmodern perspective. We have developed a framework that we have termed a 'regime of power' that acknowledges and fully appreciates the individual, Machiavellian machinations that may well be engaged in by individuals. Implicit to this argument is the ubiquity of power (Clegg 1989). While power is not viewed as a possession, but rather as a product of social relations, some groups will appear to have greater saliency, and as such can be regarded as being relatively powerful.

It is possible that within a discourse, a group will possess the ability to 'legislate' (Bauman 1987) over a particular domain; for instance, Said (1978) demonstrates the way in which occidental scholars, in effect, defined and categorised the orient, or the way in which Israel defines Palestine. Similarly, Foucault (1973) has demonstrated the position that a psychiatrist holds within medical health discourse as compared with the 'patient'. In terms of the workplace, Abbot (1988) has demonstrated the way in which some professions (eg medicine and law) have been able to gain full jurisdiction over their respective domains, while other groups (such as personnel management) have been less successful. While power may seem to be a 'possession', especially in terms of powerful groups, it is important to recognise that the relations of power can quickly change (see Carter and Crowther 1999), and they have a tendency to exhibit high levels of recursiveness (compare the rankings of UK universities now with 50 years ago).

We have drawn insights from the post-structural accounts of power to illustrate the power of the system. The preoccupation of Foucauldian researchers is with the techniques through which power is exercised, the most famous examples being Jeremy Bentham's plans for the panopticon and the religious confessional. The techniques of power produce 'truth' in subjects, be it the performance of an individual in an assessment centre or the financial performance of an organisation. The panoply of such techniques can be seen to pervade contemporary organisational life: for instance, schools, universities and hospitals find their identity in the wider environment constructed through performance measures. Within the private sector, for example, the spectacular collapse of Marks & Spencer has been constructed through the various techniques of power which produce truth on organisational performance such as financial data, customer surveys etc. Immanent to the power of the system is the multiplication of such techniques and the importance that they are afforded, characteristics that have led Power (1994) to raise the spectre of the Audit Society. The power of the system is therefore fundamental to the maintenance (or the displacement) of meaning systems within organisations.

The relevance of a discussion of power in relation to organisational change is that the prevailing relations of power construct that which constitutes what is sacred and what is profane. Furthermore the interstices of the power of meaning and the power of the system combine to produce effects in the workplace in terms of prioritising particular objectives over others. This is important, because to engage with an organisation is to engage with power, ie it is necessary to deconstruct an organisation in order to uncover the dominant relations of power and concomitant constructions of knowledge. In a fast-changing environment it is necessary to examine discourses that may well be appropriated by an organisation, or perhaps those that subject an organisation to a *normalising* gaze.

CONCLUSIONS

Of equal importance in this chapter have been our discussion of postmodernity and its implications for organisational theory. One of the implications of this discussion of postmodernity is that the organisation as a discrete entity with a fixed boundary has become less relevant. This has obvious implications for organisational theory. If the boundary of an organisation is less fixed and more permeable, then modes of organising are more problematic. No longer is it sufficient to consider how to organise within the organisation – organisation across the boundary of the organisation is also important. This has been considered previously (and will be so again) when we consider globalisation and such things as outsourcing. Organisation theory must inevitably be more complex in order to make suggestions for what is a more complex world.

SUMMARY

- Structuralism (metanarratives, underlying social and linguistic structures in society) is a theory within modernism.
- Post-structuralism and postmodernism contest metanarratives, eg of economic rationality and organisational boundaries – in favour of local subcultures, and societal and organisational microprocesses.
- Foucault's views on power:
  - relational rather than a commodity
  - exercised less through physical force and more through disciplinary practices, surveillance techniques and normalising discourses.

- Critique of Foucault: human agency and resistance seem impossible in the face of his analysis of power as totalising.

- Implications for power in organisations: the ubiquity of power (and resistance), as against there being solely sovereign (top-down) power.

FURTHER READING

BOURDIEU, P. (1988) *Distinction*. London: Routledge.

DANDEKER, C. (1990) *Surveillance power and modernity*. Cambridge: Polity Press.

HARVEY, D. (1990) *The condition of postmodernity*. Oxford: Blackwell.

REFERENCES

ABBOT, A. (1988) *The system of professions: an essay on the division of expert labor*. London: University of Chicago Press.

ANDERSON, P. (1998) *The origins of postmodernity*. London: Verso

BALL, K. and WILSON, D. (1998) Computer based monitoring in organisations. *Organisation Studies*, Vol. 19, 271–296.

BARNETT, N.J. and CROWTHER, D. (1998) Community identity in the 21st century: a postmodernist evaluation of local government structure. *International Journal of Public Sector Management*, Vol. 11, No. 6/7, 425–439.

BAUDRILLARD, J. (1998) *The consumer society*. London: Sage.

BAUMAN, Z. (1987) *Legislators and interpreters: on modernity, post-modernity and intellectuals*. Cambridge: Polity Press.

BAUMAN, Z. (1989) *Modernity and the holocaust*. Cambridge: Polity Press.

BERNSTEIN, B. (1961) Social structure, language and learning. *Educational Research*, Vol. 3, 163–176.

BERNSTEIN, B. (1975) *Class, codes and control: towards a theory of educational transmissions*. London: Routledge & Kegan Paul.

BOURDIEU, P. (1977) *Outline of a theory of practice*. Cambridge: Cambridge University Press.

BOURDIEU, P. (1988) *Distinction*. London: Routledge.

BOURDIEU, P. (2000) *Pascalian meditations*. Stanford, Calif: Stanford University Press.

BURRELL, G. (1997) *Pandemonium*. London: Sage.

CARTER, C. and CROWTHER, D. (1999) Unravelling a profession: the case of engineers in a British regional electricity company. *Critical Perspectives on Accounting*, Vol. 11 No. 1, 23–49.

CARTER, C. and GRIECO, M. (2000) New deals, no wheels: social exclusion, tele-options and electronic ontology. *Urban Studies*, Vol. 37, No. 10, 1735–1748.

CASTELLS, M. (2000) *The rise of the network society*. Oxford: Blackwells.

CLEGG, S. (1989) *Frameworks of power*. London: Sage.

CROWTHER, D., COOPER, S. and CARTER, C. (2001) Regulation – the movie: a semiotic study of the periodic review of UK regulated industry. *Journal of Organizational Change Management*, Vol. 14, No. 3, 225–238.

DANDEKER, C. (1990) *Surveillance power and modernity*. Cambridge: Polity Press.

DELANTY, G. (1997) *Social science: beyond constructivism and realism*. Buckingham: Open University Press.

DERRIDA, J. (1978) *Writing and difference* (trans A Bass). London: Routledge & Kegan Paul.

DU GAY, P. (1994) Colossal immodesties and hopeful monsters: pluralism and organisational conduct. *Organization*, Vol. 1, No. 1, 125–148.

FEATHERSTONE, M. (1988) In pursuit of the postmodern: an introduction. *Theory Culture and Society*, Vol. 5, No. 2/3, 195–215.

FISH, S. (1985) Is there a text in this class? In W.T.J. Mitchell (ed) *Against theory*. Chicago: University of Chicago Press.

FOUCAULT, M. (1972) *The archaeology of knowledge*. London: Tavistock.

FOUCAULT, M. (1973) *Madness and civilisation* (trans R. Howard). London: Tavistock.

FOUCAULT, M. (1977) *Discipline and punish*. Harmondsworth: Penguin.

FOX, C.J. and MILLER, H.T. (1995) *Postmodern public administration: towards discourse*. London: Sage

GIDDENS, A. (1984) *The constitution of society*. Oxford: Polity Press.

GOFFMAN, E. (1967) *The presentation of self*. Harmondsworth: Penguin

GREY, C. (1998) On being a professional in a 'big six' firm. *Accounting, Organizations and Society*, Vol. 23, No. 5–6, 569–587.

GRIECO, M. (1987) *Keeping it in the family: social networks and employment chance*. London: Tavistock.

GRIECO, M. (1996) *Worker's dilemmas: recruitment, reliability and repeated exchange*. London: Routledge.

HARDY, C. and PHILLIPS, N. (1998) Strategies of engagement: lessons from the critical examination of collaboration and conflict in an interorganizational domain. *Organization Science*, Vol. 9, No. 2, 217–230.

HARVEY, D. (1990) *The condition of postmodernity*. Oxford: Blackwell.

HECKSCHER, C. (1994) Defining the post-bureaucratic type. In C. Heckscher and A. Donnellon (eds) *The post-bureaucratic organisation* (pp14–62). London: Sage.

HODGSON, D.E. (2000) *Discourse, discipline and the subject: a Foucauldian analysis of the UK financial services industry*. London: Ashgate.

JACQUES, R. (1996) *Manufacturing the employee*. London: Sage.

JAMESON, F. (1991) *Postmodernism, or the cultural logic of late capitalism*. London: Verso.

JAMESON, F. (1998) *The cultural turn*. London: Verso.

KNIGHTS, D. (1997) Organization theory in the age of deconstruction: dualism, gender and postmodernism revisited. *Organization Studies*, Vol. 18, No. 1, 1-19.

LACLAN, E. (1990) *New reflections on the revolution of our time*. London: Verso.

LAVE, J. and WENGER, E. (1991) *Situated learning: legitimate peripheral participation*. Cambridge: Cambridge University Press.

LEVI-STRAUSS, C. (1949) *Elementary structures of kinship*. Boston, Mass: Beacon.

LYOTARD, J.F. (1984) *The postmodern condition* (trans G. Bennington and B. Massumi). Minneapolis: University of Minneapolis Press.

MILLS, A. (1995) Man/aging subjectivity, silencing diversity: organizational imagery in the airline industry. *Organization*, Vol. 2, No. 2, 243–270.

NEWTON, T. (1996) Postmodernism and action. *Organization*, Vol. 3, No. 1, 7–29.

NOHRIA, N. and BERKLEY, J.D. (1994) The virtual organisation. In C. Heckscher and A. Donnellon (eds) *The post-bureaucratic organisation* (pp108–128). London: Sage.

POSTER, M. (ed). (1988) *Jean Baudrillard: selected writings.* Cambridge: Polity Press.

POWER, M. (1994) T*he audit explosion* (Paper no. 7). London: Demos.

RABINOW, P. (ed). (1986) *The Foucault reader: an introduction to Foucault's thought.* London: Penguin.

RADHAKRISHNAN, R. (1994) Postmodernism and the rest of the work. *Organization*, Vol. 1, No. 2, 305–340.

REED, M. (1989) *The sociology of management.* Hemel Hempstead: Harvester Wheatsheaf.

SAID, E. (1978) *Orientalism: Western conceptions of the Orient.* London: Penguin.

SARTRE, J.-P. (1960) *Critique of dialectical reason.* London: Verso.

SAUSSURE, F. (1916) *Course on general linguistics.* Glasgow: Collins.

SEWELL, G. and WILKINSON, B. (1992) Empowerment or emasculation? Shopfloor surveillance in a total quality organization. In P. Blyton and P. Turnbull (eds) *Reassessing human resource management.* Sage: London.

TOWNLEY, B. (1994) *Reframing human resource management: power, ethics and the subject at work.* London: Sage.

WILSON, D. (1992) *A strategy of change.* London: Routledge.

ZUBOFF, S. (1988) *In the age of the smart machine: the future of work and power.* Oxford: Heinemann Professional.

Social constructionism

INTRODUCTION

Social constructionism is a set of ideas with roots in both critical theory and postmodernism. The main assumption behind social constructionism is that nothing is predetermined, neutral, fixed or necessarily the best possible of all alternatives in terms of structures, systems or processes. Rather they are 'socially constructed' by people, through institutional systems and practices, and for various reasons – for what is seen as the 'best' way of organising things, for convenience, or for other reasons such as self-interest. It challenges long-established concepts such as truth, objectivity, reason, authority and progress, including scientists' claims that knowledge is absolute and uninfluenced by societal contexts such as history, culture and ideology (Gergen 2001a). Moreover the structures, systems and processes that are in place are further 'constructed' in terms of the meanings people give to them, their understandings and interpretations, and the actions they take in regard to them. What is usually at issue are different conceptions of the 'real', and what is rational and good. Contested too are patterns of action, made all the more lively and profuse through facilitation by modern technologies of communication. This is as relevant to organisations as to wider society.

Gergen, who is a leading writer on social constructionism, does not deny the relevance and usefulness of concepts such as 'real', 'true' and 'objective'. Within a community, he argues, they are a glue that binds the traditions, trust and values of a community and enables co-operative action within that community. The problem arises when these values are extended and universalised to apply to everyone. This can lead to the denigration of others who don't share the same traditions and rationalities, and has led to contemptuous attitudes to different cultures. Where physical power lay behind these attitudes, as with the colonising Western powers, this resulted in the superimposition of Western cultures and economic, political and social systems on communities the world over at the expense of their own local traditions and practices (Gergen 2001b).

SOCIAL CONSTRUCTIONS OF PEOPLE

Social constructionists reject universalising ideas and judgements being applied to people as well. They reject any essentialist views that orthodox organisation as well as mainstream psychology theorists might suggest about people having 'essential' characteristics that are core to their personalities and capabilities, and which explain their achievements, including the positions they reach in organisations. Rather, they see people's personalities and opportunities for developing their capabilities as resulting from factors other than those regarding 'intrinsic' qualities in the person themselves. People's identities and fortunes, moreover, change in different circumstances – according to the broader context they are in and whether or not they are affirmed in their strivings and ambitions, for example. People's individual experience too is not privileged by social constructionists as it might be by humanists. This is regarded as 'a naive version of human freedom' (Alvesson and Deetz 2000, p96). Social constructionism represents a move away from 'mental paraphernalia' in individuals' heads to a position where their experience and actions are understood and enacted in an historic and social context (Parker 1998).

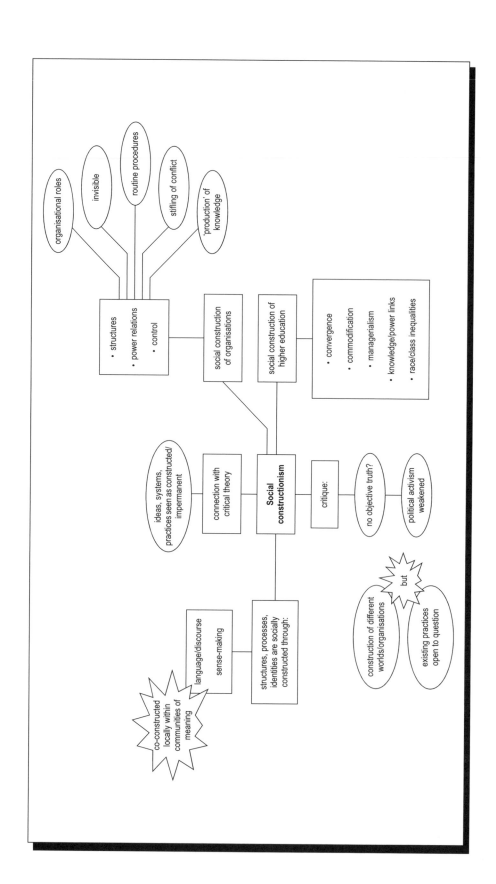

People are regarded as independent agents, rather than passive objects, albeit governed by their culture and other contextual influences (Sarbin and Kitsuse 1994). If attitudes to what people do can be separated from what people are, Gergen (2001b) argues, there can be a productive interchange between individuals. In such circumstances the way can be opened for people to see others' attitudes and activities in their particular context rather than condemning them as, say, 'evil' for doing what is seen by the outsider as unjust, inhumane or morally tainted.

THE ROLE OF LANGUAGE

Language is regarded as fundamental to constructions in social life. Social constructionists emphasise how language affects the way people relate to their environment and society. Neither the identities of the social world, including organisations, nor those of the people interpreting them and acting within them are fixed. They are subject to change and development because of the movement and development of ideas and opinions within communal interchange (Shotter and Gergen 1989). Focusing on language has helped constructionists deny certainty and objectivity as well as unitary, autonomous identities. Rather, they are in a social and politically linguistic framework that will influence their experience and their understandings of it (Alvesson and Deetz 2000, p96). To put this in a different way, such understandings are constructed within 'culturally-specific narratives, regimes of truth, patterns of power or forms of ideology' (Parker 1998, p7). Shotter (1993, p2) was very interested in how people construct their environments through language:

> For, although our surroundings may stay materially the same at any one moment in time, how we make sense of them, what we select for attention or to act upon, how we connect those various events, dispersed in time and space, together and attribute significance to them, very much depends on our use of language.

A SOCIAL CONSTRUCTIONIST STYLE OF THINKING

Social constructionism can be said to share an emphasis on language as 'forming', performing or constructing (rather than representing) social realities. Language is generally recognised as fundamentally social – as something people do together; there is no such thing as a private language (see eg Wittgenstein 1963). Language then becomes viewed as a social process in which social realities – of 'people' and 'worlds' – are made; some call this sense-making[1] (eg Weick 1995). This said, social constructionist accounts differ in very important ways. First, most emphasise socially constructed 'products' whilst some give more explicit attention to *processes* of construction. Terms employed for these purposes include 'discourses'[2] (Burr 1995), 'narratives'[3] (Barry 1997), 'accounting'[4] (Harré 1979) and 'enactment'[5] (Weick 1995). Second, many focus on individual sense-making whilst others centre on *communal* construction processes and view 'people and things' (as social realities) as constructed in these processes. Third, some theorists make much of the reflexive

1 A term intended to keep action and cognition together rather than separate.

2 'A discourse refers to a set of meanings, metaphors, representations, images, stories, statements and so on that in some way together produce a particular version of events ... each discourse claims to say what the object really is, that is, claims to be the truth' (Burr 1995, pp48–49); '.. anything that can be read for meaning can be thought of as being a manifestation of one or more discourses' (p51).

3 Viewed as > or < collective sense-making stories that (the) narrators 'inhabit', which may be more or less empowering, ... and which may "open(ing) space for the authoring of alternative stories"' (Barry 1997, p32); 'narrative (or textual) models emphasise "opening space for the authoring of alternative stories"' (p32).

4 'by accounting an actor can create and recreate actions and acts by use of publicly, socially intelligible speech to give specific meanings to human activity' (Harré 1979, p273).

5 A reference to constructing reality through authoritative acts (see Weick 1995).

recognition that 'the knower' – *including themselves as theorists* – is part of (rather than apart from) construction processes and 'products'[6] (see eg Pearce 1992). To put the point slightly differently, constructions of Other include constructions of Self – and constructions of Self are always in relation to some Other(s): Self and Other are co-operative and co-defining. This means, for example, that any discourse of Other will include the voice of the particular Self who constructed it. Further, since Self is relational there is a sense in which we construct as many identities as we do social relations (Hosking and Morley 1991).

As will be seen, a constructionist position acknowledges the familiar ego-logical world view that constructs person apart from, and dominating, nature – at the 'centre of the universe', so to speak. In addition, this constructionist style of thinking opens up another possibility: an ego-logical 'world view' that sees Self as participating in Other and Other as participating in Self (see eg Reason 1994).

CONSTRUCTING AS JOINT ACTION

Talk of 'relational' approaches and talk of sense-making are becoming more widespread in many discussions of managerial and organisational work. However, individual entities usually are presumed, such that talk of relating is a reference to what goes on 'between' entities (in contrast to what goes on 'within'). Another possible 'starting point' is with sense-making as a social process, centring language and action. One view of language is that it stands in for, or represents, how things really are. However, another and not necessarily contradictory view is that language is performative, ie that it brings people and things into being. This gives action centre stage, joining what often is separated, ie talk, action, things and events. Action now is seen to include written and spoken words, formulae and statistics, non-verbal gestures, voice tone, and artefacts of human activity such as an annual report, business accounts, dead animals, pollution ... Sense-making is ongoing when some *action (including some artefact [arti-fact]) is co-ordinated with by another act – so constructing a social process.* For example, a website is accessed and read.

By these arguments sense-making (a) becomes understood as co-constructed rather than an individual affair, and (b) becomes talk of social processes rather than meanings, so to speak, 'inside someone's head'. We should add that, in this view, social realities are co-constructed, even when acts are separated in time and/or space – as in the above examples. Furthermore, many simultaneous co-ordinations are implicated in any given construction. For example, for someone to turn away on reading the farmer's sign would require that they are able to reference English language texts and conventions, along with narratives, eg about organisation. To talk of what is co-ordinated with what we use the tools of 'act' and 'supplement' (Gergen 1994, 1995) or 'text' and 'context' (Dachler and Hosking 1995). Of course 'supplementing' some act or text also offers an act that, in turn, might be supplemented – nothing is *either* an act *or* a supplement but is *both* text *and* context.

ACTS INVITE POSSIBLE SUPPLEMENTS

For any given act, a great many co-ordinations are possible. However, not all are equally probable since much of the time certain co-ordinations become conventional – become taken-for-granted conventions. When there is no locally available convention, or when some convention is called into question, some accounting might be offered as an argument or justification. The account may, for example, refer to scientific studies, to some religious text,

---

6 This could be called the postmodern variant of social constructionist thinking.

to crossing bones or inspecting tea leaves. However, depending on other community or cultural narratives, some accounts, relative to others, are (a) more likely, and (b) more likely to be socially validated. Each of these supplements would give a different meaning to a knowledge claim and each would differently constrain how the social process might continue.

In other words, social realities are not inherently orderly – we make them orderly. The conventions of our native tongue, mathematical conventions, accounting practices, science – these may seem natural – but only to 'the locals' – to participants in that particular culture or community of practice. Conventions such as distinctions between eg observer and observed, theory and data, fact and fiction may seem 'obviously true'. But our constructionist arguments suggest that the possibility of changed supplements, of different constructions of what is 'real and good', is ever present. The subdominant voice, so to speak, offers accounts expressed in qualitative terms, offers a narrative way of knowing, particularistic and feeling. We shall suggest that such accounts – though unconventional in some communities – are vital to multi-voiced, ethical social processes.

PROCESSES ARE LOCAL-SOCIAL AND LOCAL-HISTORICAL

No universal, transcendental, or natural laws have to be invoked to explain social construction processes (Bass and Hosking 1998). They involve *what works in some here-and-now performance*, ie we are speaking of local and pragmatic issues. People show themselves to be locals, act knowingly, by co-ordinating their actions in ways that (locally) are deemed appropriate and natural, ie conventional. For example, I send a research paper to a journal, and the referees accept or reject it. However, as our constructionist arguments have indicated, the 'subdominant' text is that other possibilities and conventions are excluded. For example if, as a professional accountant, I depart too far from local-cultural conventions (eg by offering qualitative, narrative accounts and no numbers) my actions may well be rejected as those of an outsider – as ill-informed and/or as just plain wrong. In this context it is epitomised by the rise of positive accounting theory (Watts and Zimmerman 1986) and the way in which the acceptance of this theoretical view of accounting knowledge had the effect of silencing alternatives. This effect has been chronicled by Tinker and Puxty (1995) in their book *Policing Accounting Knowledge*.

'Local' has both social and historic aspects. This reference to 'local' is intended to contrast with general/universal presumptions about what is real and what we can know (ontology and epistemology). Further, a 'here-and-now' and ongoing quality is intended, but not as 'a present' in relation to conventional constructions of past, present and future. Rather, any act *references ways of co-ordinating already in place* and, in principle, is *open to new supplements* and changed ways of going on. This view of processes makes non-sense (literally) of questions about beginnings and ends and makes a (more or less) temporary punctuation of all claims to closure.

Relational constructionist arguments do not mean that anything goes – as some critics of social constructionisms have claimed (see discussion by Gergen 1994; Burr 1995). On the contrary, setting aside[7] the presumption that nature – viewed as how things really are – sets limits on human forms of life[8] makes prominent the limits constructed and reconstructed in

---

7 Note, *not* declaring false – we have no warrantable basis for such a claim and have no need to make it. In the present view, social constructionism is silent about relativism – it is not an issue that arises within this style of thinking.
8 Please note the careful form of words. We do not claim that the presumption is false – we have no sure foundations for doing so and would undermine our own arguments by such a claim. We merely note that it is a presumption that we neither care to nor need to centre in the context of our present interests.

social relations, ie *how things really are made*. In a relational constructionist approach, the limits to what might 'go' are conventional and in ongoing (re)construction in relational processes. *They are none the less limiting* – as all will know who have tried to change conventional practices.

PROCESSES MAKE PEOPLE AND WORLDS

The co-ordinations of which we have spoken make and remake social constructions as 'products'. By this we mean to include *everything we know*. We have said that the way someone or something can be known involves co-ordination with particular discourses – referenced as contexts, and that these include discourses of self, differentiated in (some) relation to (some particular) Other(s). And of course there always are many potential constructions – from multiple, Self–Other 'locations' – from multiple, moving 'standpoints', so to speak (Harding 1986). These arguments imply *multiple realities* – not as variants around some transcendental truth, or as individual subjective knowledge[9] – but as emergent products of multiple co-ordinations.

These are what some call subject–object relations (eg Fine 1994; Dachler and Hosking 1995). This 'subject' construction constructs some self as knowing about and as having warrants to achieve 'power over' (Gergen 1995) other – people, objects and events – constructed (from the subject's standpoint) as knowable and serviceable. Such conventions commonly are referenced, for example, in relation to narratives of scientific authority, ownership, formalised hierarchical position (eg government), perhaps locally accepted as validating a claim to know better and better able to decide how to continue. Social constructionism, by viewing brute 'facts' and scientific discourses as constructions, opens up other possible constructions. So for example subject–object relations, hierarchy and power over now are just *possible*, not necessary. Exploration of other possibilities then is invited, including, for example, Self and Other as different but equal, heterarchical relations between multiple voices (multi-loguing), and 'power to' rather than 'power over' (Dachler and Hosking 1995; Gergen 1995; Hosking 1995; Hosking and Bass 1998).

CRITICAL AND POSTMODERN INFLUENCES

One of the most important approaches critical theorists share with social constructionists is their unwillingness to accept ideas and institutions and what goes on in them unthinkingly, or see them as neutral or inevitable. Critical theorists would prefer to turn assumptions on their head, as mentioned in Chapter 9, and ask questions which cut across 'common sense' ideas and taken-for-granted norms of behaviour. Social constructionists, as we have seen, see everything as constructed in the sense of there being meanings invested in institutions, systems, processes, roles and people, which could be different for different 'actors' in organisations or groups of actors, and which could change in different contexts or circumstances. The fact that these constructions are seen as impermanent, changeable and changing is akin to postmodern and post-structuralist approaches in their unwillingness to accept the reality and permanence of formal and ostensibly clear and working systems and structures in organisations as well as in the wider society. Critical theorists who derive their basic position from radical theorists see social constructions primarily as a means of maintaining dominant power structures in organisations as well as in the broader society.

9 In other words, we are not speaking of subjective knowledge when objective knowledge also exists. Like relativism, subjective and objective knowledge belong to another style of thinking and not the present version of social constructionism.

WHAT IS SOCIALLY CONSTRUCTED IN ORGANISATIONS?

Theorists would see everything as socially constructed from ideas, institutions, structures and processes within institutions, positions and roles of people in authority and subject to authority, and the identities of people generally. Claims to knowledge and truth, they argue, are not objectively true, but rest within 'communities of meaning' (Gergen 2001a, p2). This will be discussed later with regard to educational practices. Within organisations, there is an 'embeddedness' of systems, practices and ideas that lead to the social construction of a wide range of factors, from the more impersonal and tangible, such as structure, to the more personal and ostensibly more ephemeral, such as identity. To take again the example from Preston's (1986) research (see Chapter 8), one can show that the 'construction' of the organisation structure and lines of communication as envisaged by senior management and believed to be operational in the organisation he studied is different from that 'constructed' and enacted by the lower-level managers Preston researched. Just as meanings in this case were constructed by a level of management different from those of senior management about the efficacy of the formal structure, so meanings can be, and are, constructed about everything else to do with organisations and the people in them (as well as those outside).

POWER

Social constructionists conceive of power relations as having been achieved in various contingent ways, including historic systems such as lines of communication and chains of command. They regard language (or, to put it in postmodern language, discursive practices) such as organisational stories and myths to be important in the representation and legitimation of power relations in organisations. They also see the ways organisational roles and people as individuals have been constructed lead to some people being included and some excluded from decision-making processes.

More subtle constructions of power have been identified by Foucault (1980a). Rather than looking at the explicit exercise of power through force and coercion, Foucault is interested in socially constructed but invisible types of control. Routine practices and procedures, he argues, constitute hidden power relations, as do moral and psychological norms, perceptions, judgements, acts, conformity, common sense observations, determinations of propriety and structural arrangements resulting in co-ordination and consent.

Another way of reinforcing power relations is in the stifling of conflict, as this disables people in their attempts to promote their views, interests and creativities. Critical theorists argue that conflicts are concealed through routine procedures, the way decisions are made, the discourses that are engaged with and discursive closures, and presumed 'neutrality' in organisational dealings (Deetz 2003).

For many critical and postmodern theorists, an important mechanism for reproducing domination is the way knowledge is 'produced'. Knowledge is socially constructed in how it is selected and discussed, and the beliefs and values embedded in this knowledge. (See the section on Higher Education below and Chapters 9 and 10 for discussions about knowledge.) The ways the wide range of institutional arrangements and discourses in organisations are constructed, many critical theorists argue, serve to reinforce dominant–subordinate relationships in various ways.

PARTICIPATION

Participation is regarded by critical theorists as embedded in social/political/historical systems of domination. They question how much effective communication there is with others and the extent to which this is real in terms of being constructed so as to allow truly free discourse and the development of alternative interests and practices, participation and consent. Is this translated in the institution in terms of seeing alternative possibilities or into action, or, more probably, does it result in closure – reproducing dominant social norms and responses? Group participation in decision-making can in an unequal system of power relations be a form of surveillance – people may have to watch what they say, as it could come back and cause them problems, and the wider the group, the less safe people might feel (Deetz 2003).

IDENTITY

Social constructionists, as already mentioned, do not regard individuals as independent, autonomous beings separated from their organisational context. Like other postmodern theorists, they see people as changeable, with shifting identities interrelating with contextual and other factors. They also reject the idea that organisation processes are neutral or apolitical, but see them as having an important role in 'identity production' (Deetz 2003, p30). They see identities as being produced through a set of organisational practices. Organisational discourse, as mentioned above, is one important channel. Discourse, they argue, is not neutral or transparent but carries with it a power-laden agenda that influences the identities of people in organisations. So, discursive practices can legitimate or disaffirm employees' identities through systems of distinctions, such as job titles, grades, functions and responsibilities, through the ways instructions are given and people are represented and through the stories and myths surrounding them. Similarly, social constructionists are interested in the way subject positions are 'embedded' in organisational systems and structures – these determine who and what is important, how things are distinguished and what in essence is 'real' and valid (Deetz 2003, p31).

The argument can be taken further to investigate to what extent and in what ways the identities of people in organisations are deliberately constructed in order to produce a specific type of person, such as a 'well-integrated worker'. Casey's (1996) analysis of Hephaestus (see Chapter 5) demonstrates an attempt by senior management to gear its employees' loyalties and identities to the company rather than to their previous identifications with their professional occupations and trade union affiliations. Of course, as Deetz points out, such identifications may be mere imitation with people hiding their beliefs and values, and other aspects of themselves. An opposite policy would be to allow people to feel 'other' in terms of organisational practices and processes, thereby allowing alternative possibilities outside existing political and social systems to emerge. Similarly, idealised pictures of workers can be constructed, such as how a 'well-integrated worker' should be, which people might then feel obliged to imitate even if this involved hiding their beliefs, values and other aspects of themselves.

HIGHER EDUCATION AS SOCIALLY CONSTRUCTED

An example of how values, principles and practices are socially constructed can be seen by considering the higher education system – how, through institutional routines and processes and through national regulation, the principles and implementation of courses in higher education have been constructed in a particular way. Many would argue that educational 'managers' as well as academic staff have in some important respects been governed in their policies and decision-making by structures and practices embedded in the system and, according to critical theorists, by the system itself.

There have been pressures for the convergence and commodification of knowledge owing to resource and structural constraints, which challenge traditional criteria for learning. For example, semesterised systems where subjects or courses span 12 teaching weeks, plus the pressure of relatively heavy assessment loads, invite questions about the effectiveness of the learning process, as do modularised systems where disparate subjects can be studied without necessarily constituting building blocks for higher levels of study. The influence of 'proximal forces' – including learning cultures and regulatory frameworks – is one of the key questions raised by the ESRC (2002).

There has been increasing emphasis in university curricula of an approach originating from the USA where learning and assessment are itemised and categorised. It includes the concept 'learning outcomes', taken from Bloom's (1956) taxonomy (Jewett and Kling 1996). At their worst, learning outcomes constitute predetermined conclusions about precisely what it is students should have learned. These might have their place in learning a skill such as driving or typing, but are more difficult to justify in an arena where critical, divergent thinking might be given priority.

This official view of learning and the language in which it is couched derives from a managerialist ideology where the discourse is based on market values (Trowler 2001). The epistemological assumptions behind such concepts lead, as Trowler (p185) points out, to the 'commodification' of knowledge. The implication is that teachers can decide what it is that students have to learn, and no allowance might be made for the possibility that students' prior knowledge and experience might reasonably lead to different outcomes. The assumption generally is that teachers have the knowledge and students do not. Chia (cited in Sadler-Smith 2001, p300) has described management education as having an atomistic and reductionist approach encouraging a 'convergent, consequential mental attitude that privileges consensus and uni-vocality'.

Thus from the start knowledge and therefore learning are at risk of being predetermined by people in power – possibly at global, governmental, institutional, managerial and tutor level. Students of course also have the possibility of influencing what counts as learning. Foucault (1984, p92) has highlighted the existence of power at various levels 'within the social body', rather than its being exercised only from above, and thus points to resistance at many points in organisations (Foucault 1980b, p39). Students who are socially and politically aware may challenge the paradigms and parameters set, whereas others may restrict their influence to challenging the pace or the amount of work required.

Critical theorists take the argument further in that they see not only the way knowledge and learning are imparted as being socially constructed, they see knowledge itself as being politically constructed through being set in the framework of relations of domination and subordination, and closely interrelated with existing power structures. Radical writers such as Alvesson and Deetz (1996) are aware of the material context in which the education system is embedded. They see ideas right down to consciousness being heavily influenced by the ideologies that support the dominant economic, political and social structures in society. Flyvbjerg (1993, p4) argues that:

> Power defines ... what counts as knowledge, and, ultimately, what counts as reality. Power does not limit itself to defining a certain conception of reality. Power defines physical, economic, ecological and social reality itself.

Power is more concerned with the defining of reality than with understanding how reality is, otherwise, constructed.

RELATING POWER AND KNOWLEDGE

Teacher–student relationships are an important manifestation of links between power and knowledge. Teachers play a prominent role in the social construction of learning. Through their considerable control of the discourse of learning and knowledge they mark out the legitimate (and by omission, illegitimate) fields of knowledge. They structure teacher–student relationships through their discourse, as that defines the way knowledge and understanding are to be approached – its rules and procedures (Linstead 2001). Thus what counts as knowledge for our students may depend on the power structures they are part of and the types of power relations they are subject to. Tutors and the requirements of their courses are likely to play a crucial role in what is regarded by students as epistemologically valid.

Dangers of dependence on tutors and the difficulties in achieving critical, independent thinking became apparent in a recent focus group discussion with four MBA students (Green *et al* 2002). They expected knowledge to come from or be facilitated by the tutor. Even those who were keenest on class/group participation and saw the role of the tutor primarily as a facilitator conceived of their own participation in terms of applying the knowledge they were learning rather than contributing their own knowledge.

The teacher–student power relationships described above are reinforced by the ways in which educational achievement is assessed and measured. There is an assumed objectivity which is legitimated through the requirements and procedures mentioned above. Postmodern theorists such as Alvesson and Skoldberg (2000) challenge the notions of a universalised objectivity and rationality by pointing to the existence of people with diverse cultural backgrounds in Western societies and to the existence of a broad dichotomy between a transcendent rationality versus multiple, different, subjective rationalities. Labov's work, described below, shows how the legitimation of inequalities in Western societies can be perpetuated by the narrowing of epistemological criteria to universalised standards dependent on the perspectives and values of the dominant culture, and applied indiscriminately to people of diverse cultures and backgrounds.

If we consider tests or diagnostic instruments, which are determined *ab initio* and used on a wide range of subjects, transcendence is assumed through the claim of equal validity for all respondents. What is assumed and is also crucial to the validity of the research is agreement as to the meaning of linguistic terms (Seale 1999). However, shared meaning is problematic. Labov (1972) demonstrated: that language can differ between people of different classes and ethnicities; how the research process itself can be differently interpreted according to the cultural values, assumptions and personal interest of the informants; and also how meanings attributed to research results can be influenced by the researchers' own constructs, values and world views.

Labov's work showed how Afro-American children were discriminated against in the education system through 'standard' diagnostic methods, and what the consequences were for their rated performance. He analysed the responses of a white middle-class American and an Afro-American working-class child regarding the concept of God. What he found was that the former spoke in 'grammatical', coherent prose, the latter in more local language without conventional grammar. Yet the content of what was said by the Afro-American had more depth, greater logic and more interest – not easily seen on a first reading of a transcription of their statements. In another study, Labov (1972) showed how a black youth from Harlem, when having to answer questions put by a white middle-class teacher across a table, remained largely silent. It was an entirely different story when done in the boy's youth club, in comfortable surroundings, with familiar faces and snacks – and with marked differences in outcome!

CRITIQUE

Many scholars in particular have disagreed with many social constructionist ideas, and even found them threatening. The idea most contested is the idea that 'truth' is not objective, but exists within a community of meaning. Some scientists have felt that their work is thereby undermined and that scientific claims to objectivity and the research methods used are regarded as no more valid than, say, mythology. Similarly, some have interpreted social constructionist attacks on the possibility of objective ideas as 'relativistic' and an attack on moral certainty.

Some radical theorists have likewise felt that their political values are undermined by relativist approaches, and some have found social constructionist scholarship too focused on critique and not enough concerned with contributing to social understanding (Gergen 2001b). The emphasis on diversity, fragmentariness and the localness of experience and subjectivities has led some theorists to wonder whether this invalidates people's experiences – those of black women, for example – and whether it leads to the denial of collective interests and consequently to political paralysis (Burr 1998).

There have been criticisms too of the apparent refusal by social constructionists to accept the reality of the material world outside of discourse. Lannamann (cited in Gergen 2001b, p10) likened social constructionists' attitudes to the body with that of Christian Scientists' refusal to accept the practice of modern medicine. In his case this was true of his parents and led to the tragic and needless death of his brother. Gergen himself sympathises with this view. In his defence he acknowledges that he does not ignore the physical, and has used medical support when needed. Where the relevance of social constructionism comes in, he argues, is at the point of this 'sure knowledge' (as about the medical condition of the body). It is then that a space can be opened up for reflection, with the possibility of stepping outside conventional ways of seeing and allowing for alternative understandings of 'what is the case', possibly leading to reconsideration and reconstruction (Gergen 2001b, p10). Health and illness themselves are concepts that are socially constructed and derive their meanings only within communities of relationships.

CONCLUSIONS

Social constructionism has raised exciting ideas – the potentially infinite number of ways one can understand events and people, including the possibility of constructing oneself differently. It also opens up the possibility of representing differently social issues such as disability, illness, gender and race (Burr 1998). The power of social constructionism, especially for those with radical inclinations or with postmodern understandings is that 'things could be different' and 'be done differently' (Willig 1998, p94).

Of particular significance in the context of our discussion of organisation theory is the fact that, according to social constructionism, all theory is both context-dependent and based upon language and the way that it is used. It is also based upon a shared construction (and assumed understanding) between the parties involved. Thus a hierarchy of seniority in an organisation is based upon the acceptance of its existence by all concerned. The power relationships we have mentioned several times in this book are social constructions. This might seem an anarchic position but social constructionists merely point out that, as social constructions, nothing is fixed. At the same time it is implicit in this theory that shared understandings are necessary in order for society, and organisations, to function. It will be apparent that from this perspective there is no question of an absolute best way of organising – merely a suitably convenient and/or accepted way of doing so. This viewpoint therefore is quite different from that held by much of the theory we have considered.

SUMMARY

- Systems, structures and processes are 'socially constructed' by people rather than being natural, neutral, objective or unalterable.

- People's identities are relational and socially constructed rather than being their essential core.

- Language is important in constructing social and political realities.

- Social realities are validated or rejected through social relationships within a 'community of meaning'.

- Organisational social constructions: ideas, structures, processes, roles, identities, power relations, knowledge.

- Values, principles and practices in higher education are analysed as social constructions.

- Critique: highly contested is the idea that truth is not 'objective' but exists within communities of meaning; radical theorists have felt their political values thereby undermined; non-acceptance of the reality of the material world – refuted by Gergen who argues that what is constructed is reflections about that world.

FURTHER READING

BURR, V. (1995) *An introduction to social constructionism*. London: Routledge.

DACHLER, H.P. and HOSKING, D.M. (1995) The primacy of relations in socially constructing organizational realities. In D.M. Hosking, H.P. Dachler and K.J. Gergen (eds) *Management and organization: relational alternatives to individualism*. Aldershot: Avebury.

GERGEN, K.J. (1995) Relational theory and the discourses of power. In D.M. Hosking, H.P. Dachler and K.J. Gergen (eds) *Management and organization: relational alternatives to individualism*. Aldershot: Avebury.

GERGEN, K.J. (2001a) Introduction. In K.J. Gergen *Social construction in context*. London: Sage.

GERGEN, K.J. (2001b) Constructionism and realism: a necessary collision? In K.J. Gergen *Social construction in context*. London: Sage.

REFERENCES

ALVESSON, M. and DEETZ, S. (1996) Critical theory and postmodernism approaches to organizational studies. In S. Clegg, C. Hardy and W.R. Nord *Handbook of organization studies*. London: Sage.

ALVESSON, M. and DEETZ, S. (2000) *Doing critical management research*. London: Sage.

ALVESSON, M. and SKOLDBERG, K. (2000) *Reflexive methodology: new vistas for qualitative research*. London: Sage.

BARRY, D. (1997) Telling changes: from narrative family therapy to organisational change and development. *Journal of Organisational Change Management*, Vol. 10, No. 1, 30–46.

BASS, A. and HOSKING, D.M. (1998) *A changed approach to change* (Research Paper Series RP9808). Birmingham: Aston Business School.

BLOOM, B.S. (ed) (1956) *Taxonomy of education objectives handbook: cognitive domain*. New York: McKay.

BURR, V. (1995) *An introduction to social constructionism*. London: Routledge.

BURR, V. (1998) Overview: realism, relativism, social constructionism and discourse. In I. Parker (ed) *Social constructionism, discourse and realism*. London: Sage.

CASEY, C. (1996) Corporate transformations: designer culture, designer employees and 'post-occupational' solidarity. *Organization*, Vol. 3, No. 3, 317–339.

DACHLER, H.P. and HOSKING, D.M. (1995) The primacy of relations in socially constructing organizational realities. In D.M. Hosking, H.P. Dachler and K.J. Gergen (eds) *Management and organization: relational alternatives to individualism*. Aldershot: Avebury.

DEETZ, S. (2003) Disciplinary power, conflict suppression and human resources management. In M. Alvesson and H. Willmott (eds) *Studying management critically*. London: Sage.

ESRC. (2002) *Review of current pedagogic research and practice in the fields of post-compulsory education and lifelong learning*. London: Tavistock Institute.

FINE, M. (1994) Working the hyphens: reinventing self and other in qualitative research. In N.K. Denzin and Y.S. Lincoln (eds) *Handbook of qualitative research*. London: Sage.

FLYVBERG, B. (1993) *Power has a rationality that rationality does not know*. Aalborg: Dept. of Development and Planning, Aalborg University.

FOUCAULT, M. (1980a) *The history of sexuality*. New York: Vintage.

FOUCAULT, M. (1980b) *Power/knowledge: selected interviews and other writings 1972–1977*. New York: Pantheon Books.

FOUCAULT, M. (1984) *The history of sexuality: an introduction*. London: Penguin Books.

GERGEN, K.J. (1994) *Realities and relationships*. Cambridge, Mass: Harvard University Press.

GERGEN, K.J. (1995) Relational theory and the discourses of power. In D.M. Hosking, H.P. Dachler and K.J. Gergen (eds) *Management and organization: relational alternatives to individualism*. Aldershot: Avebury.

GERGEN, K.J. (2001a) Introduction. In K.J. Gergen, *Social construction in context*. London: Sage.

GERGEN, K.J. (2001b) Constructionism and realism: a necessary collision? In K.J. Gergen *Social construction in context*. London: Sage.

GREEN, M., PHEIFFER, G., ANDREW, D. and HOLLEY, D. (2002) *How do we know what we mean when we talk about learning?* Paper presented at the Discourse, Power and Resistance in Post-Compulsory Education and Training Conference, April 2002, University of Plymouth.

HARDING, S. (1986) *The science question in feminism.* Milton Keynes: Open University Press.

HARRE, R. (1979). *Social being: a theory for social psychology.* Oxford: Basil Blackwell.

HOSKING, D.M. (1995) Constructing power: Entitative and relational approaches. In D.M. Hosking, H.P. Dachler and K.J. Gergen (eds) *Management and organization: relational alternatives to individualism.* Aldershot: Avebury.

HOSKING, D.M. and BASS, A. (1998) *Constructing changes through relational dynamics* (Aston Business School Research Paper Series No RP9813). Birmingham: Aston Business School.

HOSKING, D.M. and MORLEY, I.E. (1991). *A social psychology of organising.* Chichester: Harvester Wheatsheaf.

JEWETT, T. and KLING, R. (1996) *Teaching social issues of computing: challenges, ideas and resources.* Orlando: Academic Press Inc.

LABOV, W. (1972) Academic ignorance and Black intelligence. *Atlantic Monthly*, June.

LINSTEAD, S. (2001) Rhetoric and organizational control: a framework for analysis. In R. Westwood and S. Linstead (eds) *The language of organization.* London: Sage.

PARKER, I. (1998) Realism, relativism and critique in psychology. In I. Parker (ed) *Social constructionism, discourse and realism.* London: Sage.

PEARCE, W.B. (1992) A 'camper's guide' to constructionisms. *Human Systems: The Journal of Systemic Consultation and Management*, Vol. 3, 139–161.

PRESTON, A. (1986) Interactions and arrangements in the process of informing. *Accounting, Organizations and Society*, Vol. 11, No. 6, 521–540.

REASON, P. (ed). (1994) *Participation in human inquiry.* London: Sage.

SADLER-SMITH, E. (2001) A reply to Reynold's critique of learning style. *Management Learning*, Vol. 32, No. 3, 291–304.

SARBIN, T.R. and KITSUSE, J.I. (1994) A prologue to constructing the social. In T.R. Sarbin and J.I. Kitsuse (eds) *Constructing the social.* London: Sage.

SEALE, C. (1999) *The quality of qualitative research.* London: Sage.

SHOTTER, J. (1993) *Conversational realities: constructing life through language.* London: Sage.

SHOTTER, J. and GERGEN, K.J. (1989) Preface and introduction. In J. Shotter and K.J. Gergen *Texts of identity.* London: Sage.

TINKER, T. and PUXTY, A.G. (1995) *Policing accounting knowledge: the market for excuses affair.* London: Paul Chapman.

TROWLER, P. (2001) Captured by the discourse? The socially constitutive power of new higher education discourse in the UK. *Organization*, Vol. 8, No. 2, 183–201.

WATTS, R.L. and ZIMMERMAN, J.L. (1986) *Positive accounting theory.* Englewood Cliffs, NJ: Prentice Hall.

WEICK, K. (1995). *Sensemaking in organisations.* London: Sage.

WILLIG, C. (1998) Social constructionism and revolutionary socialism: a contradiction in terms? In I. Parker (ed) *Social constructionism, discourse and realism.* London: Sage.

WITTGENSTEIN, L. (1963). *Philosophical investigations.* Oxford: Basil Blackwell.

Environmentalism

CHAPTER 12

INTRODUCTION

During the 1970s there arose a general recognition and acceptance that any actions an organisation undertakes will have an effect not just upon itself but also upon the external environment within which that organisation resides. In considering the effect of the organisation upon its external environment it must be recognised that this environment includes both the business environment in which the firm is operating, the local societal environment in which the organisation is located and the wider global environment. An organisation can have a very significant effect upon this external environment and can actually change it through its activities. These changes can either be viewed as beneficial or be viewed as detrimental to the environment; indeed the same actions can be viewed as beneficial by some people and detrimental by others. This is why any regulatory body considering planned activity of an organisation will find a range of views amongst interested parties, with some in favour and others opposed. This is of course because the evaluation of the effects of the actions of an organisation upon its environment are viewed and evaluated differently by different people.

Recognition of the rights of all stakeholders and the duty of a business to be accountable in this wider context has been largely a relatively recent phenomenon.[1] The economic view of accountability solely to owners has only recently been subject to debate to any considerable extent. It is recognised however that some owners of businesses have always recognised a responsibility to other stakeholders, and this is evident from the early days of the Industrial Revolution. Thus, for example, Robert Owen (1816) demonstrated dissatisfaction with the assumption that only the internal effects of actions need be recorded through accounting. Furthermore he put his beliefs into practice through the inclusion within his sphere of industrial operations the provision of housing for his workers at New Lanark. Others went further still and Jedediah Strutt of Belper and his sons, for example, provided farms to ensure that their workers received an adequate supply of milk, as well as building accommodation for their workforce which was of such high standard that these dwellings remain highly desirable in the present.[2] Similarly the Gregs of Quarry Bank provided education as well as housing for their workforce. Indeed Titus Salt went further and attempted to provide a complete ecosphere for his workers. Thus there is evidence from throughout the history of modernity that a self-centred approach to managing organisational activity was not universally acceptable and was unable to satisfactorily provide a basis for human activity.

THE GAIA HYPOTHESIS

While theorists of organisations were developing the notion of greater accountability to stakeholders during the 1970s, other developments were also taking place in parallel. Thus in

---

1 Mathews (1997) traces its origins to the 1970s, although arguments (see Crowther 2002) show that such concerns can be traced back to the Industrial Revolution.

2 Indeed the earlier workers' accommodation provided by Richard Arkwright, arguably the instigator of the Industrial Revolution, at Cromford, Derbyshire, remain equally desirable – see Crowther (2002).

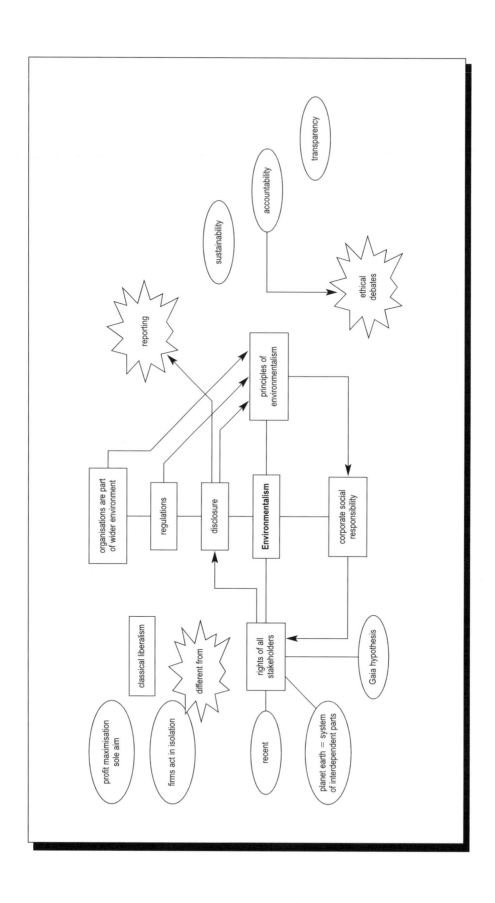

1979 Lovelock produced his Gaia hypothesis, in which he proposed a different model of the planet Earth; in his model the whole of the ecosphere, and all living matter therein, was co-dependent upon its various facets and formed a complete system. According to this hypothesis, this complete system, and all components of the system, was interdependent and equally necessary for maintaining the Earth as a planet capable of sustaining life. This Gaia hypothesis was a radical departure from classical liberal theory, which maintained that each entity was independent and could therefore concentrate upon seeking satisfaction for its own wants, without regard to other entities. This classical liberal view of the world forms the basis of economic organisation, provides a justification for the existence of firms as organs of economic activity and provides the rationale behind the model of accounting adopted by society. The Gaia hypothesis however implied that interdependence, and a consequent recognition of the effect of one's actions upon others was a facet of life. This consequently necessitates a different interpretation of accountability in terms of individual and organisational behaviour.

Given the constitution of economic activity into profit-seeking firms, each acting in isolation and concerned solely with profit maximisation, justified according to classical liberalism, it is perhaps inevitable that organisation theory developed as organisation-centric, seeking merely to manage the activities of the firm insofar as they affected the firm. Any actions of the firm that had consequences external to the firm were held not to be the concern of the firm. Indeed enshrined within classical liberalism, alongside the sanctity of the individual to pursue his own course of action, was the notion that the operation of the free market mechanism would mediate between these individuals to allow for an equilibrium based upon the interaction of these freely acting individuals, and that this equilibrium was an inevitable consequence of this interaction.[3] As a consequence, any concern by the firm with the effect of its actions upon externalities was irrelevant and not therefore a proper concern for its managers.

The Gaia hypothesis stated that organisms were interdependent[4] and that it was necessary to recognise that the actions of one organism affected other organisms and hence inevitably affected itself in ways that were not necessarily directly related. Thus the actions of an organism upon its environment and upon externalities was a matter of consequence for every organism. This is true for humans as much as for any other living matter upon the planet. It is possible to extend this analogy to a consideration of the organisation of economic activity taking place in modern society and to consider the implications both for the organisation of that activity. As far as profit-seeking organisations are concerned, therefore, the logical conclusion from this is that the effect of the organisation's activities upon externalities is a matter of concern to the organisation, and hence a proper subject for the management of organisational activity.

While it is not realistic to claim that the development of the Gaia theory had a significant impact upon organisational behaviour, it seems perhaps overly coincidental to suggest that a social concern among business managers developed at the same time that this theory was propounded. It is perhaps that both are symptomatic of other factors that caused a re-examination of the structures and organisation of society. Nevertheless, organisational theory

---

3 This assumption of course ignores the imbalances in power between the various parties seeking to enact transaction through the market.

4 In actual fact Lovelock claimed in his hypothesis that the Earth and all its constituent parts were interdependent. It is merely an extension of this hypothesis to claim the inter-relationship of human activity, whether enacted through organisations or not.

has, from the 1970s, become more concerned with all the stakeholders of an organisation, whether or not such stakeholders have any legal status with respect to that organisation.

THE DEVELOPMENT OF STAKEHOLDER APPROACHES

Implicit in this concern with stakeholders is an acceptance that it is not just the owners of the organisation who have a concern with the activities of that organisation, and more significantly the effects of those actions. Additionally there are a wide variety of other stakeholders who justifiably have a concern with those activities, and are affected by those activities. Those other stakeholders have not just an interest in the activities of the firm but also a degree of influence over the shaping of those activities. This influence is so significant that it can be argued that the power and influence of these stakeholders are such that they amount to quasi-ownership of the organisation.

Nevertheless, the performance of businesses in a wider arena than the stock market and its value to shareholders has become of increasing concern. Gray *et al* (1987) consider social reporting in terms of responsibility and accountability. Gray (1992) argues that there is a need for a new paradigm, with the environment being considered as part of the firm rather than as an externality and with sustainability and the use of primary resources being given increased weighting. Rubenstein (1992) goes further and argues that there is a need for a new social contract between a business and the stakeholders to which it is accountable. The concept of the social contract is not of course new. It was first introduced in the seventeenth century by Hobbes (1651). It was extended by Rousseau (1762) to explain the relationship between a government and its citizens. It has been extended recently, however, to argue about the relationship between organisations and their stakeholders and society.

Although the disclosure of the actions of the firm in terms of their impact upon the external environment is essentially voluntary in nature this does not necessarily mean that the actions themselves are always voluntary. Nor does it mean that all such disclosure is necessarily voluntary. The regulatory regime operating in the UK means that certain actions must be taken by firms that affect their influence upon the external environment. Equally certain actions are prevented from being taken. These actions and prohibitions are controlled by means of regulation imposed by the government of this country – both the national government and local government. For example, all proposed building of new industrial premises is controlled by planning regulations, and when this proposed planning involves designated green belt land then this can also involve public enquiries. Such enquiries also arise when the proposal is for new mining, either open-cast or deep mining. Acceptance of any such proposals is generally dependent upon the plans, including proposed actions to protect local communities and the environment, and, in the case of mining, steps required to be taken to repair the environment once the activities have ceased. Equally, regulations govern the type of discharges that can be made by organisations, particularly when these are considered to cause pollution. Such regulations govern the way in which waste must be disposed of and the level of pollutants allowed for discharges into rivers, as well as restricting the amount of water that can be extracted from rivers.

THE ENVIRONMENT AND REGULATION

The regulatory regime operating in this country is continuing to change and become more restrictive as far as the actions of an organisation and its relationship with the external environment are concerned.[5] It seems reasonable to expect these changes to continue into

5 In other words the extent of regulation in this area has increased in recent years and is continuing to increase.

the future and concern for the environmental impact of the activities of organisations to increase. These regulations tend to require reporting of the activities of organisations, both to satisfy regulatory requirements but also to meet the internal needs of the organisation. Managers of an organisation, in both controlling current operations and in planning future business activities, must have data to help manage the organisational activities in this respect. The growth of environmental data, as part of the management information systems of organisations, therefore can be seen to be, at least in part, driven by the needs of society at large, as reflected in the regulations imposed upon the activities of organisations. As the extent of regulation of such activities can be expected to increase in the future the more forward-looking and proactive organisations might be expected to have a tendency to extend their environmental impact reporting in anticipation of future regulation, rather than merely reacting to existing regulation.

It cannot reasonably be argued, however, that the increase in stature and prominence accorded to environmental concerns among organisations is driven entirely by present and anticipated regulations. Organisations which choose to report externally upon the impact of their activities on the external environment do so voluntarily, and in doing so they must expect to derive some benefit from this kind of disclosure. The kind of benefits organisations can expect to accrue through this kind of disclosure will be considered later in this chapter. At this point, however, we should remember the influence of stakeholders upon the organisation, and it can be suggested that increased disclosure of the activities of the organisation is a reflection of the growing power and influence of stakeholders, without any form of legal ownership, and the recognition of this influence by the organisation and its managers.

Thus the objective of this concern is to incorporate the effect of the activities of the firm upon externalities and to view the firm as a network extending beyond just the internal environment to include the whole environment. In this view of the organisation it does not stop at the organisational boundary but extends beyond, to include not just the business environment in which it operates but also the whole social environment. Environmentalism therefore provides a recognition that the organisation is an integral part of society, rather than a self-contained entity with only an indirect relationship with society at large. This self-containment has been the traditional view taken by an organisation as far as their relationship with society at large is concerned, with interaction being only by means of resource acquisition and sales of finished products or services. Recognition of this closely intertwined relationship of mutual interdependency between the organisation and society at large can help bring about a closer, and possibly more harmonious, relationship between the organisation and society. Given that the managers and workers of an organisation are also stakeholders in that society in other capacities, such as consumers, citizens and inhabitants, this reinforces the mutual interdependency.

ENVIRONMENTALISM AND STAKEHOLDERS

Environmentalism also provides an explicit recognition that stakeholders other than the legal owners of the organisation have power and influence over that organisation and also have a right to extend their influence into affecting the organisation's activities. This includes the managers and workers of the organisation who are also stakeholders in other capacities. Environmentalism therefore provides a mechanism for transferring some of the power from the organisation to these stakeholders, and this voluntary surrender of such power by the organisation can actually provide benefits to the organisation. Benefits from increased disclosure and the adoption of environmental accounting can provide further benefits to the organisation in its operational performance, beyond this enhanced relationship with society at large. These benefits, it is argued, can include:

- an improved image for the organisation which can translate into additional sales
- the development of environmentally friendly or sustainable methods of operation which can lead to the development of new markets
- reduced future operational costs through the anticipation of future regulation and hence a cost advantage over competitors
- decreased future liabilities brought about through temporal externalisation
- better relationships with suppliers and customers which can lead to reduced operational costs as well as increased sales
- easier recruitment of labour and lowered costs of staff turnover.

It needs to be recognised however that there are increased costs of instituting a regime of environmental accounting and that these additional costs need to be offset against the possible benefits to be accrued. These increased costs are concerned with the development of appropriate measures of environmental performance and the necessary alterations to the management information and accounting information systems to incorporate these measures into the reporting system. This is particularly problematical for the organisation in terms of justification, because the increased costs are readily quantifiable but the benefits are much more difficult to quantify.

This leads to one of the main problems with the accounting for externalities through social and environmental accounting. This problem is concerned with the quantification of the effects of the activities of the organisation upon its external environment. This problem revolves around four main areas:

- determining the effects upon the external environment of the activities of the organisation
- developing appropriate measures for those effects
- quantifying those effects in order to provide a comparative yardstick for the evaluation of alternative courses of action, particularly in terms of an accounting-based quantification
- determining the form and extent of disclosure of those quantifications so as to maximise the benefits of that disclosure while minimising the costs of the disclosure and minimising the possibility of knowledge of the firm's operational activities being given to competitors.

THE PRINCIPLES OF ENVIRONMENTALISM

There are three basic principles to environmentalism, which together comprise organisational concern with the environment (see Figure 12.1).

Sustainability

Sustainability is concerned with the effect which action taken in the present has upon the options available in the future. If resources are utilised in the present, then they are no longer available for use in the future, and this is of particular concern if the resources are finite in quantity. Thus raw materials of an extractive nature, such as coal, iron or oil, are finite in

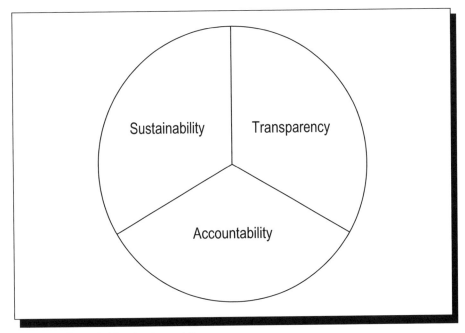

Figure 12.1 *Three principles of environmentalism*

quantity and once used are not available for future use. At some point in the future, therefore, alternatives will be needed to fulfil the functions currently provided by these resources. This may be at some point in the relatively distant future, but of more immediate concern is the fact that as resources become depleted then the cost of acquiring the remaining resources tends to increase, and hence the operational costs of organisations tend to increase.[6]

Sustainability therefore implies that society must use no more of a resource than can be regenerated. This can be defined in terms of the carrying capacity of the ecosystem (Hawken 1993) and described with input–output models of resource consumption. The paper industry for example has a policy of replanting trees to replace those harvested, and this has the effect of retaining costs in the present rather than temporally externalising them. Similarly, motor vehicle manufacturers such as Volkswagen have a policy of making their cars almost totally recyclable. Viewing an organisation as part of a wider social and economic system implies that these effects must be taken into account, not just for the measurement of costs and value created in the present but also for the future of the business itself.

Measures of sustainability would consider the rate at which resources are consumed by the organisation in relation to the rate at which resources can be regenerated. Unsustainable operations can be accommodated for either by developing sustainable operations or by planning for a future lacking in resources currently required. In practice, organisations mostly tend to aim towards less unsustainability by increasing efficiency in the way in which resources are utilised. An example would be an energy efficiency programme.

6 Similarly once an animal or plant species becomes extinct (Topal and Crowther 2004) then the benefits of that species to the environment can no longer be accrued. In view of the fact that many pharmaceuticals are currently being developed from plant species still being discovered this may be significant for the future.

Accountability

Accountability is concerned with an organisation recognising that its actions affect the external environment, and therefore assuming responsibility for the effects of its actions. This concept therefore implies a quantification of the effects of actions taken, both internal to the organisation and externally. More specifically, the concept implies a reporting of those quantifications to all parties affected by those actions. This implies a reporting to external stakeholders of the effects of actions taken by the organisation and how they are affecting those stakeholders. This concept therefore implies a recognition that the organisation is part of a wider societal network and has responsibilities to all of that network rather than just to the owners of the organisation. Alongside this acceptance of responsibility therefore must be a recognition that those external stakeholders have the power to affect the way in which those actions of the organisation are taken and a role in deciding whether or not such actions can be justified, and if so at what cost to the organisation and to other stakeholders.

Accountability therefore necessitates the development of appropriate measures of environmental performance and the reporting of the actions of the firm. This necessitates costs on the part of the organisation in developing, recording and reporting such performance, and, to be of value, the benefits must exceed the costs. Benefits must be determined by the usefulness of the measures selected to the decision-making process and by the way in which they facilitate resource allocation, both within the organisation and between it and other stakeholders. Such reporting needs to be based upon the following characteristics:

- understandability to all parties concerned
- relevance to the users of the information provided
- reliability in terms of accuracy of measurement, representation of impact and freedom from bias
- comparability, which implies consistency, both over time and between different organisations.

Inevitably, however, such reporting will involve qualitative facts and judgements as well as quantifications. This qualitativeness will inhibit comparability over time and will tend to mean that such impacts are assessed differently by different users of the information, reflecting their individual values and priorities. A lack of precise understanding of effects, coupled with the necessarily judgemental nature of relative impacts, means that few standard measures exist. This in itself restricts the interorganisation comparison of such information.

Transparency

Transparency, as a principle, means that the external impact of the actions of the organisation can be ascertained from that organisation's reporting and that pertinent facts are not disguised within that reporting. Thus all the effects of the actions of the organisation, including external impacts, should be apparent to all from using the information provided by the organisation's reporting mechanisms. Transparency is of particular importance to external stakeholders, as these users lack the background details and knowledge available to internal users of such information. Transparency therefore can be seen to follow on from the other two principles and equally can be seen to be a part of the process of recognition of responsibility on the part of the organisation for the external effects of its actions and equally part of the process of transferring power to external stakeholders.

SOCIAL RESPONSIBILITY AND ORGANISATIONAL PERFORMANCE

There have been many claims that the quantification of environmental effects and costs, and the inclusion of such costs into business strategies, can significantly reduce operating costs by firms; indeed this was one of the main themes of the 1996 Global Environmental Management Initiative Conference. Little evidence exists that this is the case, but Pava and Krausz (1996) demonstrate empirically that companies they define as 'socially responsible' perform in financial terms at least as well as companies that are not socially responsible.[7] Similarly, in other countries efforts are being made to provide a framework for the quantification of environmental effects (Abreu and David 2004) and the certification of accountants who wish to be considered as environmental practitioners and auditors.[8] Azzone *et al* (1996), however, suggest that despite the lack of any regulatory framework in this area a degree of standardisation, at least as far as reporting is concerned, is beginning to emerge at an international level. If this is the case then it can be expected to become reflected in the regulatory frameworks at national levels in due course. It can equally be argued that firms regarding themselves as successful can afford to devote more effort towards being socially responsible as they progress upwards through a form of Maslow's hierarchy.

Jones (1996) suggests that any method of managing for biodiversity should be based upon the concept of stewardship rather than ownership. Similarly Ranagnathan and Ditz (1996) state that when environmental issues are quantified they are more likely to be included in the business decision-making process and can therefore help to improve the performance of firms. As well as a concern with environmental effects from the point of view of the internal use of such information for decision-making purposes, of equal concern is the use of environmental information for external reporting purposes. In this respect it can be argued that the incorporation of environmental information into the annual reports of firms reflects the concern with the wider scope of organisational activity. Such concern can be seen to be reflected in the discourse concerning environmental issues that is taking place in society at large and is reflected in the media. Equally, however, it can be argued that the inclusion of such information into the corporate reporting system, as manifest in the annual reports, is a reflection of the desire of firms, and their managers, to address a wider audience through their reports. This wider audience can be considered to be those members of society at large who are concerned with the environment and with environmental issues. This will include environmental pressure groups and their individual members as well as other individual members of society. At one level it can be argued that this reflects a recognition by the firm and its managers that the wider external stakeholder community has an interest in the firm and the effect of its actions upon the environment.

At another level, however, it can be argued that these individual members of society, whether members of environmental pressure groups or not, may also be stakeholders in the firm in other roles; for example they may well be customers, or potential customers, or suppliers or employees. Because stakeholders may well have multiple roles in their interaction with an organisation it becomes impossible to separate out the reasons for an organisation desiring to increase the extent of its environmental concern. Nevertheless, as Jones (1996) reports, the extent of environmental reporting, in terms of the number of firms engaged in such

---

7 It is accepted however that different definitions of socially responsible organisations exist and that different definitions lead to different evaluations of performance between those deemed responsible and others.

8 For example, the Canadian Institute of Chartered Accountants is heavily involved in the creation of such a national framework.

reporting, has grown rapidly since 1990 and continues to grow. Similarly KPMG (*Management Accounting* 1996) confirms this growth in environmental reporting but states that it differs considerably in terms of just what is reported. They argue that a lack of standards, coupled with an uncertainty as to whom such reporting is directed, has led to this wide variation in environmental reporting. Gamble *et al* (1996) on the other hand argue, based upon empirical research, that environmental reporting is not increasing in coverage but that there are national differences. Beaver (1989), however, has identified some changing trends in reporting and highlights a rapid growth in reporting requirements and changes in existing requirements, with which Eccles (1991) concurs.[9]

ETHICS

One component of this change to a concern with social responsibility and accountability has been the recognition (or reinstatement) of the importance of ethics in organisational activity and behaviour. In part this can be considered to be a recognition of the changing societal environment[10] of the present time and in part a recognition of the problems brought about through corporate activity taken without any account of ethical implications. Among such activity can be seen the many examples of pollution (for example Union Carbide at Bhopal, India or the Exxon Valdiz oil spill) and greed (such as the Enron incident). These have caused a rethinking of the role of ethics in organisation theory.

Ethics is however a problematical area, as there is no absolute agreement as to what constitutes ethical (or unethical) behaviour. For each of us there is a need to consider our own ethical position as a starting point, because that will affect our own view of ethical behaviour. The opposition provided by deontological ethics (see below) and teleological ethics (regarding the link between actions and outcomes), and by ethical relativism and ethical objectivism (regarding the universality of a given set of ethical principles) represents key areas of debate and contention in the philosophy of ethics. This provides a starting point for our consideration of ethics.

Deontological ethics

According to deontologists certain actions are right or wrong in themselves and so there are absolute ethical standards that need to be upheld. The problems with this position are concerned with how we know which acts are wrong and how we distinguish between a wrong act and an omission. Philosophers such as Nagel argue that there is an underlying notion of right that constrains our actions, although this might be overridden in certain circumstances. Thus, there may be an absolute moral constraint against killing someone, which in time of war can be overridden.

Teleological ethics

Teleological theory distinguishes between 'the right' and 'the good', with 'the right' encompassing those actions which maximise 'the good'. Thus it is outcomes that determine what is right, rather than the inputs (ie our actions), in terms of ethical standards. This is the viewpoint promoted by Rawls (1973) in his *A Theory of Justice*. Under this perspective, one's duty is to promote certain ends, and the principles of right and wrong organise and direct our efforts towards these ends.

---

9 These changes are principally concerned with the use of a broader range of measures of performance together with an increasing recognition of the social implications of organisational activity.

10 This is in keeping with our discussion of social constructionism.

Utilitarianism

Utilitarianism is based upon the premise that outcomes are all that matter in determining what is good, and that the way in which a society achieves its ultimate good is through each person pursuing his or her own self-interest. The aggregation of all these self-interests will automatically lead to the maximum good for society at large. Some Utilitarians have amended this theory to suggest that there is a role for government in mediating between these individual actions to allow for the fact that some needs can best be met communally.

Ethical relativism

Relativism is the denial that there are certain universal truths. Thus, ethical relativism posits that there are no universally valid moral principles. Ethical relativism may be further subdivided into 'conventionalism', which argues that a given set of ethics or moral principles is valid only within a given culture at a particular time, and 'subjectivism', which sees individual choice as the key determinant of the validity of moral principles.

According to 'conventional' ethical relativism, it is the mores and standards of a society that define what moral behaviour is and what ethical standards are set – not absolutely, but according to the dictates of a given society at a given time. Thus, if we conform to the standards of our society then we are behaving ethically. We can see however that ethical standards change over time within one society and vary from one society to another; thus the attitudes and practices of the nineteenth century are different from our own, as are the standards of other countries. A further problem with this view of ethics is how we decide upon the societal ethics to which we seek to conform. There are the standards of society at large, the standards of our chosen profession and the standards of the peer group to which we belong. For example, the standards of society at large tend to be enshrined within the laws of that society. But how many of us rigorously abide (eg) by the speed limits of this country? Different groupings within society tend to have different moral standards of acceptable behaviour, and we have a tendency to behave differently at different times and when we are with different groups of people. Equally, when we travel to a foreign country we tend to take with us the ethical standards of our own country rather than change to the different standards of the country we are visiting. Thus it becomes very difficult to hold to a position of ethical relativism because of the difficulty of determining the grouping to which we are seeking to conform.

Ethical objectivism

This philosophical position is in direct opposition to ethical relativism; it asserts that although moral principles may differ between cultures, some moral principles have universal validity whether or not they are universally recognised. There are two key variants of ethical objectivism: 'strong' and 'weak'. Strong ethical objectivism or 'absolutism' argues that there is one true moral system. Weak ethical objectivism holds that there is a 'core morality' of universally valid moral principles, but also accepts an indeterminate area where relativism is accepted.

We can see that each of these theories of ethics is problematical and that there is no overarching principle determining what is ethical or what is not. Nevertheless a concern with ethics has been introduced explicitly into organisation theory in recent years. This has led to an interest in corporate social responsibility, as we considered in Chapter 7.

CORPORATE SOCIAL RESPONSIBILITY

There appears to have been a resurgence of public interest and concern about the environment in recent years. Adams (1992, pp106–107) explains this resurgence of interest as follows:

> In Britain during the last four decades, within a market economy driven by consumer preference and purchasing capacity, greater economic leisure has provided the opportunity to both analyse and reflect on the underlying nature and direction of a demand-led economic system. There is an increasing requirement for information on the social and environmental impact of corporate policy and appraisal effects. The movements for healthy eating, ethical investment and, above all, environmental concern have played a big part in awakening the consumer's social awareness ... The very process by which the majority in the West have become affluent is increasingly being questioned by some of its beneficiaries. Can we go on like this? Is it sustainable? Is the whole system flawed and ultimately self-destructive? These questions are being asked not just by pressure groups but also by individuals, by business, by governments and global institutions.

These concerns have led to the general opinion that there is something different about environmental information that deserves reporting in its own right rather than being subsumed within the general corporate reporting and lost in the organisation-centric norm of corporate reporting. This opinion is based upon a recognition that:

> The environment (which is a free resource to individual businesses) is increasingly being turned into a factor that does carry costs. Primarily as a result of requirements imposed by current or probable future government regulation on pollution control, but also to some extent because of the wider concern of the public, who can affect a business's profitability by their behaviour as consumers, employees, and investors, there is a financial impact that needs to be accounted for.
>
> (Butler *et al* 1992, p60)

This general concern with the social and environmental effects of organisational activity has recently become known as corporate social responsibility (CSR). CSR has gained prominence in recent years (Abreu *et al* 2003) in practically every sector of society: this includes business, civil society and other areas. Actually defining CSR is difficult, however, as it is a broad and elastic concept. The concept continues to expand to embrace new problems associated with corporate activities. For example, some topical problems that are today associated with corporate activities (eg global warming) were virtually unknown to the corporate world in the early days of the concept. The fragmented and elastic nature of CSR means that any problems that are remotely connected with corporate activity can properly be brought within the ambit of the concept. Thus not only is CSR concerned with the company's relationship with its employees, its consumers and others in close proximity with the company, as might have been expected in the early days of the concept, but it also encompasses such new corporate problems as the exploitation of child labour, which implicates corporate activity located thousands of miles away from the problem.

There is therefore a general assumption that CSR is recognised globally as an issue that will have equal concern throughout the world, albeit with differing emphases according to the perspectives of the countries concerned. Although Abreu and David (2004) demonstrate that this is an issue of concern throughout the countries of the European Union (EU), but with diverse aspects being focused upon in different countries, the reality is that the impetus for this concern stems from the Anglo-Saxon world and is arguably predicated in the corporate misbehaviour manifest within this world. Arguably it is only within the Cartesian world of Anglo-Saxon hegemony – which is increasingly dominating the global market – that the separation of rights from responsibilities (Crowther 2004) has allowed such corporate misbehaviour to occur and thereby necessitate this concern with CSR. One of the dominant discourses concerning CSR is concerned with accountability, and this accountability implies reporting to the various stakeholders of the corporation.

SUMMARY

- Organisations affect the external environment – businesses and the wider global environment.

- Gaia hypothesis: whole ecosphere forms a complete system, unlike classical liberal theory, which postulates the independence of each entity.

- From 1970 there have developed theories and regulations to include all stakeholders inside and outside the organisation.

- Environmentalism provides mechanisms for transferring some of the managers' power in organisations to other stakeholders.

- Ethics has been reinstated as a standard for organisational activity.

- Corporate social responsibility (CSR) as a subject indicates concern with the social and environmental effects of organisational behaviour.

FURTHER READING

ACKERMAN, R.W. (1975) *The social challenge to business*. Cambridge, Mass: Harvard University Press.

CROWTHER, D. (2002) *A social critique of corporate reporting*. Aldershot: Ashgate.

CROWTHER, D. and RAYMAN BACCHUS, L. (eds). (2004) *Perspectives on corporate social responsibility*. Aldershot: Ashgate.

REFERENCES

ABREU, R., CROWTHER, D., DAVID, F. and MAGRO, F. (2003) Corporate social responsibility in Portugal. *The Corporate Citizen*, Vol. 3, No. 2, 7–15.

ABREU, R. and DAVID, F. (2004) *Corporate social responsibility: exploration inside experience and practice at the European level*. In D. Crowther and L. Rayman Bacchus (eds) *Perspectives on corporate social responsibility* (pp109–139). Aldershot: Ashgate.

ADAMS, R. (1992) Green reporting and the consumer movement. In D. Owens (ed) *Green reporting*. London: Chapman & Hall.

AZZONE, G., MANZINI, R. and NOCI, G. (1996) Evolutionary trends in environmental reporting. *Business Strategy and Environment*, Vol. 5, No. 4, 219–230.

BEAVER, W. (1989) *Financial reporting: an accounting revolution*. Englewood Cliffs, NJ: Prentice-Hall.

BUTLER, D., FROST, C. and MACVE, R. (1992) Environmental reporting. In L.C.L. Skerratt and D.J. Tonkins (eds) *A guide to UK reporting practice for accountancy students*. London: Wiley.

CROWTHER, D. (2002) *A social critique of corporate reporting*. Aldershot: Ashgate.

CROWTHER, D. (2004) Limited liability or limited responsibility? In D. Crowther and L. Rayman Bacchus (eds) *Perspectives on corporate social responsibility* (pp42–58). Aldershot: Ashgate.

ECCLES, R.G. (1991) The performance evaluation manifesto. *Harvard Business Review*, Vol. 69, No. 1, 131–137.

GAMBLE, G.O., HSU, K., JACKSON, C. and TOLLERSON, C.D. (1996) Environmental disclosure in annual reports: an international perspective. *International Journal of Accounting*, Vol. 31, No. 3, 293–331.

GRAY, R. (1992) Accounting and environmentalism: an exploration of the challenge of gently accounting for accountability, transparency and sustainability. *Accounting, Organizations and Society*, Vol. 17, No. 5, 399–425.

GRAY, R., OWEN, D. and MAUNDERS, K. (1987) *Corporate social reporting: accounting and accountability*. London: Prentice-Hall.

HAWKEN, P. (1993). *The ecology of commerce*. London: Weidenfeld & Nicolson.

HOBBES, T. (1651) *Leviathan*. Many editions.

JONES, M.J. (1996) Accounting for biodiversity: a pilot study. *British Accounting Review*, Vol. 28, No. 4, 281–303.

LOVELOCK, J. (1979) *Gaia*. Oxford: Oxford University Press.

MATHEWS, M.R. (1997) *Twenty-five years of social and environmental accounting: is there a silver jubilee to celebrate?* Paper presented at the British Accounting Association National Conference, March 1997, Birmingham.

OWEN, R. (1816) *A new view of society and other writings*. Many editions.

PAVA, M.L. and KRAUSZ, J. (1996) The association between corporate social responsibility and financial performance: the paradox of social cost. *Journal of Business Ethics*, Vol. 15, No. 3, 321–357.

RANAGNATHAN, J. and DITZ, D. (1996) Environmental accounting: a tool for better management. *Management Accounting*, Vol. 74, No. 2, 38–40.

RAWLS, J. (1973) *A theory of justice*. Oxford: Oxford University Press.

ROUSSEAU, J.-J. (1762) *The social contract*. Many editions.

RUBENSTEIN, D.B. (1992) Bridging the gap between green accounting and black ink. *Accounting, Organizations and Society*, Vol. 17, No. 5, 501–508.

TOPAL, R.S. and CROWTHER, D. (2004) Biodiversity practice and the social responsibility concept. In D. Crowther and L. Rayman Bacchus (eds) *Perspectives on corporate social responsibility* (pp186–202). Aldershot: Ashgate.

Current ideas of organisation

INTRODUCTION

In recent years some new concepts have been introduced into organisation theory, which we will examine in this chapter. The first of these is the concept of change management. This is predicated in a recognition that in the modern turbulent environment organisations are faced with a rapidly changing environment and need to respond by undergoing change themselves. Change management is based upon the assumption that this change can be managed.

The second new concept we will consider in this chapter is known as knowledge management. This is based upon a recognition that knowledge is the key resource for a modern organisation and that this too can be managed.

At the present time most organisations are faced with the prospect of their environment becoming increasingly susceptible to competitive and global pressures. This has resulted in many business organisations finding themselves having to adjust many of their operational features in order to cope, and in many cases just to survive. Indeed one of the few constants in business today is the issue of change, and how it can be managed to best effect to optimise business performance. Another observable phenomenon is how this subject spans the management disciplines, from personnel to finance, from operations to marketing; all of them cannot fail to be touched in some way by this issue of change. The clearest indication of the change phenomenon and of the importance of time can be found in the imperatives that many customers are placing upon business organisations. Whereas 20 years ago the emphasis might have been on cost, and 10 years ago on quality, today the emphasis has swung decidedly towards time-based issues. As an indication of this, Stalk and Hout (1991) provide a temporal analysis of strategy through these concepts, arriving at a supposition that time is now paramount as the competitive factor in business.

THE NATURE OF CHANGE

Change is probably the single most important factor of successful business management in the present. Organisations have to change in order to remain successful in today's increasingly competitive and global markets. Thus, organisations have to change not just what they provide to customers, in order to keep abreast of their customers needs, but also how they provide their goods or services. This is necessary not just for a business to be successful and to grow in size, profitability or market share but simply just to survive in the modern environment. Businesses are now faced with dynamic and ever more highly complex operating environments. This is true not just of the internal environment of the business and how it is organised and uses technology to achieve its objectives but is also true for its external environment. The market that a business serves is also becoming more complex as customers become more sophisticated in their needs and more demanding in what they want and how that is provided.

Some of this change is brought about by changes in technology. Thus, production methods for cars have changed dramatically since Henry Ford introduced the assembly line. Now

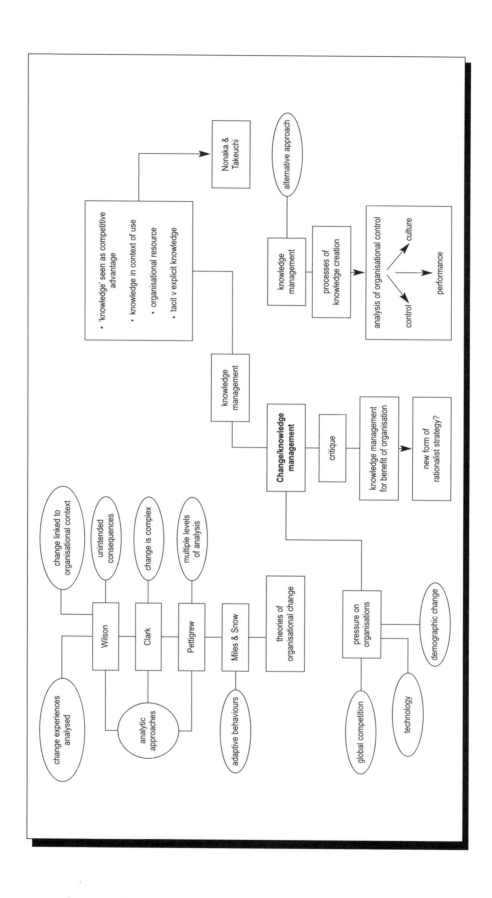

robots and computers are used extensively in the manufacturing process. Equally, information technology, particularly through the advent of the Internet, has changed the way people communicate and hence how businesses operate and customers make purchases. These changes can be expected to continue into the future.

Change is not just brought about by technology, however: businesses are continually trying to improve their products or services and the level of service they offer to their customers. This results in changes to operational processes, procedures and systems. Thus, the way a business is organised is also subject to change on a regular basis. Because businesses are subject to change, this means that the people who work in those businesses are also subject to change. So there are three factors involved in organisational change:

- technological change
- organisational system change
- people-oriented change.

Technology and systems and processes can be changed at will without any adverse reaction from the technology or systems. Reaction to change comes from the people involved, and dealing with those people to secure effective, managed change is the most difficult part of the change management process. The management of that aspect of change is the most challenging and most rewarding aspect of change management, and the one of which you must be most aware.

UNDERSTANDING CHANGE

Change is the way in which organisations stay competitive and seek to grow. For the people in organisations, however, this change can be both an opportunity and a threat. It is an opportunity to learn new skills, to enjoy personal growth and to enrich career opportunities. New activities undertaken by an organisation bring with them opportunities for promotion, but they also bring along with them problems. Equally, departmental or factory closures bring about dismissals, as do deteriorating markets and bankruptcies. These are threats to people, and all change has within it the risks of both gain and loss. It is also a threat to people in having to learn new skills and new ways of working. People are inherently conservative and are more comfortable maintaining the status quo rather than seeking change for its own sake. Indeed an old Chinese curse is 'May you live in a time of change!'

Nevertheless, all people experience change. Often, change takes place as a gradual process as they grow up and mature, and as their career progresses. People deal with these kinds of change as a matter of course – it is only sudden change that causes a problem for people. This should tell us that the planning of change is a crucially important part of the change management process. It should also tell us that the communication process is an equally important part of the change management process. Keeping people informed of what is planned reduces rumour, reduces fear and increases support and motivation.

As far as people are concerned, there are three strategies for dealing with change that can be adopted. These are:

- *Resistance.* This is about the rejection of change and trying to maintain the status quo. We have seen, however, that change is inevitable, and so resistance merely delays change rather than preventing it.

- *Following.* This is about being open to change and willing to go along. Followers, however, never initiate change themselves; instead, following is always about trying to catch up with the leaders.

- *Leadership.* This is a successful response to change. Leaders develop strategies for change and succeed in their goals. This benefits both themselves through job satisfaction and other rewards, and also the organisation by which they are employed.

THE CAUSES OF CHANGE

We have seen that change is a constant process in organisations. If you are going to deal effectively with change, it is important that you understand the underlying causes of change. It is these causes which tend to create the imperative for change, and understanding them will help you to both recognise what changes are necessary and to develop strategies for managing the necessary change. These causes affect the external markets of organisations but can also affect the internal structures and processes of an organisation. We can classify these underlying causes into three distinct types:

- economic causes
- social causes
- technological causes.

Economic causes

The most talked-about economic change taking place at the present is the trend towards globalisation as markets converge. Globalisation means that customers can now purchase their requirements from a firm which may be based anywhere in the world. Equally, businesses are competing against other businesses that might be located anywhere in the world. No longer do national boundaries have any effect upon the patterns of trade. Thus markets and the level of competition have changed dramatically in recent times and this change is still continuing. This has affected the size of markets and the level of competition but it has also had a significant effect upon established patterns of demand as customers gain access to new products and services and new ways of doing business. Globalisation has also had an effect upon the financing of both businesses and governments as the flows of finance around the world are subject to change.

Other patterns of economic change are also important, taking place at a more national level. The economic cycle of an individual country can create a powerful cause for change in a business. In times of recession a business must change in order to survive. Conversely in times of growth a business must change in order to take advantage of the new conditions. This economic cycle tends to take place at a national or even regional level and can affect a business but not its competitors. This gives an added imperative to the understanding of the economic causes of change and the need to react to them.

Social causes

Social, political and demographic changes affect everyone, and they also affect organisations. During the 1960s and 1970s we saw a boom in youth culture and the development of new products and markets to meet the needs of these young affluent people. During the 1980s we witnessed a change from a community- to an individual-centred society. During the 1990s and the early years of the twenty-first century we have been witnessing an increasingly ageing population with a consequent change in patterns of demand and purchasing. These changes have affected businesses and the types of products and services demanded. These socio-demographic changes have caused businesses to change to meet the needs of society. Over the last 50 years we have also seen many political changes: firstly towards state ownership and the provision of social benefits to individuals, then towards privatisation and the need for individuals to make provision for their own health and pensions requirements; now we are seeing a move towards a community-based individualism. Throughout all this period there has been one other change, which is in terms of fashion. Fashions change for a variety of reasons, some of which are socio-demographic, but these changes affect many, if not all, businesses.

Businesses cannot affect these changes in the political environment to any great extent, but they affect those businesses and the patterns of demand for their goods and services. Thus we have seen a big increase in demand for financial products such as pensions and healthcare insurance and new types of products such as personal pensions and savings schemes. At the same time we have seen a reduction in demand for such things as public transport – although this trend is now being reversed. All of these changes are a result of the changing political climate, but they also provide a cause for change within organisations to which they must respond.

Technological causes

We have already mentioned technological changes. These have brought about new processes in businesses, new organisational structures, new products and services and new demands from customers. All of these have demanded change for businesses to such an extent that most businesses now are unrecognisable from what they were 25 years ago. Indeed many new businesses have come into existence, while others no longer exist. There is a big demand now for computers and software, for example, which barely existed 25 years ago. This demand could not have been anticipated only a few decades ago. When the computer was invented by what is now IBM, it was forecast that the total world demand for computers would be for fewer than 50 machines. Soon, nearly everyone will want their own computer. At the same time the demand for products such as mechanical calculating machines (which were in common use 30 years ago) has completely disappeared. On a smaller scale, few people now want a black-and-white television – almost everyone owns a colour television, and quite possibly more than one. Technological change is ongoing, and it is difficult to imagine what will happen in the next 25 years. Nevertheless, this technological development will require organisations to continue to change.

The underlying causes of change are not always easy to predict. They are, however, a root cause of the necessity for change in businesses. An awareness of them is therefore essential for any manager in a business, and being aware of changes in society can help a manager be aware of the possible necessity for change in the organisation in which she or he is employed. This anticipation is one of the ways of being a leader in change management rather than a follower.

ORGANISATIONAL ATTITUDES TO CHANGE

Most people would consider that organisations are complex and individualistic, being a composite of the various interacting interests. Attempts have, however, been made to categorise organisations according to their patterns of behaviour and approaches to change. Miles and Snow (1978) believe that organisations can be grouped into four distinct types depending upon the adaptive behaviour used to maintain an effective alignment with their environment. The basic ideas leading to this categorisation are that:

- Organisations act and bring about change in order to create their environment.
- Management's strategic choices shape the structure and processes of the organisation.
- The selected structure and process constrain strategy.
- Thus organisational behaviour and response to change are based upon the strategic choices made by managers.

We can then therefore see that managers have a crucial role to play in the change management process. Miles and Snow describe the process of organisational change as a process of adaptation. They consider it as being concerned with the solving of three problems:

- The *entrepreneurial* problem, which is concerned with the acceptance of the product and market domains of the organisation.
- The *engineering* (or technological) problem, which is concerned with the creation of systems for the organisation to achieve its objectives.
- The *administrative* (or procedural) problem, which is concerned with reducing uncertainty.

Based upon these premises they identify four types of organisation:

- *Defenders* perceive the environment as stable, are finance- and production-dominated, and aim to grow incrementally through market penetration. For them change is concerned with planning, and this planning is about problem-solving, and performance evaluation is achieved by comparing present performance with that of previous time periods.
- *Prospectors* are concerned with finding and exploiting new product and market opportunities; they are creators of change. They are people-centred, with a low degree of structural formalisation. Marketing and research and development are the dominant functions. Planning is concerned with problem-finding, and performance evaluation is achieved by comparison with similar organisations.
- *Analysers* are followers of change rather than initiators and undertake extensive market surveillance to achieve this. They tend to operate a matrix structure, with marketing and production being the dominant functions. Planning for these organisations is all-important and therefore intensive and comprehensive, and performance evaluation tends to be by means of comparison of actual performance against plans and budgets.
- *Reactors* tend not to have a clearly articulated strategy, and the strategy–structure relationship does not change to meet changing environmental conditions. They are therefore viewed as unsuccessful organisations, with failure being their ultimate destination.

TYPES OF CHANGE

Change can be slow and gradual or it can be rapid and radical. This is overly simplistic, and a wide variety of types of change exist. All types of change can be either reactive or proactive.

Reactive change is when a business is forced to change because of external pressures, such as a declining demand for its core product, while proactive change is voluntary, in anticipation of market changes. In practice change often involves both proactive and reactive elements. Thus for example a financial crisis will cause reactive change but it will also be proactive in that the managers of the business need to decide what and how to change in order to maximise the chances of successful change. Understanding the type of change you are dealing with will help you to manage it effectively. It will also help you understand how other people will respond to the change.

We can classify change into five distinct types:

- gradual change
- radical change
- crisis
- organic change
- response to competitors.

Gradual change

A gradual change is one that takes place slowly over a period of time. As we stated previously, all organisations and all people are undergoing gradual change all the time. Gradual change can however be an important part of a change management programme when it is planned. Such a change may involve many people or few but can be effective as a programme to improve the quality of products and processes, to reduce costs and to raise productivity. The Japanese approach through the use of quality circles is an example of such a gradual change programme.

Radical change

A radical change is a sudden or dramatic change that has a major effect upon the business. An example would be a decision to move the manufacture of a product to a new location. Radical change can be either commercial (such as the example above) or structural, and it is very often accompanied by cultural changes. Radical change is more risky than gradual change, but the benefits as well as the problems can be much greater. Radical change is harder for people to accept and requires careful planning before it is implemented.

Crisis

Crisis is an inevitable cause of change, and that change is nearly always radical. Crisis management is always urgent and is best managed by a single person or a small group who are able to respond rapidly. Full, but rapid, analysis of the situation is necessary for successful change even in these circumstances, and drastic action is often called for. Managed change is still however the key to successful change. Examples could be the closing of a business unit or even the relocation (or elimination) of headquarters operations. It is easy to say, but crisis management should be avoided if at all possible. An awareness of the features of change that we have considered in this chapter will help to avoid the necessity of crisis management.

Organic change

All organisations move through a life cycle from newness to maturity as they grow. As they grow and mature, change is inevitable within the business as more people are employed, new skills are needed, and new systems and processes come into being. A large business needs more people, more managers and more systems to manage operations than does a small business. This change is referred to as organic because it is inevitable with growth. It is often gradual, but sometimes a period of radical change can take place as the business readjusts to its new needs. Radical change can be reduced through careful planning and management of the change process.

Response to competitors

This type of change is often caused by a business adopting a follower approach to change – an analyser business, according to Miles and Snow (1978). This may not always be the case, however. If a rival business suddenly launches a new product or embarks upon a price-cutting campaign, then a response is needed to obviate the threat. A good manager will react to this and seize upon it as an opportunity to re-examine his or her own business's products or markets or price structure and will look to manage change which will improve upon the competitor. Even better of course is the anticipation of the actions of competitors, and awareness of all the factors involved in change will help to achieve this.

Although change is both ubiquitous and necessary, its management is not a simple process. Moreover, in order to be successful, change management programmes need to be built upon a theoretical understanding. It is worth, at this point, reflecting on a report prepared in the late 1970s by the British Economic and Social Research Council which lamented that much theorising about organisations was in fact atheoretical, acontextual and lacking in an empirical base. A number of theorists have sought to address these deficiencies, and moreover they have made significant contributions to the extant knowledge on organisational change. In this chapter we will look at some of the key theorists and consider what they have had to say about change and its management.

The approach taken by those we will consider can be considered as being 'analytical' approaches to change. Broadly speaking, the analytical school of change considers organisational change an inherently complex process. It seeks to unravel the multiple analytical levels of organisational change, trying to make sense of change experiences. This perspective does not seek to prescribe change recipes; rather it considers organisational change processes as being far too complex to allow generalised, universal science-like prescriptions accompanied by an emphasis on the appreciation of context sensitivity. The organisational change process is viewed as being inextricably linked to the organisation's contextual environment.

Perhaps of necessity, the prevailing empirical feature of the analytical school is to study a single or small number of organisations in depth, over time, allowing the construction of a rich, historically contextualised picture of the organisational change process. There have been a number of important contextual contributions in the last two decades. In this chapter it is my intention to focus upon the work of three key theorists – Pettigrew, Wilson and Clark – in terms of their contribution to the study of organisational change. The concerns they raise, as we will see, pose important questions for organisational change theory.

ANDREW PETTIGREW: THE CONTEXT AND PROCESS OF ORGANISATIONAL CHANGE

Pettigrew's early work highlighted the non-rational nature of organisation and clearly demonstrated the highly politicised nature of organisational life. Such ideas now form the assumptions that underscore contemporary organisational theory, but this was not always the case. Pettigrew (1973) described the decision-making process in an organisation, demonstrating the way in which a gatekeeper – Kenny – was able to exert large amounts of control over the organisation through controlling information about alternatives and, by extension, introducing his own favoured alternatives. Kenny's sphere of influence extended over the purchase decisions of information technology systems. Over a quarter of a century later, Pettigrew's findings seem less than remarkable. Yet this is a sign of how his insights into the non-rational, dysfuntional possibilities of technocracy have moved to the centre stage of organisational theorising.

The findings from Pettigrew's work on decision-making were to resurface once again in his extensive study of the organisational change process in ICI. This book has been highly influential in terms of theorising about organisational change. It was from studying the actions, both in the here and now as well as looking at the organisation's history, that Pettigrew was able to argue for the importance of context, content and process in terms of understanding organisational change. The model proposed by Pettigrew (1985) is an analytical device for thinking about organisational change and stresses its iterative nature. From Pettigrew's model, the context of change is the 'why' of change, ie what the pressures are that trigger change. In general terms Pettigrew (1985) highlights the fact that generic change triggers from within the realm of the external environment may come from:

- economic/business factors
- political factors
- social factors.

As Pettigrew's work on Sir John Harvey-Jones notes, pressures for change may also come from within the organisation, from organisational factions dissatisfied with the status quo, and wanting to 'think the unthinkable'. Pettigrew's interest in 'change triggers' is sustained in his later work (see Pettigrew and Whipp 1991), where he gives a number of practical examples of pressures for organisational change emerging from the external environment.

The content of change is the 'what' of change; quite literally what is it the organisation is attempting to change? The organisation might want to change its 'culture', or its 'structure', or embark on a programmed change such as total quality management (TQM). In all of these cases, the content is essentially a labelling exercise – to give the change initiative a name. Integral to exploring the content of change is questioning the objectives behind the change, and the assumptions behind the change. The process of change examines 'how' the change is introduced, studying the implementation of the changes and the process of change through time. The actions and reactions of managers, workers and other stakeholders are central to this analysis. Key to understanding the implementation of organisational change is an appreciation of the power relations at play within the organisation (and outside the organisation, in the wider social system).

It is for his identification with process that Pettigrew is best known. His conception of process is informed by an understanding of the micro-political: the actions undertaken by the people within the organisation. As such, Pettigrew's notion of process is linked to events. It is the analysis of such events that take primary consideration over other context and content. More recently, Pettigrew has extended this area of interest into examining the dynamics of boardrooms, with a particular focus on the impact of non-executive directors on the politics of

185

decision-making. The charting of the dramas in and around the boardroom is clearly a fruitful line of analysis in terms of engaging with the rationales – the constructions – of particular initiatives.

Yet by concentrating on this, Pettigrew could be accused of persistently ignoring the issue of the preconfigured context of the organisation, ie to what extent is change possible? The sense of organising within his account of process is absent. This is problematic, for without a sense of organising it is difficult to know whether organisational change has actually occurred – that is, change beyond the surface fripperies of mission statements and corporate egos. This lack of a sense of the pre-existing has been a criticism levelled at Pettigrew by Clark (1996, 2000) and by Rowlinson and Proctor (1999). The former argues that a characteristic of Pettigrew's work is to recount the founding conditions of an enterprise, and then to helicopter to the present to discuss organisational changes. Similarly, Grieco (1996) has referred to this as birthmarking. Rowlinson and Proctor's (1999) critique is that Pettigrew's processual analyses lay claim to being historical but in fact demonstrate a poor understanding of historical narrative; they are, therefore, 'bad history'.

The timeline analyses pursued by Pettigrew reach their apogee in his collaboration with Whipp (1991), which saw them try to determine whether the way in which organisational change was managed actually made a difference to organisational success. They found it did, although it was far from a simple, causal relationship. Rather, it was a complex combination of the following factors:

- coherence
- leading change
- human resources as assets and liabilities
- environmental assessment
- the link between strategic and operational change.

The interconnectedness of the different variables is emphasised, likening it to a hologram and invoking analogies with Chinese medicine. The prerequisite factors for 'successful change' identified by Pettigrew and Whipp (1991) do not offer easy-to-follow, prescriptive steps. Pettigrew and Whipp have been criticised for attempting to do too much, and on the basis of their empirical material, their theoretical claims are not sustainable. This reflects Wilson's position (see below), when he suggests that through their model they are trying to explain the world, an ambition that ultimately results in a model of limited capacity. Pettigrew's work, however, raises many questions, and with it reveals problems to his approach. Yet whatever these difficulties, his importance in terms of highlighting the need for analysing the politics of organisation change needs to be acknowledged.

DAVID WILSON: STRATEGIES OF CHANGE

Wilson's most significant contribution to the study of organisational change came in his 1992 book *A Strategy of Change*. In the context of 1992, when managers and employees alike were being exhorted to love change, he was problematising many of the normative exhortations of the so-called gurus. Chapter by chapter, he highlights deficiencies in many of the assumptions underpinning the management of change. He argues that there is more to change than the simple belief that an organisational blueprint, effective communication and good leadership will bring about the desired results.

According to him, much of the influential thinking on organisational change has been bedevilled by such ideas. Wilson questioned this agenda and therefore problematised it. He demonstrates the way in which, rather than resembling anything new, much of the theorising on organisational change is underscored by a heavy dose of Taylorism: the one best way being reanimated to act as the *leitmotif* of contemporary approaches to the management of change. With the benefit of hindsight, the prescience of Wilson's theorising can be seen clearly. In the first instance, the consulting industry and programmed change initiatives are now taken for granted; at the time of writing, this was far from clear. In this sense he identified that consultants are important players in the actor network of disseminating and supplying management ideas – programme change initiatives – and that this is a recent phenomenon.

Wilson's particular targets were the most exalted ideas of the day – namely, those of corporate culture and TQM. Wilson identified what he was to term the programmed change initiative, ie a package of change, an ideology complete with tools, techniques and practices. In broader terms, and of greater relevance to our understanding, is Wilson's approach. He seeks to analyse initiatives on their own terms: empirically and theoretically do the ideas stand up? Do they match their own criteria for success? This pragmatic approach yielded considerable fruit, for he was able to demolish the ideas that 'quality' is critical and that 'having the right culture' is a cornerstone to a corporate nirvana. Moreover, he demonstrated the way in which a particular worldview – with all of its assumptions and prejudices (white, male, middle-class and Anglo-Saxon) – get passed off as commonsensical fact. This is nowhere more vivid than in his analysis of Sir John Harvey-Jones's consultant-corporate doctor, *Troubleshooter* television series, which saw the esteemed former chairman of ICI provide advice to organisations at critical junctures in their corporate histories. While the advice was rhetoric-intensive, coming as it did from the man who allegedly awoke ICI, Wilson strips away its veneer, exposing it as the rigid application of a particular homespun logic that ignores the specificity of particular organisational contexts.

PETER CLARK: FOCUS UPON PROCESS

The parallels between some of Clark's early theorising and the work of Wilson on programmed change initiatives are striking. Clark, in 1972, conjectured that there was the potential for programmed approaches, although he was unsure as to how they would come about. Wilson, writing in 1992, provides an excellent commentary on how pervasive programmed change approaches had become, and, importantly, he identified the infrastructure that was supporting the programmed change movement.

Clark, in his analysis of organisational change, starts with first principles by arguing that one has to take a view as to what constitutes organisational change: 'clarifying the concept of change is an essential requirement as it has been used very loosely' (Clark and Starkey 1988, p50). He takes it to be 'events occurring in organisations which might be theorised as organisational change' (Clark 1996). In his opinion there are two broad types of organisational change:

- dislocation
- the development of robust, viable organisational forms.

This distinction is worth exploring: he is suggesting that many change initiatives actually constitute attempts at creative destruction, ie removing practices from the organisation. An implication of this would be to look at a programmed change initiative in order to question whether it constituted creative destruction or an attempt to build new organisational capabilities. Allied to this point is Clark's assertion that building new practices may require exnovation – the removal of existing practices – a point distinct from creative destruction.

The nature of Clark's work is to study organisational change from a perspective that takes a sophisticated angle on organisations as entities. It is a task-based approach to the study of change. The implication of his work is that much of the theorising on organisational change is flawed because of the problematic nature of the position taken on organisations. According to him the 'characteristic of organisational theory has been to concentrate on durable features such as organisational structure rather than oscillations and process' (Clark 1996). The corollary of the 'obsession' (Clark and Mueller 1996) with structure is a suppression of process. This results in 'confusion of what ought to become with the assumption that "the becoming" was not too problematic' (Clark 1996, p6). This is in stark contrast to the exhortations of Kanter. It is Clark's (1972) contention that greater attention needs to be paid to process in order to gain a richer understanding of attempts to enact organisational change.

The first concern of Clark is to look at the existing organisation attempting to undergo change; it is his contention that the pre-existing form is vital in terms of analysing change. Clark posits that there is no *tabula rasa*: rather the antecedents of the organisation are of vital importance to attempts at organisational change. The three features that Clark argues are important for grasping the antecedents of an organisation are:

- the configuration of the forces in the organisation
- organisational recursiveness
- organisational repertoires.

Configuration

The first feature, the configuration of forces in the firm, broadly reflects the views held by both Wilson and Pettigrew. The idea here is that it is important to have a sense of the 'configuration of forces and relations between pre-existing social and individual groups' (Clark 1996). Pertinent questions become, therefore, which groups are relatively powerful and why? Are there conservatives v modernisers involved in the change process? In Clark's early work (1972) he discusses problem ownership, and it is 'crucial to have a sense of the organisational power balances and politics within an organisation in order to make sense of an organisational strategy'. Clark has demonstrated the changing power dynamics in supply chains, especially the case of Marks & Spencer, which saw Cora become relatively powerless as it was locked into a relationship as a junior to Marks. The intrigue and strategising that are immanent to Pettigrew's is absent from Clark's theorising.

Recursiveness

The second part of the shadow that antecedents cast over attempts at organisational change is in terms of recursiveness. Clark suggests that without recursiveness social life would not exist. The idea here is that the ingrained forces in the firm, the way things are, have a tendency to be 'recursive', ie an organisation and its patterns of activities and ways of thinking reproduce themselves over time. In terms of taking the discussion on recursiveness from the realm of the abstract to the practical, it is sustained through factors that *inter alia* include: 'Standards of procedures'; sagas, myths and ideologies; political coalitions; single loop learning; and founding coalitions. Recursiveness acts as a pivotal difference between a task approach (ie what it is that an organisation does) and an event approach (such as the kind preferred by Pettigrew).

An example of recursiveness given (Whipp and Clark 1986) is the insurmountable difficulties that Rover faced in attempting to transform itself from being a niche manufacturer, in the class-ridden British society of the 1930s to 1970s, to a mass car producer of 250,000 units, as was attempted with the SDI project in the 1970s. Put simply, according to the analysis proposed by Whipp and Clark (1986), the problems that stymied Rover's attempts to become a leading European car manufacturer were attributable to the absence of particular capabilities within their structural repertoire. This, given the recent experiences at Rover and the subsequent buyout by the Phoenix group, poses the question as to whether recursiveness might, in terms of organisational outcomes, prove to be chronic. Clark would suggest that Phoenix's attempts to transform Rover will fail because of the difficulties of developing structural poses in the repertoire. The notion of the repertoire is in need of further elaboration.

Repertoires

In close relation to the concept of recursiveness is the notion of repertoire. The premise is that organisations have a 'repertoire'; this can be thought of as the organisational capacity for carrying out particular activities. This will consist of:

- its standard operating systems (people, technology, layout, tacit knowledge)
- its ability to deal with events out of the ordinary
- its ability to deal with crisis situations (see Clark and Staunton 1989).

In one sense, a parallel can be drawn between the work of Clark and that of the work on routines by Nelson and Winter (1982), although arguably Clark has a richer sense of organisation. What are we to make of the notion of the chronic recursiveness of an organisation's repertoire? A danger is that it is overbearingly deterministic, for it predicts the failure of attempts at transformation. Moreover, it is difficult to see where successful transformation can come from. This has led Scarbrough and Swan (1999) to comment about the 'conservative' nature of Clark's conception of change.

If we look at Gearing's (1958) schematic, its significance is that it highlights the importance of temporality to the notion of an organisational repertoire. It highlights the fact that temporality is not homogeneous and linear but rather that heterogeneous temporalities exist. Within the realm of organisational theorising, traditional assumptions behind temporality have been questioned (Clark 1978). For Clark, organisational studies generally can be considered to be time-free analyses, ignoring the 'formidable problems of time and structure' (Whipp and Clark 1986, p55). Clark argues that, in order to conduct an adequate treatment of temporality in the process of organisational change, the analysis must commence with the treatment of recursiveness and structural pose repertoires. Moreover, it needs to escape the tyranny and linearity of clock-time, and Clark demonstrates that there are other forms of time, such as event time. For instance, Clark and Starkey (1988, p55) argue that:

> events occur serially and that the events define time. It is often the enactment of future events by key decision makers – the strategic time keepers – and their capabilities in politicking for the activation of the repertoire which shapes the tasks that the organisation management undertake.

The insights provided by the concept of the repertoire are highly significant for considering organisational change, and given that an organisational repertoire can only be firm-specific, it adds to the cogency of the case for a contextual perspective. Taking the earlier insights on recursiveness, it would be the essence of Clark's position that an organisation's repertoire is likely to be robust for the future.

The difficulties that Clark has identified in terms of the capacity for learning is something that emphasises the constraint that the past places on the present. The corollary of the limits placed on an organisation by its preconfigured repertoire that is recursive is that the 'zone of manoeuvre' open to an organisation is limited. The easy part, according to Clark, is to develop a strategy, the difficulty comes in trying to enact it. Therefore the strategic choice is open but limited by the organisational repertoire and also by the interdependencies that an organisation faces. In terms of realising a set of changes, Clark (1996) alerts us to the possibilities of unintended consequences of the actions embarked upon.

THE CONTINGENT NATURE OF THE CORPORATE WORLD

Clark (1996, 2000) alerts us to the contingent nature of the corporate world by highlighting the fact that unintended consequences abound in any attempt at corporate transformation. Put simply, a particular programme of change may well have far-reaching effects, but perhaps not those that were intended! In terms of the UK, an unintended consequence of the successive Conservative governments of the 1980s and early 1990s was to open up questions about the legitimacy of the British polity (see Charter 88). These doubts were in part a result of the grievance felt by many regions of the UK (eg Scotland) of being subject to New Right policies despite having resoundingly rejected them at the ballot box. The 'winner takes all' feature of the 'first past the post' system allowed the Thatcher governments to win large majorities on the basis of a minority of the popular vote (see Hutton 1995). The Thatcherite message generally proved popular in the South of England; more importantly it held considerable appeal in the crucial 'marginal' constituencies. However, in the North of England and in Scotland and Wales alternative political messages were supported with a growing sense of disillusionment. The Labour Government's changes to the electoral system since assuming office in 1997 have had significant impact on the regions, in that they have given added legitimacy and a heightened level of autonomy to Scotland, Wales and London.

In drawing this section to a close, we need to examine the work of these theorists. Each has something important to say, but the overall message is that managing change in an organisation is a complex process. Each in his own way critiques the assumptions that change is something that can be managed through a series of steps, that managers can be trained to manage, and that organisations must be able to change. For Clark the idea of change revolves around a task-based approach, but at the same time his treatment of power is implicit and therefore somewhat understated. In contrast, Pettigrew's account of change, perhaps through its concentration of events, is far too focused on the 'here and now' and has serious limitations in its treatment of organisation. Yet the contribution that Pettigrew has made to theorising the micro-dynamics of organisational change should not be underestimated. Wilson focuses his work in the area of programmed change, and we have considered this in Chapter 3.

KNOWLEDGE MANAGEMENT

Knowledge management (KM) has fast become one of the master concepts of contemporary organisational thinking. As a practice, there is strong evidence to suggest that it is becoming more and more pervasive throughout the corporate world. In brief, the argument is that 'knowledge' is increasingly becoming the source of competitive advantage in a globalised economy. As such, the analytical leverage of knowledge management rests in its claim to be able to both (a) 'mine' the existing knowledge assets of the firm and (b) create new knowledge. In this sense, KM can be considered a useful example of mode 2 knowledge production (Lyotard, 1984; Gibbons *et al* 1994), ie where knowledge is produced outside the ivory towers of the universities, directly in the context of use. As such it is noteworthy that many of the leading contributors to thinking on KM are members of consultancy organisations.

While concerns have been expressed as to whether KM is merely the latest in a long line of organisational 'fashions', such fears have been allayed through pointing to the likely enduring nature of how twenty-first century organisations are to go about managing their knowledge base. As such it is argued that there is a validity regarding a concern with knowledge in organisations that extends beyond the mere vicissitudes of fashion. In terms of situating KM, it is useful to reflect upon its antecedents. It has been argued that KM, as a theoretical area of enquiry, has been constituted through the coalescence of a number of management subjects (see Figure 13.1).

It would be misplaced, however, to suggest that the domain of KM constitutes a synthesis between the different disciplines. Instead, each perspective brings with it particular analytical concerns. It would also be erroneous to suggest that each discipline has an equal bearing on KM.

For instance, Swan (1999) has argued that there has been a concerted attempt by the information systems (IS) community to colonise KM, while there has been considerable concern among the HR profession that KM is fast developing a people management gap

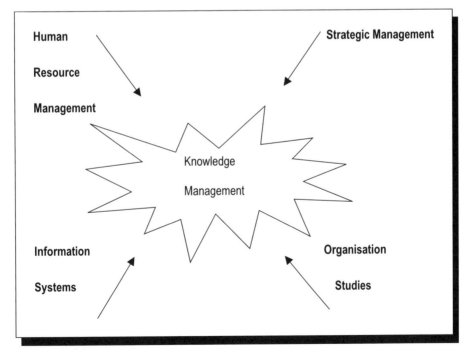

Figure 13.1 *The making of knowledge management*
Source: Scarbrough and Carter (2000, p20)

(Scarborough and Swan 1999). The preponderance of the IS community in KM initiatives has led some writers to sound the caveat that KM must be seen as more than a technicist fix, reducible to the implementation of a company intranet, such as through Lotus Notes or Groupware. From the perspective of strategy, issues of knowledge have acted as the foundation stone of the influential 'resource-based theory' approach. Resource-based theory emerged as a critique of the Harvard-based 'design school', a perspective that has been influentially criticised as not sufficiently concerned with process and too much with rational planning and market analysis. The resource-based view (RBV) in strategic management has put issues of path dependency, the role of (organisational) history, firm-specific resources, appropriability and politics on the agenda. Undoubtedly, the RBV has emerged as an influential alternative to approaches that were more concerned with market positioning, segmentation, and acquisition and diversification strategies. The appeal of RBV is that it places emphasis on what the organisation 'can do' as opposed to what Clark (2000, p214) has termed 'the strategic fantasies of formal, written mission statements'. It is this concern with 'what an organisation can do' that has fuelled the interest of strategists into knowledge management.

This is a relevant starting-point for acknowledging the recent emergence of the discourse of knowledge management. From our perspective, one of the most striking features of this discourse is the debt to the resource-based approach in the way that knowledge is presented as an endogenous, if sometimes elusive, organisational resource. The shift towards looking at the organisation and its immediate supply chain is a cornerstone of approaches to KM. The spread of the discourse seems to be driven by claims that this hitherto hidden but highly valuable resource is now accessible to management and exploitation. In order to make sense of intangible assets, there have been a number of attempts to introduce concepts that help clarify the nature of 'knowledge in organisations'. Perhaps most famously, Nonaka and Takeuchi (1995) in their highly influential book, *The Knowledge Creating Company*, have claimed that the insights of KM mean that the 'knowledge creating process is no longer an enigma' (p236). They have argued that knowledge can be distinguished in terms of whether it is 'tacit' or 'explicit', and whether it is held collectively – such as in a team – or individually. For instance, Lam (1997), drawing on Nonaka's work, argues that organisations possess a key knowledge agent, such as an 'individual', a 'team' etc. This work has been developed more extensively within the teamworking literature, where issues of the distribution and value of knowledge have been placed at centre stage.

Critiquing knowledge management

Reservations have been raised as to whether the perspective promulgated by Nonaka and Takeuchi (1995) pays sufficient attention to process. While their contribution has been critiqued as holding an overly static view of knowledge, it has nonetheless been profoundly influential. The root metaphor of the discourse – exemplified by references to data-mining, for example, or 'drilling down into the knowledge base' – represents knowledge as a quasi-natural resource that requires conversion into more explicit forms. Through the use of the mental maps and practical tools of KM, managers are able to achieve the 'quintessential knowledge-creation process', namely 'when tacit knowledge is converted into explicit knowledge' (Nonaka and Takeuchi 1995, pp230–231). This privileging of tacit knowledge presumes that knowledge can be abstracted and reified from individuals. This understanding has fuelled the development and growth in intranet facilities and other such data-mining techniques. The corollary of the importance of such techniques to the discourse of KM has led to the nascent discipline being largely dominated by technicist approaches, which seek to provide the means of making tacit knowledge explicit.

More recently, there have been calls for a less technically determinist view of KM, ie a second generation of KM (Blackler 2000). Such a view of KM demands greater attention to the processes through which knowledge is codified and created. This emphasis on knowledge necessitates a review of the way in which organisation performance and control is dealt with in organisations. In particular, it is likely to have profound institutional, cultural implications within organisations. For example, it is our contention that the current knowledge debate is likely to have significant ramifications for CIMA (Chartered Institute of Management Accounting) practitioners. As Crowther *et al* (2001) have noted:

> An important, if not fundamental, feature of all approaches to performance management is the alignment of objectives, measures, strategic decision making and rewards intended to promote value creation at all levels of the business

Therefore, as organisations attempt through KM to transform themselves into 'knowledge-creating companies', there is an urgent need to consider how performance is to be measured. For instance, recent studies have illustrated how inadequate attention to a holistic view of performance had injurious consequences in terms of the knowledge creation and long-term financial viability. This is mirrored by reports of the failure of many KM projects because of poor co-ordination and measurement (Scarbrough and Swan 1999).

Whatever one's view concerning the techniques of knowledge management, it is clear that the intention is to arrive at codified knowledge, what Nonaka and Takeuchi (1995) have described as being the very quintessence of knowledge creation, such that this knowledge can be applied by anyone with access to the intranet. To use an intranet does not need an expert, with his or her associated cost, in order to apply the knowledge. The position taken in this review is that this 'knowledge' is in fact data that has been captured for subsequent use – thus it is possible to consider data warehousing as a mechanism for knowledge management. It is only when this data is actually extracted, manipulated and interpreted that we enter the domain of knowledge and can consider its management.

CONCLUSIONS

Organisation theory continues to change, and in this chapter we have considered two recent developments that are a focus of the development of such theory. Each has relevance to the changing world of business. Change management is a reflection of the fact that the environment in which organisations operate is not static but rather is radically changing, and so organisations need to change with their environment. All change management theory is based on the premise that change is more effective if it is planned.

Knowledge management on the other hand is a reflection of the increasing use of information technology and its vast storage ability. The aim is to capture the extensive knowledge that people possess and thereby use it for the benefit of the organisations that employ them. However, critics of the knowledge management approach argue that it is a rerun of the scientific rational approaches with which we started this book – another method of treating people in the organisation as commodities to be used for the benefit of the organisation rather than as people. So these critics would argue that organisation theory is evolving through a concern with more issues but it is certainly not developing.

SUMMARY

- Successful change management is crucial to organisations because of competitive global markets, demographic changes and technological developments.

- Change can be technological, or systems- or people-oriented.

- There are different types of change, and organisations adapt differently to change.

- Key theorists of organisational change:

  - Pettigrew: the 'why', 'what' and 'how' of change; focuses on organisational processes, at the expense, some argue, of the prefigured context of the organisation.

  - Wilson: problematises many of the assertions of management 'gurus'; sees programmed change inititatives as replicating 'one best way' approaches underpinned by a functionalist ideology.

  - Clark: studied the destruction as well as the development of organisational forms; concentrates on organisational process for a richer understanding of change; looks at the pre-existing organisational form to analyse change.

- Knowledge management (KM) theories claim to 'mine' existing knowledge in organisations and develop new knowledge.

- Critique: rather than the technically determinist view of KM, and rather than treating people as commodities to be used as in rationalist approaches; critics have suggested looking at the processes through which there is control in the organisation and knowledge is codified and created.

FURTHER READING

CLARK, P. (2000) *Organisations in action*. London: Routledge.

GRIECO, M. (1996) *Worker's dilemmas: recruitment, reliability and repeated exchange*. London: Routledge.

NELSON, R. and WINTER, S. (1982) *An evolutionary theory of economic change*. Cambridge, Mass: Harvard University Press.

NONAKA, I. and TAKEUCHI, H. (1995) *The knowledge creating company*. New York: Oxford University Press.

WILSON, D. (1992) *A strategy of change*. London: Routledge.

REFERENCES

BLACKLER, F. (2000) Knowledge management. *People Management*, 22 June.

CLARK, P. (1972) *Action research and organisational change*. London: Harper & Row.

CLARK, P. (1978) *Study of time: Vol. III. Time reckoning in large organisations*. Berlin: Verlag-Springer.

CLARK, P. (1996, September) *Structural activation, recursiveness, temporal duality and national specificities in a strategy for organisational change*. Paper presented at the British Academy of Management conference, Aston Business School, Birmingham, September 1996.

CLARK, P. (2000) *Organisations in action*. London: Routledge.

CLARK, P. and MUELLER, F. (1996) Organisations and nations: from universalism to institutionalism. *British Journal of Management*, Vol. 7, No. 2, 125–140.

CLARK, P. and STARKEY, K. (1988) *Organisation transitions and innovation design*. London: Frances Pinter.

CLARK, P. and STAUNTON, N. (1989) *Innovation in technology and organisation*. London: Routledge.

CROWTHER, D., COOPER, S., DAVIS, T. and DAVIES, M. (2001) Shareholder or stakeholder management: strategies for performance optimisation. Paper presented at EAA Congress, Athens.

GEARING, T. (1958) Dysfunctional consequences of organisational goals in strategic leadership. *Administrative Science Quarterly*, Vol. 3, No. 2, 240–247.

GIBBONS, M., LIMOGES, C., NOWOTNY, H., SCHWARTZMAN, S., SCOTT, P. and TROW, M. (1994) *The new production of knowledge: the dynamics of science and research in contemporary societies*. London: Sage.

HUTTON, W. (1995) *The state we're in*. London: Cape.

LAM, A. (1997) Embedded firms, embedded knowledge: problems of collaboration and knowledge transfer in global cooperative ventures. *Organisation Studies*, Vol. 18, No. 6, 973–996.

LYOTARD, J.-L. (1984) *The post modern condition: a report on knowledge*. Manchester: Manchester University Press.

MILES, R.E. and SNOW, C.C. (1978) *Organisational strategy, structure and process*. New York: McGraw-Hill.

NELSON, R. and WINTER, S. (1982) *An evolutionary theory of economic change*. Cambridge, Mass: Harvard University Press.

NONAKA, I. and TAKEUCHI, H. (1995) *The knowledge creating company*. New York: Oxford University Press.

PETTIGREW, A. (1973) *The politics of organisational decision-making*. London: Tavistock Publications.

PETTIGREW, A. (1985) *The awakening giant: continuity and change in Imperial Chemical Industries*. Oxford: Blackwell.

PETTIGREW, A. and WHIPP, R. (1991) *Managing change for competitive success*. Oxford: Blackwell.

ROWLINSON, M. and PROCTER, S. (1999) Organizational culture and business history. *Organization Studies, Berlin*, Vol. 20, No. 3, 369–396.

SCARBROUGH, H. and CARTER, C. (2000) *Investigating knowledge management*. London: Chartered Institute of Personnel Development.

SCARBROUGH, H. and SWAN, J. (1999) *Case-studies in knowledge management*. London: IPD.

STALK, G. and HOUT, T.M. (1991) *Competing against time*. London: Free Press.

SWAN, J. (1999) *Knowledge management and the people management gap*. Keynote presentation given to the BPRC, Warwick Business School, June 1991.

WHIPP, R. (1991) Human resource management, strategic change and competition: the role of learning. *International Journal of Human Resource Management*, Vol. 2, No. 2, 165–192.

WHIPP, R. and CLARK, P. (1986) *Innovation and the auto industry*. London: Frances Pinter.

WILSON, D. (1992) *A strategy of change*. London: Routledge.

Conclusions

CHAPTER 14

THE COMPLEXITY OF THEORY

In this book we have sought to show the diversity and complexity of the theories that exist about organising and their relevance to the modern world of business. We have sought to show that different strands of theory have developed at different times, but new theory has not replaced older theory – rather it has taken its place alongside that theory. So we are left with a situation where multiple theories exist which sit alongside each other, and all continue to develop and to have relevance. We recognise, however, and have sought to illustrate, that different strands of theory have gained prominence at particular points in time. This is in part a reflection of the fact that the concerns and priorities of society change over time and so the focus of theory reflects this. For organisations cannot sit outside society – they are an integral part of that society. In part it is also a recognition that the problems of organising have not been solved despite the extensive development of theory. Each of these theories contains a partial solution – hence their continued use and relevance – but none contains the complete answer.

This in itself suggests that the postmodernists are correct in saying that there is no single answer. Organisations are too complex and too varied for there to be a single correct way of organising that applies to them all – or even to one single organisation at all points in time. More importantly, organisations are made up of people, and people are too varied for theory to cope. Those who reject postmodernism would concur that organisations are complex and varied but would deny that this means that a comprehensive theory is not possible. They would argue that theory continues to develop and improve and that eventually a comprehensive theory will be developed which will incorporate the best parts of the existing theories but with other developments, as yet unknown.

We do not intend to take sides in this debate. Rather, throughout this book we have sought to show the various strands and developments in organisation theory. Equally we have sought to show that all have some relevance to the modern business world. We are confident that it will continue to develop but would not wish to make ourselves hostages to fortune by attempting to forecast in what directions those developments will take place. Instead we would wish to conclude by considering some important issues we have not yet discussed.

WHY THEORISE?

What is theory? The answer to this question is not as simple or as straightforward as might be expected, since there is little consensus in the social sciences as to what actually constitutes 'theory'. Furthermore, the word is used so loosely that it threatens to render it meaningless. In recognising the lack of agreement about 'what theory is', Sutton and Staw (1995) take a different approach, attempting to build consensus around 'what theory is *not*'; in doing so they make explicit five elements of academic articles that are generally regarded as not constituting theory. These are as follows:

1 *References to theory developed in earlier work* is not theory, unless the author attempts to explicate the concepts and causal arguments in this work, and makes explicit the link to the 'stream of logic' being developed or tested.

2 *Data* are not theory. While data or empirical evidence play an important role in confirming, revising or discrediting existing theory, as well as guiding the development of new theory, observed patterns are not theory. Sutton and Staw (1995) argue that 'Data describe *which* empirical patterns were observed and theory explains *why* empirical patterns were observed or are expected to be observed'. Mintzberg (1979, p584) is more succinct, positing that 'the data do not generate theory – only researchers do that'.

3 *Lists of variables or constructs* are not theory. While variables and constructs are important components of theory, on their own they do not constitute theory, since they must also elucidate why they are connected and how they come about.

4 *Diagrams and figures* are not theory. Again these can play a useful part in elucidating theory in research papers, but rarely constitute theory on their own. This is because even though such graphical representations can help bring order through explicitly mapping patterns and causal relationships, they rarely explain why these connections are being made.

5 *Hypotheses* are not theory. Hypotheses are concise and explicit statements about the relationships that might be expected to exist or outcomes that are likely to occur, but they do not throw light on why. Nevertheless, hypotheses can provide crucial bridges between theory and data.

Weick (1995) is less convinced by the endeavour of Sutton and Staw (1995), preferring to focus on the 'process' rather than the 'product' of theorising. For him 'what theory is *not*, theorising *is*'. By this, Weick means that in the process of theorising researchers rarely emerge with a 'full-blown' theory, but the resulting 'approximate' theory may well be expressed as any of the five elements discussed above. For Weick (1995, p386):

> Products of the theorising process seldom emerge as full-blown theories, which means that most of what passes for theory in organizational studies consists of approximations. Although these approximations vary in their generality, few of them take the form of strong theory, and most of them can be read as texts created 'in lieu of' strong theories. These substitutes for theory may result from lazy theorizing in which people try to graft theory onto stark sets of data. But they may also represent interim struggles in which people intentionally inch toward stronger theories. The products of laziness and intense struggles may look the same and may consist of references, data, lists, diagrams, and hypotheses. To label these five as 'not theory' makes sense if the problem is laziness and incompetence. But ruling out those same five may slow inquiry if the problem is theoretical development still in its early stages

DiMaggio (1995) adds a further interesting twist to the idea of theory as process rather than product, arguing that 'theories are not just constructed, they are socially constructed after they are written. Theoretical ideas take on a life of their own ... To some extent, the quality of a theory is a function of the quality of the people who employ it.'

ASPECTS OF THEORY

When scientists build theory they start from the premise that the present situation is knowable and that it is possible to use this known present to build a theory with predictive capability. Indeed for them, the point of theory-building is its predictive utility, and a theory without that predictive utility has no value. In the social sciences in general, and in management or organisational theory in particular, things are a little different. Our basic building blocks of theory are all concerned with people, and not only do different people behave differently, but the same person behaves differently in different circumstances or in the same situation at different times. Unlike hydrogen and oxygen atoms, which always react to each other in a certain limited number of ways, the ways in which people react to each other is complex, multifaceted and variable. Indeed the interactions of people are so complex that we are unable in the social sciences to build any theory that provides a complete explanation of the current situation – let alone have any certainty attached to its predictive ability. This makes the utility of any theory we build more problematic.

We therefore need to consider further just what the purpose is of any theory that is built concerning organisation. Any theory must be more than a simple description of an isolated incident. It must also have a generalisability built into it so that the understanding derived from one set of circumstances can be extended to other circumstances. Thus when we consider theory it does not necessarily have the same purpose as it would in science and we need to think of its utility in terms of both its descriptive ability and its predictive ability.

From our starting point that any situation involving people is complex, we can go on to say that we are unable to narrow down our theory to such an extent that we can completely capture all the aspects of the situation in order to come up with a complete description of that situation. In building theory we necessarily limit our observations and data to enable us to develop theory, but this means that we have created an artificial boundary around our area of research. It is always possible to draw that boundary differently and therefore deal with a different set of data. This may mean that any theory we develop from this different data-set could be different. Indeed from the same data-set it is possible to develop different explanations and so develop different theories that explain the phenomena observed in the data. This is partly because we, as people, are a part of the data we are studying and partly because our explanations of the phenomena depend upon our own ontology and epistemology.

As the theory we develop is limited, we are unable to completely describe any given situation. This means that other theories are possible that describe the situation, and these other theories may provide different understandings of the situation. Thus in management research we have different and competing theories which seek to create an understanding of any problem. It also means that the creation of theory that has a descriptive power, as long as that descriptive power is generalisable, can be an aim of the research itself, and there is not necessarily a requirement for our theory to have predictive power. Increasing our understanding of the present through offering different explanations of the present is one of the aims of management research. In developing a different theory describing the present we are not necessarily seeking to replace existing theories but merely to add alternative explanations.

Any theory that extends our understanding will of course have some predictive ability, as it enables us to find common themes in differing situations. It should therefore enable us to seek remedies to problems through the transfer of useful solutions from one set of problems to another set that appear superficially to be different. This is why *descriptive* theories are useful research. When we talk about *predictive* theories, however, what we generally mean is a theory which enables us to say that if we do *x* then *y* will happen. In management research this is more problematic but nevertheless is an essential part of theory-building, which is attempted by management researchers all the time.

We must remember however that our predictive theories are unlike those of the sciences. In chemistry, for example, we can develop a theory which states that a certain set of chemicals when combined in certain proportions will react in a certain way that we can predict with certainty – indeed this is the test of a robust scientific theory. In management research, because we are dealing with the unpredictability of people, that certainty of the predictive power of our theory eludes us. Our predictive theories are necessarily probabilistic and therefore subject to statistical error.

Thus we can only ever develop theory which states that we have identified factors which account for a percentage of the explanation and thus we can only ever predict in the form of stating that we are z per cent certain that y will happen if we do x. We can never predict with certainty, but this does not invalidate our theory any more than the creation of theory with descriptive utility but little predictive utility. Indeed it is the utility of theory that determines its validity. This is determined by its explanatory power, which is partly descriptive and partly predictive. This in itself enables our research to add to knowledge and enables our insights to be passed on to other people. In the longer term good theory may replace existing theory, and this is the way in which knowledge is built and extended.

THE CASE AGAINST MORE THEORY

A number of prominent researchers argue against the development of more theory, at least in the short term, and some argue against theory in itself:

1   Some have argued that the field of organisational studies needs more descriptive narratives on organisational life based on intense ethnographic work, rather than more theory-building. Some academics have even called for a moratorium on theoretical papers in order for existing and future theory to be 'grounded in a well-crafted set of organizational narratives'.

2   More direct voices against theory can be found amongst those who rely exclusively on quantitative methods. Those taking an extreme position have argued that it is more important to identify correlations between variables than to understand the underlying causal nuances.

3   Those advocating a meta-analysis view argue that the mission of social science is the accumulation of empirical findings rather than the ebb and flow of theoretical findings.

In summary, however, we can say that theory is important because it aids our understanding. It allows us to generalise and to transfer the knowledge gained from one situation to another situation. In general, therefore, we can be better managers in organisations if we have an awareness of appropriate, relevant theory.

WHO DEVELOPS THEORY?

It is normally thought that theory about organisations has been developed by academics, and it is certainly true that a significant part of the theory discussed in this book has been generated in this way. It is equally true that some of the theory we have discussed has been developed by practising managers using their experience and observations in order to generalise about situations and expected outcomes. Other theory we have discussed has been developed by management consultants based upon their wide experience of a large number of organisations. Each has its merits and concomitant problems.

Academics have an element of impartiality in their theorising, as impartial seekers after truth. It can therefore be expected that their theory is better, as they have no particular reason to promote one brand of theory over another. Equally, however, these academics can be divorced from reality and fail to develop appropriate and relevant theory. Crowther and Carter (2002) have been critical of such theorising, describing it as a legitimation of irrelevance. Conversely, practising managers can be expected to be concerned with solving their own immediate problems rather than seeking generalised applications of theory.

Management consultants on the other hand have an element of impartiality from their wide experience, as well as an element of practical experience. But management consultants also have an imperative to sell their services – which effectively negates any claim to impartiality. Indeed Carter and Crowther (2000) have been equally critical of management consultants and their creation of fashions in organisational theory. They describe some of this theory as little more than nostrums.

So who develops good theory? The answer is that none of these groups has the prerogative in this respect. Some of the longest-lasting (and therefore presumably better) theory has been developed by members of each of these groups. It is not who develops any theory that matters. Rather it is the utility of the theory in explaining and/or predicting which really matters.

GLOBALISATION

One factor we have mentioned several times in previous chapters that has an effect upon organisation theory is globalisation. Globalisation is a factor affecting all organisations and all markets. One of the most important factors affected by globalisation is the significance of culture to organisations, making it both more important and less important. It is less important because the dominant culture of any society becomes less significant to an organisation. Similarly the organisational culture becomes less important because of the way it must necessarily change in an era in which the organisational boundary is less important and more subject to change. It is more important because of the need to recognise different cultures around the world and the way they affect established mores of organising. Organisation theory must – and is – adapting to this changed environment.

CONCLUDING THOUGHTS

We have sought to show that organisation theory is a complex subject that continues to develop. Various factors are ensuring that this development continues. Equally we have sought to show that no single perspective has primacy over others. Rather, each of the strands of theory we have discussed is still relevant and has something to offer. Which of these you prefer depends upon your own perspective, and the preferences of the authors are to some extent apparent from this book. So we finish by reiterating the message that none of these should be ignored. Neither should any be adopted to the neglect of others.

REFERENCES AND FURTHER READING

CARTER, C. and CROWTHER, D. (2000) Organisational consumerism: the appropriation of packaged managerial knowledge. *Management Decision*, Vol. 38, No. 9, 626–637.

CROWTHER, D. and CARTER, C. (2002) Legitimating irrelevance: management education in higher education institutions. *International Journal of Education Management*. Vol. 16, No. 6, 268–278.

DIMAGGIO, P. (1995) Comments on 'What Theory is *Not*'. *Administrative Science Quarterly*, Vol. 40, 382–384.

MINTZBERG, H. (1979) Patterns in strategy formation. *Management Science*, 581–560.

SUTTON, R. and STAW, B. (1995) What theory is *not*. *Administrative Science Quarterly*, Vol. 40, 371–381.

WEICK, K. (1995) What theory is *not*, theorising *is*. *Administrative Science Quarterly*, Vol. 40, 385–390.

Index